Working in Class

Working in Class

Recognizing How Social Class Shapes Our Academic Work

Edited by Allison L. Hurst and
Sandi Kawecka Nenga

ROWMAN & LITTLEFIELD
Lanham • Boulder • New York • London

Published by Rowman & Littlefield
A wholly owned subsidiary of
The Rowman & Littlefield Publishing Group, Inc.
4501 Forbes Boulevard, Suite 200, Lanham, Maryland 20706
www.rowman.com

Unit A, Whitacre Mews, 26-34 Stannary Street, London SE11 4AB,
United Kingdom

British Library Cataloguing in Publication Information Available

Library of Congress Cataloging-in-Publication Data
Names: Hurst, Allison L., 1969- editor of compilation. | Nenga, Sandi Kawecka, editor of compila-
tion.
Title: Working in class : recognizing how social class shapes our academic work / edited by Allison
L. Hurst and Sandi Nenga.
Description: Lanham : Rowman & Littlefield, [2016] | Includes bibliographical references and index.
Identifiers: LCCN 2015043660 (print) | LCCN 2015047222 (ebook) | ISBN 9781475822526 (cloth :
alk. paper) | ISBN 9781475822533 (pbk. : alk. paper) | ISBN 9781475822540 (electronic)
Subjects: LCSH: Education, Higher—Social aspects—United States. | Low-income college stu-
dents—United States. | Educational mobility—United States. | Social classes—United States.
Classification: LCC LC191.94 .W67 2016 (print) | LCC LC191.94 (ebook) | DDC 378.1/9826942—
dc23
LC record available at http://lccn.loc.gov/2015043660

∞ ™ The paper used in this publication meets the minimum requirements of American
National Standard for Information Sciences Permanence of Paper for Printed Library
Materials, ANSI/NISO Z39.48-1992.

Printed in the United States of America

Contents

Acknowledgments

We would like to acknowledge the Associated Colleges of the South for the grant in 2013–2014 that made this project possible. We are also thankful to Furman University and the Shi Center for Sustainability for providing such a welcoming space for our interdisciplinary workshop on innovative social class research in June 2014.

We are grateful to each of our home institutions—Furman University in Greenville, South Carolina, and Southwestern University in Georgetown, Texas, for supporting us during this project. We thank all those who attended the momentous workshop, whose scholarship and insights were invaluable to the creation of this volume. In addition to ourselves, they are Penny Lewis, Sean McCloud, Jessi Streib, Jenny M. Stuber, Deborah Warnock, Alma Billingslea-Lee, Gretchen Braun, Andrea Lewis, Monica Melton, Kolawole Olaiya, Michael Svec, and Beau Weston.

We would like to thank Sarah Jubar at Rowman & Littlefield for her immediate receptivity to the goals of this book and editorial stewardship of the project. Thanks to Carlie Wall and Christine Fahey of Rowman & Littlefield as well. We are indebted to Krista Soria for allowing us to borrow her phrase "working in class" for the title of this book.

Allison would like to thank, as always, Jason Tanenbaum for being the patient (and sometimes not so patient) recipient of innumerable conversations, lectures, and questions about Bourdieu. He is an honorable sociologist many times over.

Sandi would like to thank Lalena and the LASSes (Katy Hadley, Jeni Loftus, Robyn Ryle and Carla Shirley) for their unwavering support.

Introduction

Allison L. Hurst and Sandi Kawecka Nenga

A book is written a few words at a time. This book began with a short e-mail from Allison Hurst to Sandi Nenga written in June 2013. In it, Allison proposed creating a mini-conference for social class scholars and trying to highlight the cutting-edge scholarship on social class going on in the Southern region of the United States. Allison wrote, "There are a few people whose work with class really interest me—yours included. I thought it would be nice to have a chance to meet with the idea of a possible book collection at the end. . . . My ambition is to have southern colleges associated with cutting-edge interesting work on class."

A few hundred e-mails later, Allison and Sandi had obtained funding from the Associated Colleges of the South (ACS) to host an interdisciplinary workshop entitled "Innovative Approaches to Social Class Research" at Furman University in Greenville, South Carolina. We invited five rising scholars of social class: Penny Lewis (City University of New York), Sean McCloud (University of North Carolina, Charlotte), Jessi Streib (Duke University), Jenny M. Stuber (University of North Florida), and Deborah Warnock (who was at the time at the University of Louisville).

In addition, several faculty members from ACS schools participated: Alma Billingslea-Lee (Spelman College), Gretchen Braun (Furman University), Andrea Lewis (Spelman College), Monica Melton (Spelman College), Kolawole Olaiya (Furman), Michael Svec (Furman), and Beau Weston (Centre College). This was truly an interdisciplinary group, with members representing English, religious studies, history, women's studies, anthropology, education, and, of course, sociology.

For two days in June 2014, we met at Furman University in Greenville, South Carolina, to discuss how we all approached social class in our research. We realized that our own social class locations (past and present) critically informed not just our research, but *all* the work we did in the academy. Our social class also powerfully shaped our work in classrooms, field sites, professional conferences, advising sessions, and committee meetings.

Other volumes have acknowledged the critical role a social class location plays in shaping the academic work of professors (see Dews and Law 1995; Tokarczyk and Fay 1993; Grimes and Morris 1997; Ryan and Sackrey 1984; hooks 2000; Oldfield and Johnson 2008), but no volume that we knew of had focused on all three aspects of our work as professors—teaching, research, and service.

What the ACS workshop participants began to do, spontaneously, was to make connections between our own class positions, our academic work, and published scholarship about social class. What the ACS workshop participants did, in essence, was to exercise their "sociological" imaginations.

THE "SOCIOLOGICAL" IMAGINATION

Sociologist C. Wright Mills ([1959] 2000) developed the term *sociological imagination* to describe how one might go about trying to explain social problems. For Mills, the only way to truly understand an individual's situation was to look at the ways that individual's life unfolded against a larger historical, economic, political, and social backdrop. By making the connections between an individual's biography and the history of the larger society, Mills argued, we could begin to move away from the oppressive idea that a poor situation was exclusively the result of an individual's choices.

Despite its disciplinary name, Mills's concept of the sociological imagination was inherently interdisciplinary. In a footnote, Mills wrote:

> One other point: I hope my colleagues will accept the term "sociological imagination." Political scientists who have read my manuscript suggest "the political imagination"; anthropologists, "the anthropological imagination"—and so on. The term matters less than the idea, which I hope will become clear in the course of this book. By use of it, I do not of course want to suggest merely the academic discipline of "sociology." Much of what the phrase means to me is not at all expressed by sociologists. (Mills [1959] 2000, 19)

Regardless of whether the ACS workshop participants were scholars of education, English, religion, women's studies, or sociology, everyone practiced this analytical move between the individual and the larger social, historical, and discursive context. To understand our academic work, analyses moved between our individual class biographies, the research literature on social class, and our experiences working in the academy.

This, then, became the focus of this volume. Cutting-edge scholars of social class (many of whom—but not all—are still working at universities in the American South) share the insights they have developed by placing their individual experiences working in the academy in a broader context. Throughout the volume, scholars draw upon a variety of scholarly literatures and theories (such as literary criticism of the *Bildungsroman*, research into classed patterns of language use, or Bourdieu's concepts of *habitus* and cultural capital) in order to make sense of their scholarship, their teaching, and their working conditions in the academy.

THE LIVED EXPERIENCE OF SOCIAL CLASS

We asked all the contributors to critically reflect on how their class backgrounds affected their place and work in the academy. Throughout the volume, you will have the opportunity to read sometimes very personal stories that anchor and inform the more objectively "academic" passages. We thought it would be only fair to say a few words about our own social background and how these have motivated the compilation of this volume.

Sandi Kawecka Nenga

In graduate school, I remember asking a mentor for advice about how to handle a sticky situation with the professor for whom I was a teaching assistant. The professor worked me well beyond the twenty hours per week noted in my contract. He asked me to sit in his office while I created and graded the class exams, and then asked me to perform hours of petty, pointless tasks on top of that. I was frustrated that the terms of the contract were being violated. My mentor listened sympathetically and then said, "You have to stop being a secretary, Sandi. You're an academic now and you need to start acting like it."

If my mentor explained this comment more, I did not hear it. I was too busy trying to stop the rage-filled epithets from escaping my mouth. What, I wondered, was WRONG with being a secretary? (I had worked as one for five years before starting my doctoral program.) If I had a contract with a set number of hours listed on it, why should I have to ignore it in favor of acting like an academic? And what on earth did I have to do in order to properly "act like an academic"?

My mentor's comment suggested that I needed to consider my time too valuable to waste on menial tasks and that I should act less subservient. But it took me a while to decode that suggestion because, as so often happens, messages about social class are buried in the substrata of a conversation. Statements about social class seem to erupt from the ground up in vague, emotionally encrypted statements—and I am perpetually two box tops and a stamp short of what I need to send away for the decoder ring.

Instead, I thought more about the ways social class shaped my teaching experiences and my working conditions in academia. And I started to plot a research project about how social class shaped women's childhood experiences (Nenga 2003) because I realized that there were too few pieces of scholarship about the lived experience of social class. Without a body of research to draw upon, I realized, conversations with many academics about social class would remain vague, uninformed, and potentially explosive.

Allison L. Hurst

I am a working-class academic. I say this proudly and somewhat defensively, because for many academics, the idea that there could be something "working-class" about me is absurd, unimaginable, unlikely, or just plain wrong. We who grew up poor, who grew up witnessing the myriad indignities and humiliations visited upon our parents, our brothers, our sisters, our communities, can never forget our pasts, as much as many of us would like to do so.

One of Bourdieu's many definitions of class is that each member "is more likely than any member of another class to have been confronted with the situations most frequent for the members of that class" (Bourdieu 1977, 85). That is a bit wordy but it rings true for me. I have had many bonding moments with other working-class academics over the eating of government cheese, fixing things with string, feeling an outsider in graduate school, being "exceptional" (like a freak) at school, and not quite feeling at home anymore, once being educated.

I became a sociologist, I am convinced, in large part to understand my experience and others like me, and to find ways to break down class barriers so that our experiences no longer separate us but rather bring us together. But even more than that, my doing sociology has also been suffused with the need to bring justice to my family and my community (a word that means what I say even if the community doesn't recognize itself). And I have become convinced, over the years, that bringing justice requires first raising awareness of class matters.

There are many people who inhabit academia who have never gone to bed hungry. Many there who doubt that there are thousands of Americans who will go to bed hungry tonight. When I was in graduate school I took a sociology of work course. We read a book about low-income workers at a fast food restaurant.

When I was reading the book I remembered my own experiences at McDonald's, and the older black man named Derry who walked two miles to work every day, in his polyester blue uniform, in the scorching heat of the Inland Empire desert. I remembered, too, one of our managers (white) who had gone to college but who lived precariously in a one-bedroom apartment and whose ambitions reached no higher than a lateral move to a store in Orange County. Lastly, I remembered the franchise owner (Latino) in his sleek black Cadillac, who was rumored to own five other stores in the county, a local boy who had made it big.

My memories of work and my experience of growing up in the working class did not fit with our classroom discussion of low-wage workers. To my peers, low-wage work was aberrant, not normal. It affected primarily immigrants, women, people of color, and people with little education (often in combination). No one in my class, other than myself, had relatives who worked for so little pay they could not afford decent housing, who had to choose between paying the utilities and buying groceries. That, to me, was "normal." Having the privilege of not having to make choices: that was aberrant.

But what was "normal" for academia was that social class shaped, and continues to shape, the conversations we hold about our work and our lived experiences in the academy. We may not share the same reference points but we live and breathe class as part of our work every day. It is thus crucially important that this conversation about class be multivocal, so that the varied effects of class be recognized for what they are.

THE BOOK TITLE: WORKING IN CLASS

We titled the book *Working in Class* in order to capture multiple facets of what it means to recognize the ways that social class shapes our academic work.

At its simplest, "working in class" refers to one of the places academics work: the classroom. As instructors, we work in class by performing lectures, moderating discussions, modeling problem solving, running simulations, leading writing activities, reviewing material, and explaining assignments. Though the classroom is one worksite, it is by no means the only place where academics teach.

For many academics and the contributors to this volume, our teaching and mentoring work extends beyond the classroom into office hours, mentoring research at field sites, supervising student teaching, advising student groups, planned meetings with students in coffee shops, and unplanned discussions on academic malls.

In addition to working in the classroom, the phrase "working in class" evokes images of artists working in a particular medium. Much the same way an individual artist chooses to work in glass, oil paints, or metal, academics choose areas of specialization. Class is the medium in which we, as scholarly artists, work. We work ideas of social class the way a potter works clay: we knead, stretch, shape, and mold ideas of social class. We do this in our teaching, our mentoring, our research, and in our administrative duties. Ultimately, we produce images and stories of social class that help our audience to view social class in a new way.

Not every academic chooses social class for their scholarly medium; in fact, many disciplines have ignored social class or relegated it to the status of control variable. For many of the contributors to this volume, "working in class" refers to the sheer effort it takes to make social class a visible, salient part of our teaching, scholarship, and administrative work. Like the baker who works wet and dry ingredients into a dough, or the secretary who squeezes an appointment into a crowded calendar, academics sometimes have to muscle social class into our scholarly agendas and course content.

But it is not enough to work in social class once; in order to keep class in our scholarly disciplines, we need to work it in the way a woodworker stains wood: permanently coloring an object by rubbing in a stain and repeatedly pushing it into all the cracks and crevices. Through our scholarship and our teaching, we permanently work in social class by making it a central aspect of our analyses and repeatedly investigating the topic in our classes.

Finally, the phrase "working in class" reminds us that our academic work is carried out while we are surrounded by and immersed in social class. As several contributors point out, we are not always cognizant of the ways that social class shapes our language, our bodies, our behaviors, our norms, and our actions. Nevertheless, social class powerfully shapes our interactions with our students, our research participants, and our colleagues. We work in academic settings immersed in social class. Recognizing the ways that social class shapes those environments can be a powerful tool in the arsenal of social justice.

OVERVIEW OF BOOK

The volume is divided into three sections, representing the three areas of an academic's work: research, teaching, and service. We have taken some liberties with the contributions to the final section, reading service widely to mean both how class affects the labor we do in and for our disciplines as well as how our class affects our position in the academy.

In chapter 1, Sean McCloud shows us how our class background has an impact not only on the types of research we engage in, but also on how others read the research we do. Grounded in the rich theoretical terrain of Pierre Bourdieu, McCloud describes how his class position shaped his own research into Pentecostalism and analyzes the class biases of early twentieth-century eugenicist work. These early scholars routinely and uncritically linked "depraved religions" with poor people, as in the case of Pentecostalism.

In chapter 2, Irene López and Olivia Legan discuss the problems of controlling for class in psychological research as well as the presumed classlessness of psychological research subjects. They argue that this is problematic because class has its own important and independent effects on outcomes. An emphasis on controlling for class can also erase people who are poor from psychological research. They then show how, over the course of López's research on skin color and ethnic identity, class can be operationalized and deployed in research to provide much more accurate results.

In chapter 3, Sara Appel, a white woman, investigates the connections between class and place, and the privileged position of locating oneself as a "global" scholar, noting that research outside one's national borders may be more easily conducted, even considered, by those with travel experience (of a particularly privileged kind). She argues for a form of global subjectivity grounded in situated relational intimacies rather than an individually based "desire for the world" that so easily elides into another form of class privilege.

The final chapter of this section confronts the issue of location in academic hierarchies and how this affects "success" in the academy. After describing the ways that gender and class operate to keep working-class women out of top positions, Lynn Arner provides some very useful strategies for working-class women to navigate this rough terrain. Although the focus is on the discipline of English, we expect that her suggestions and observations are relevant to most disciplines today.

The second section of the volume addresses the complicated relationships between our social class background and our teaching. Most, but not all, of our contributors here are professors in education programs, so they have particular insights into the ways in which class may affect teaching practices.

In chapter 5, Andrea D. Lewis focuses on the complicated intersections between class and race in the classroom. Raised in a solidly middle-class, even upper-middle-class mostly white neighborhood, Lewis, a black woman, was unable to secure a teaching position in her home community. Instead, she was offered a job in a low-income neighborhood teaching mostly African American children. What this meant for her practices and her understandings of her own position are the vehicles through which she conveys important information about how race and class operate today.

In chapter 6, we move from the public school system to the world of colleges and universities. Sociologist Jessi Streib draws upon sociological research into classed language patterns and socialization practices in order to understand how particular teaching practices place working-class students at a disadvantage and reproduce class privilege for affluent students. Streib then considers ways to provide all students in a college classroom with the same educational resources in the pursuit of academic justice.

In chapter 7, Melissa Quintela expands the focus from how class affects how we teach in the classroom to how it also affects our mentoring and service outside of the classroom. Quintela, a working-class academic, teaches at a private liberal arts college. She outlines specific pedagogical techniques and mentoring practices that have been effective in this context.

In chapter 8, Dwight Lang extends the discussion of mentorship by describing his work with the First-Generation College Students@Michigan group. The students Lang mentors at a large public university have different needs and responses than those Quintela teaches in the small private liberal arts college. The contrast of the two chapters helps us see how our own social class backgrounds operate in particular contexts with consequential effects on our teaching styles, practices, and effectiveness.

The issue of training college students who come from families of privilege to teach children in poverty is the focus of chapter 9, by Michael Svec and P. L. Thomas, which concludes our section on teaching. In some ways, this chapter brings us full circle to the issues raised by Lewis at the outset of this section. Among other topics, Svec and Thomas address the myth of meritocracy and the pernicious and pervasive deficit view of poor children that are too often functioning as important mechanisms for the reproduction of social class.

Our final section addresses how our social class backgrounds and current locations affect our work in the academy, broadly speaking. This includes service but also issues of power and voice. In chapter 10, Krista Soria describes the overlap between her working-class background and her work as an adjunct in the academy, in terms of expectations, behaviors, and reward. Echoing some of the points made by Arner, Soria argues that adjunct faculty today represent the working class within a very hierarchical system of higher education.

Following up on some of the themes described by Soria, in chapter 11, Timothy Haney reports the findings of a mixed methods study of the Canadian professoriate. He finds that class background plays a significant role in how professors approach their scholarly, pedagogical, and administrative work. Interestingly, professors from advantaged backgrounds tend not to see class operating in their lives and their work, while professors from less privileged backgrounds are much more aware of the salience and effects of class in the academy. Studies such as Haney's are a good first step toward understanding class inequalities among today's professoriate.

One of the disciplines hardest hit by the "adjunctification" of the academy is English. In chapter 12, Gretchen Braun suggests that when academics in the humanities discuss the ongoing "job crisis," their discourse is influenced by the narrative traditions that are their objects of scholarly study. Braun argues that the use of the *Bildungsroman*, the novel of self-development, to narrate the job market experience has classed implications, and may impede productive, concrete, and systemic responses to the growing inequality within the professoriate.

In the final chapter, Deborah Warnock provides a big-picture view of some troubling changes in higher education that are affecting access and outcomes of college students from less privileged backgrounds. These include the overuse of contingent labor so well described in the chapters by Arner, Soria, and Braun, but also the shriveling of public financial support for higher education. More students today are financing college through debt, but the burdens of debt are not equally shared. The least privileged students are those most encumbered and the least able to repay. All of this has implications for those who work in academia, especially those who are themselves from less advantaged backgrounds. Warnock argues that it is difficult to reconcile the goals of facilitating upward mobility for students from similar backgrounds while being aware that the goals of many colleges and universities stand in contrast to the recruitment and support of these students. This, combined with the fact that campuses are increasingly reliant on adjunct labor, makes it difficult for the contemporary tenure-track or tenured working-class academic to reconcile his or her position in the academy.

Before concluding, we would like to add a final word about Bourdieu. The reader may notice that several of the authors refer to and build upon the work of Pierre Bourdieu. Although unintentional, we believe this was no accident.

Academics who have struggled personally with the issues of class effects on their teaching, research, and general academic labor are likely to have found solace and illumination in Bourdieu's theories. We believe the frequent mention and use of Bourdieusian concepts here are a testament to the helpfulness of his work.

To some extent, the book project itself can be seen as an attempt at a sketch of a collective self-analysis (Bourdieu 2004). We must interrogate our particular positions from which we view the world and our work in the world, as part of the greater understanding of that world we seek to know, describe, and explain.

—

Part One

Research

Chapter One

Class as a Force of Habit

The Social World Embodied in Scholarship

Sean McCloud

I have been prayed over twice. The first time, when I was ten years old, occurred at a charismatic holiness church in my small, rustic and rusting, Midwestern factory/farm town. I had been invited to attend the church by my best friend at the time. Little did I know that the invitation was part of his devout family's plan to get me saved.

Coming from a nonreligious/nonsupernaturalist household (it wasn't until I was eight that I learned that Christmas was a religious holiday), I went not only because I wanted to be with my friend, but also because of a preteen version of ethnographic curiosity toward something so foreign to me.

When the pastor asked for individuals to come up front to be prayed over, my friend, his sister, mother, and father all urged me to go. I said "okay" and proceeded to the front. There, the pastor put his hand on my forehead and began saying words in an indecipherable whisper. After what seemed like an hour, but was probably less than a minute, he pushed at my head and moved away to pray over another person.

I went back to my seat and my friend's mother asked how I felt. I said, "I'm fine," and decided at that moment that I would not be going to church with my friend's family again.

The second occasion took place when I was a graduate student studying an ecumenical group that practiced Pentecostal gifts of the spirit such as speaking in tongues, divine healing, prophesy, and holy laughter. A group of five men circled me, their hands stretched toward me with palms open, saying prayers.

The goal was to "carpet" me, which entailed the subject toward whom the prayers were being directed to be "touched" by the Holy Spirit and to gently fall to the floor, thus demonstrating that they had received a spiritual blessing.

Such "carpeting" was occurring all around me, some happening after only a few seconds of prayer. I stood in the circle, holding my digital recorder and listening while the men prayed and occasionally pushed at my shoulders. After nearly thirty minutes, they decided to move on to another person.

In both cases, as a nonreligious person, I had not learned how to respond to such situations, nor was I at points in my life in which I was open to new ways of acting, responding, moving, gesturing, and thinking. But for my friend's family and the men praying over me, such religious gestures, emotions, and the proper responses to them had been historically inculcated by their social locations, becoming habits that moved them to act and feel certain ways.

This chapter offers one way to think of class, viewing it as a "force of habit" that influences the way we act, think, and feel. It also provides a brief case study of pre–World War II social scientific theories about religious and class differences to point out the obvious: class—as a force of habit—influences scholars in their research and teaching as much as it influences the people that they study.

CLASS AS A FORCE OF HABIT

"Class" connotes a wide range of associations, from Marxist analysis to quantitative examinations of education and income. At its most basic, class has often been defined as a combination of variables:

- Income (how much money one makes)
- Occupation (what job one holds)
- Education (how much one has)
- Wealth (how much one has accumulated or inherited)

But class is much more than this. Class is certainly about money and what we consume. But it is also about how we move our bodies, how we use them, and what we put on and into them. Class concerns boundaries, those distinctions we make between ourselves and others. Because of this, class entails relationships, identities, meaning, and power. It foments comfort and discomfort. It can be explicit or hidden, conscious or unconscious. It reveals itself in our most ingrained habits.

Class is both material and representational. As noted by the historian Kathryn Oberdeck, contemporary scholars have often divided along the lines of locating class in language and culture or in "objective" material conditions

(Oberdeck 1999, 6). Yet class is "in" both, because the material and representational are not opposed, but joined.

Class is certainly a status grounded in material conditions. One is both constrained and enabled by the material circumstances in which she or he resides. One's future life trajectory, social networks, cultural preferences, habituated ways of thinking and acting in the world, and even health and well-being are related to one's socioeconomic situation. How long one lives, where they live, whom they befriend, what jobs they work, how they vote, and whom they marry are all influenced by—and help constitute—class.

The material circumstances fomented by and constitutive of class also produce demonstrable physical and psychological effects, and whether those be pain, sorrow, happiness, hunger, comfort, discomfort, illness, pride, confusion, or otherwise, they are just as "real" as one's occupation or religious affiliation. Class, among other things then, is about affect, emotion, feeling. Class foments habits. Class is a force of habit.

What is the classed "force" referred to in the phrase "force of habit"? The force is, first and foremost, social/historical/material. It is the social habituation—based in our material conditions—historically inculcated into our bodies. The religious gesture enacted during stress, the repeated phrase uttered in response to an event, the violent outburst shouted when feeling betrayed—these are the immediately available tools of reaction, the most accessible without forethought, the quickest performance in one's repertoire of possibilities.

These are responses from the force of habit. The reproduction of structures and dispositions is not automatic and inevitable, but is likely because the force of habit makes alternatives less likely, less accessible, less palpable. In suggesting this, I am influenced by the scholarship of Pierre Bourdieu and his concept of habitus.

The habitus lies at the heart of Bourdieu's theoretical framework. He devised the concept to describe how humans actively negotiate the social world that formed them. Bourdieu suggests that the habitus concept directly contests, "on the one hand, mechanism, which holds that action is the mechanical effect of the constraint of external causes; and, on the other, finalism, which, with rational action theory, holds that the agent acts freely, consciously, and, as some of the utilitarians say, 'with full understanding,' the action being the product of a calculation of chances and profits" (Bourdieu 2000, 138).

In other words, Bourdieu conceived of habitus as an alternative to both structuralist and rational actor theories of human behavior. Individuals, which Bourdieu refers to as "agents," are neither automatons trapped in society's iron cage nor autonomous individuals unaffected by material and social circumstance.

Bourdieu defined habitus many times in multiple writings. He referred to it as a "system of lasting, transposable dispositions which, integrating past experiences, functions at every moment as a matrix of perceptions, appreciations, and actions" (Bourdieu 1977, 82–83).

The habitus is thus a "product of history," formed out of our social locations, family upbringing, educational opportunities, physical placement within the society, and other "structures constitutive of a particular type of environment" (Bourdieu 1977, 82, 72).

The habitus structures what we think, how we think, how we act, and how we move and position our bodies. In this conception of habitus, one may be reminded of Karl Marx's famous line from *The German Ideology*, that "it is not consciousness that determines life, but life that determines consciousness" (Marx and Engels 1964, 74–75). And while habitus sounds similar to the idea of class consciousness, one major exception is that habitus includes much doxa, which Bourdieu defined as the socially constructed opinions, assumptions, and inclinations that are so ingrained that they seldom come to conscious recognition.

Doxa, as the religious historian Jacques Berlinerblau notes, "is what agents immediately know but do not know that they know" (Berlinerblau 2001, 346). This is why Bourdieu suggests that one might better use the term "class unconscious" to describe the material, socially locative forces of habit that make up habitus (Bourdieu 1985, 728). "The social world," Bourdieu writes, "doesn't work in terms of consciousness; it works in terms of practices, mechanisms, and so forth" (Bourdieu and Eagleton 1992, 113).

Some have suggested that Bourdieu's view of individuals and/or the social world is static (Butler 1997, Rothenberg 2010). In response to such assessments, Bourdieu asserted "habitus is not the fate that some people read into it. Being the product of history, it is an open system of dispositions that is constantly subjected to experiences, and therefore constantly affected by them in a way that either reinforces or modifies its structures" (Bourdieu and Wacquant 1992, 133). "It is durable," he writes, "not eternal!" (133).

But even though the habitus adapts and changes with new experiences, people have a statistical tendency to encounter situations, individuals, and institutions that reinforce the assumptions and habits one already has (Bourdieu 1990, 60–61). In other words, the social milieu within which one lives tends to be similar to that in which one's habitus initially developed.

In addition, Bourdieu sees individuals experiencing a certain level of comfort, and therefore attraction, to those social locations that helped form their habitus. "Guided by one's sympathies and antipathies, affections and aversions, tastes and distastes," he writes, "one makes for oneself an environment in which one feels 'at home' and in which one can achieve that fulfillment of one's desire to be which one identifies with happiness" (Bourdieu

2000, 150). Thus, while habitus is adaptable, any possibilities of change must battle a social and psychological inertia that tends to keep things as they are.

Often Bourdieu's concept works best with regard to class as a force of habit when "habitus" is understood as a set of characteristics relegated to individuals and created by one's material and social conditions. This view concurs with Bourdieu in that a similar "habitus" can be common among people living under and with similar social relations, cultural styles, and material conditions.

But in this rendering, habitus is not social relations and material conditions, but rather that which is generated by such things. Thus, social relations and material conditions (and these things must include cultural styles, mores, etc.) inculcate certain forces of habit into us—how we think, act, move our bodies. When we use the term "force of habit," we think of Marx saying that life determines consciousness, but we also think about Skinnerian experiments teaching various habits to rats and humans, the endorphin rush the obsessive compulsive receives through ritual repetition, or the anxiety release garnered by the alcoholic, drug addict, food addict, or smoker when they get their fix. Once a pattern is established, it is hard to break. How much more difficult that becomes when it is something under the radar of conscious acknowledgment and doxically shared with one's closest peers.[1]

The tension between the possibilities of change and the forces of social reproduction reveal themselves in a continuous dialectic in Bourdieu's writings. This is especially prominent in *Pascalian Meditations*, a late work in which he deals most explicitly with the subject of change. "It would be wrong to conclude that the circle of expectations and chances cannot be broken," Bourdieu writes in one section, because there is a "relative autonomy of the symbolic order, which, in all circumstances and especially in periods in which expectations and chances fall out of line, can leave a margin of freedom for political action aimed at reopening the space of possible" (Bourdieu 2000, 234).

But elsewhere he asserts that "symbolic action cannot, on its own, without transformation of the conditions of the production and transformation of dispositions, extirpate bodily beliefs, which are passions and drives that remain totally indifferent to the injunctions or condemnations of humanistic universalism" (Bourdieu 2000, 180).

Because the habitus is not merely intellectual, but fully embodied, Bourdieu suggests that "only a thoroughgoing process of countertraining, involving repeated exercises, can, like an athlete's training, durably transform habitus" (Bourdieu 2000, 172). But even given such countertraining, the possibilities of change may still be muted, as "dispositions are subject to a kind of permanent revision, but one which is never radical, because it works on the basis of premises established in the previous state" (161).[2]

Using Bourdieu's concept of habitus to think about how class is a force of habit can provide a means for understanding how one's social location/class background plays a role in one's interactions with and understandings of the social world in which she resides. This is just as much the case for scholars as it is for the people they study, and it is especially notable in eugenics-influenced social scientific theories about class and religious differences in the pre–World War II era.

EXPLAINING RELIGIOUS AND CLASS DIFFERENCES IN THE AMERICAN AGE OF EUGENICS

Now rightfully seen as a discredited pseudoscience, recent scholarship suggests that eugenics held much more appeal in the early twentieth century among elites, academics, religious leaders, and the masses than previously thought (Kevles 1985, Carlsen 2001). Involving things as varied as rural family studies, state fair "fitter family" contests, and forced sterilization laws for those considered "unfit," the movement proved a pervasive current in American culture from the 1880s up to the beginning of World War II.

Eugenics was intertwined with and influenced by evolutionary anthropology, nativism, racism, progressivism, and the professionalization of fields such as sociology. As a malleable and inconsistent form of biological determinism, the eugenics movement may be seen as part of a larger early twentieth-century discourse concerned with explaining differences and inequalities among humans. Through the use of photographs, Mendelian genetics, and social Darwinism, eugenicists claimed to offer scientific proof that some individuals, families, and entire races of people were more or less advanced than others.

Social class plays a role in this narrative in that it was frequently explained—like religion—through the trope of inherent biology. Social class was often an essential part of the eugenically inflected discourse on religious affiliation. But even more, one might argue that class is the force of habit that led middle- and upper-middle-class academics to theorize the lower classes they studied in ways that provided a pseudoscientific apologetics that supported class and racial hierarchies.

In the first decades of the twentieth century, during the height of the eugenics movement, a number of prominent psychologists and sociologists suggested that religious differences—like class, race, and cultural differences—could partially (and sometimes entirely) be explained by inherent human character traits. In other words, certain religious beliefs and practices naturally attracted certain races and classes of people.

This line of argumentation mirrored eugenicists' occasional references to religion. For example, in the 1933 revised edition of their popular college textbook *Applied Eugenics,* Paul Popenoe and Roswell Hill Johnson suggested that "the religion of a people corresponds to some extent to the inherent nature of the mind of that people, as well as to its national or racial traditions and economic organization" (Popenoe and Johnson 1933, 214).

Eugenicists like Paul Popenoe and Roswell Hill Johnson, Ellsworth Huntington, Leon Whitney, and William McDougall saw religious practices and beliefs—like the physical features of human bodies—as providing evidence that some people were more or less evolved or genetically endowed than others (Huntington and Whitney 1928; McDougall 1977).

Several shared themes and language consistently appeared in a selection of popular eugenics, psychology of religion, and rural church sociology writings from the early 1900s through the 1930s. First, the eugenic and social scientific writings under study similarly assumed that there were depraved religions that created depraved people. Conversely, some also suggested that depraved people were naturally attracted to depraved religions.

Second, eugenicists, sociologists, and psychologists reached nearly identical conclusions about which religious communities were the most depraved, degenerate, or unevolved: Roman Catholic, sectarian, fundamentalist, ecstatic, minority, and new religious ones.

Third, these writings frequently asserted that some modern religious practices and beliefs were inherently "primitive," but persisted among unevolved races and classes of people. Rural whites who participated in ecstatic religious revivals and the burgeoning Pentecostal movement garnered special attention from eugenicists and scholars who held this view. Their participation in supposedly "primitive" religious practices ostensibly contradicted early twentieth-century racist assumptions that white Anglo-Saxons were the most advanced race of humans.

Yet the period's popular science easily helped resolve this quandary, as seen in Frederick Morgan Davenport's 1905 work, *Primitive Traits in Religious Revivals.* In this published dissertation, the future New York state representative and Hamilton College law and politics professor used a Lamarckian version of environmental degeneracy theory, a popular idea in much of the nineteenth century but one that slowly lost favor in the early twentieth (Davenport 1905).

In the three decades after Davenport, both eugenicists and sociologists who studied rural America—Warren Wilson, Edmund Brunner, and others—offered theories of rural white population degeneracy (Wilson 1925, Brunner 1927). In brief, they suggested that the best racial "stock" had left the country for the city, leaving "morons" and other "inadequate" and "less favored" individuals who were attracted to emotional, ecstatic religious practices.

In noting that writings on religion and eugenics mirrored each other in distinguishing and ordering religious phenomena in ways that offered a scientific apologetics for existing American inequalities, no conscious, conspiratorial motivations need be suggested. Instead, one might draw from Pierre Bourdieu's model of society as a collection of groups with varying interests who, through their frequently unwitting activities, promote their own images of the world as the most natural and acceptable for all.

Bourdieu argues that the different categories and classifications used by groups and individuals wielding the most power in a society tend to symbolically reproduce—in his term homologize—that society's existing power relations. The eugenics and religion scholarship under discussion offered symbolic and cultural capital (in the form of scientific explanations and classifications) that supported existing social hierarchies (Bourdieu 1991, Bourdieu 1977).

Here it is suggested, as does the historian of science George Stocking in his work on the persistence of Lamarckianism until the 1910s, that "it may be quite illuminating to suggest that the thinking of social scientists was conditioned by assumptions which rarely came fully to their consciousness" (Stocking 1968, 237). In other words, the assumptions were, in part, forces of habit inculcated by scholars' social locations, classed, racialized, and religious identities that stood at some marked difference from those about whom they theorized.

Pentecostalism was one predominantly working-class religious movement whose activities were dubbed, by some scholars, as evolutionarily backward. Speaking in tongues, in particular, was picked out as a primitive and unevolved form of religious expression being practiced by primitive, unevolved people.

In his 1927 study *Speaking with Tongues,* Colgate University president George Barton Cutten asserted that the Pentecostal practice "could be traced to primitive times, for it is a primitive experience, a reverberation of the very early days of the race" (Cutten 1927, 2).

To explain how a twentieth-century American could practice such a primitive activity, Cutten referenced a psychology of the subconscious, arguing that "for modern man to permit himself to indulge in this form of expression means that he must put himself in a psychological state where the controlling apparatus of his mind is not functioning, and where the primitive reactions, which usually sleep in the subconscious, find their way to the surface and represent the individual" (Cutten 1927, 4).

While this seemed to explain how developmentally advanced people could speak in tongues, he was quick to add his assertion that those who spoke in tongues also possessed naturally low mentality, suffered from illiteracy, and were filled with nervous energy (Cutten 1927, 6).

The example of this pre–World War II scholarship may seem far afield from contemporary studies. Yet all scholars today—like actors in any other social arena—bring habits to their work that are not just inculcated by the training of their field, but also the social locations from which they came.

Although no formal statistics back up this claim, it probably will not sound shocking or original to readers to suggest that the scholarly habitus under discussion is largely bourgeois (as well as white, male, and mildly progressive) (Muzzatti and Samarco 2006). This can become a problem when the experiences, dispositions, and understandings of the world inculcated by that social location are naturalized as the "way things are" for everyone.

As noted by Bourdieu, scholars like to imagine themselves to be objective observers of their subjects, but in this assumption they are wrong (Bourdieu 1988, 2000, 2007). And when their subjects involve the social world (as "religion" surely does), some idioms, groups, theories, and evidences get a pass, while others get questioned.

In the study of American religion, for example, relatively few have suffered a barrage of questioning as to why they chose to examine the topics of Puritans, Methodists, abolitionists, civil rights activists, Episcopalians, and—more recently—noncharismatic evangelicals. But, as the religious historian Kelly Baker notes, those who study those groups and topics considered "insidious and unloved" (whether that be certain new religions, working-class prosperity gospel, movements, or popular culture fandoms) find themselves placed in the confessional, expected to reveal what personal peculiarity would spur them to such an "odd" subject (Baker 2012).

"Are you one of them?" seems to be one of the questions. And however you answer, you have already lost the game. If you respond in some affirmative, your study may be dismissed because you are too much an insider (i.e., "he only thinks class is important because he grew up poor," or "her arguments can be explained by the fact that she is a Taiwanese Buddhist from California"). But if you say that you have no personal stake in the subject, you still remain under suspicion.

In what Daniel Rodgers has dubbed an "age of fracture," contemporary identity politics and its accompanying personalization of everyday life worlds often means that studying something appears to be an endorsement of it, some unacknowledged therapeutic project of the self that the scholar must be working through (Rodgers 2011, Illouz 2008, Giddens 1991).

Sometimes that may be the case. As Baker notes, we are all implicated by our social locations, past histories, and the habits these have inculcated (Baker 2012). Our research interests do not come out of a vacuum cleaned of all social and psychological entanglements. But not all research topics, theoretical approaches, and the social locations that foment them are viewed as legitimate as others, particularly those that stray from the unacknowledged "default" position of the American religious studies habitus.

As researchers, we need to find ways to be more reflexive about how our past and present social locations—how our classed forces of habit—constrain what we see as legitimate and illegitimate evidence, topics, and methods.

NOTES

1. For a study that examines how such unacknowledged, classed dispositions play out in marriages between people of different class backgrounds, see Jessi Streib, *The Power of the Past: Understanding Cross-Class Marriages*.

2. I am struck here by what Bourdieu attributes to the stoics: "The stoics used to say that what depends upon us is not the first move but only the second one. It is difficult to control the first inclination of habitus, but reflexive analysis, which teaches that we are the ones who endow the situation with part of the potency it has over us, allows us to alter our perception of the situation and thereby our reaction to it. It enables us to monitor, up to a certain point, some of the determinisms that operate through the relation of immediate complicity between position and dispositions" (Bourdieu 1992, 136).

Chapter Two

Controlling for Class

Or the Persistence of Classism in Psychology

Irene López and Olivia Legan

In the field of psychological research, psychologists are trained to assess the "true" association between variables by first ruling out the effect of other extraneous variables. As such, demographic variables, such as socioeconomic status, are routinely "controlled" because they supposedly confound the relationships between our main constructs of interest. Yet what does it mean to control for these types of variables? And what does it convey about what psychology considers important to study?

In this essay, I (the first author) review my work and discuss how my understanding of class has developed and shaped my research. Over time, I have shifted from ignoring or trying to "control" or "partial out" the effects of social class to more explicitly integrating the association of class with other variables. Doing so has not only required me to learn the statistical and methodological challenges involved in assessing class, but has also helped me understand how class shapes my variables of interest. Ultimately, I have learned that when we, as psychologists, attempt to "control for class" we are, in effect, engaging in classism.

THE OMISSION OF CLASS

Open any introductory undergraduate psychology textbook and you are likely to find that psychology is routinely defined as the scientific study of behavior and mental processes (American Psychological Association [APA] 2015b). The definition stems from the field's initial study of individual differences in sense and perception. As such, the primary focus of psychology has historically been on delineating differences in bodily perceptions, cognitions, and reaction times, and not necessarily on studying the impact of larger contextual variables.

Consequently, the subject areas and "subjects"[1] studied were considered to be classless (Lott 2014). The field's early and exclusive focus on documenting individual and biological differences, therefore, did not allow for the assessment of larger structural forces (for an exception see Walsh, Teo, and Baydala 2014).

Yet social class, defined as "power, prestige, and control over resources" (Diemer et al. 2012), is related to social position and rank (Kraus and Stephens 2012), and has always been an appropriate and necessary topic of study in psychology. Social class affects individual experiences, and, in fact, shapes the totality of our lived experiences.

It influences a host of varied outcomes, from our individual perceptions, attributions, bodily reactions, brain development (Chen and Miller 2013; Gianaros and Manuck 2010; Kraus and Mendes 2014), to our health and mental health (Robertson et al. 2015; Scott 2014; World Health Organization 2014). Psychology is, therefore, more aptly defined as the scientific study of behavior and mental process *in context*, with social class being one of the most encompassing and defining of all contexts.

Still, despite its centrality and importance, social class has been woefully neglected in psychology (Fiske and Markus 2012; Kraus and Stephens 2012; Lott 2014). Indeed, psychology has been so "myopic" in its focus (Lott 2014) that a study of six APA journals, from 1970 to 1989, indicated that only 33.5% of studies contained the social class information of participants (Graham 1992). Thus, not only are the issues related to the poor underresearched, but the poor themselves are underrepresented in the research as well. Such neglect has meant that social class has been "under-theorized" in psychology (Day, Rickett, and Woolhouse 2014, 397).

The neglect of social class is readily apparent at the graduate level, where students receive little training in studying and integrating it into research and therapy—despite repeated calls to the contrary (Diemer et al. 2012; Liu 2011; L. Smith 2009). In fact, a recent content analysis of the top two journals in the field of counseling psychology found that, while class was the variable *most* likely to be mentioned in comparison to race and gender, the impact of class was the *least* likely to be further assessed or analyzed (Reimers 2007).

Thus, while multicultural training is essential, and indeed helps students acquire more compassionate and accurate structural explanations regarding poverty (Toporek and Pope-Davis 2005), class-focused discussions in graduate school remain rare. This is unfortunate because it is vital to understand how class interacts with and shapes our representations of race and gender (Liu et al. 2004b; Ostrove and Cole 2003; L. Smith 2009).

Indeed, in my own training as a clinical psychologist, I never had a class that specifically dealt with issues of economic status and power. Indeed, in my own training as a clinical psychologist, I never had a class that specifically dealt with issues of economic status and power—although this was clearly an interest of mine (Hall, López, & Bansal 2001). Instead, there was the optional class on "diversity," which was solely focused on conversations of race and gender.

When class issues were discussed, they were inevitably eclipsed by and confounded with race. For example, I specifically remember one seminar that introduced the use of the MMPI-2, a standard psychological instrument. When I inquired about the validity of this measure with less advantaged (poor) populations, I was told that, with some minimal adjustments, this measure could successfully be used with "these special populations."

However, when I pressed further about this issue, the speaker reported on some preliminary normed data that had been obtained with a small number of *racial minorities*. Apparently, race was not only synonymous with economic disadvantage, but was also being described euphemistically as "special." In later research, my professor and I were able to show that indeed the MMPI-2 did not discriminate against ethnic minorities (Hall, Bansal, & López 1999)—although we did not assess the mitigating role of socioeconomic status.

Why is it, I wondered, that in a field that prides itself on its ability to understand the nuances of psychological experience, we were so unable to consider the unique influence of class? Further, why were Whites allowed to be classed while racial and ethnic minorities were not?

The lack of specific training in class issues did not dampen my interest in these issues although it did affect how I proceeded with my work. In my first-authored publication written while in graduate school, I assessed whether monocultural involvement was a better predictor of adjustment than dual-cultural involvement among teenage Puerto Rican mothers—without considering whether this predictive relationship could vary by class (López and Contreras 2005).

I assumed, as many others did, that if my participants were low-income, their inclusion was sufficient to address class issues. Yet, while my work had real-world (face) validity, there was no explicit measurement of social class. While we found that dual-cultural involvement (biculturality) was a better predictor of well-being than monocultural involvement, the lack of social class measurement meant that we could not be sure if this relation could vary by status.

This lack of measurement was unfortunate as many of the psychological benefits often attributed to biculturality can, perhaps, be partially explained by having greater leverage or access to particular types of class privilege. In other words, if we define biculturality as the acquisition of dual-cultural norms, could it be that the benefits of biculturality may be due to the acquisition of, or access to, behaviors or values that are more highly esteemed, valued, and classed?

Also, can it be that someone who has a lower income and is bicultural may have less access to either economic or cultural resources, and thus be less adjusted, than someone who has a higher income and is bicultural? In other words, psychological well-being may not only be contingent on how biculturality is defined, but may also be explained by how biculturality interacts with class.

THE (MARGINAL) INCLUSION OF CLASS

Indeed, in my next study, which focused on adult Puerto Rican women, there was clear evidence of how cultural opportunities were limited by class. Specifically, this study assessed the moderating effect of skin color on ethnic identity and self-esteem (López, 2008a). Unlike my first study, I moved from omitting social class to including it—even though the measurement was coarse and not central to any of my analyses.

First, in this study, there were explicit measures of socioeconomic status. Specifically, the usual indicators of socioeconomic status were included, such as income, occupation, and years of educational attainment, because these three measures have been considered the triumvirate of measurement in the objective assessment of socioeconomic status (Diemer et al. 2012; Kraus and Stephens 2012).

But to make these indicators more context sensitive, participants were asked how many years of schooling they had received in the continental United States as well as on the island of Puerto Rico. Doing so acknowledged the circular migration that characterized the lives of many Puerto Ricans (Aranda 2007; Duany 2002) and assessed whether these variables could differentially predict outcome.

Additionally, familial access to resources was assessed. Findings indicated that although 70% of the sample had some college education, approximately half of the women reported that neither their fathers, nor mothers, had obtained a high school education (López 2008a). Knowing that these participants came from families with limited resources helped put in perspective the rather surprising finding that, despite their own high educational gains, close to a third of the participants still lived in subsidized housing (López 2008a).

This study, therefore, instructs us that it is key to have multiple measures of class. Doing so allows researchers to assess the degree of correlation between measures and to assess when they diverge (Diemer et al. 2012). Indeed, a growing body of research is showing that income and education are not always correlated across different ethnic and racial groups (e.g., Shavers

2007), indicating that an investment in education does not always produce the same benefits and social mobility for all (Hurst 2010).

Apart from such descriptive statistics based on covariates, correlational analyses from this study also revealed that various markers of class were associated with the outcome variable of self-esteem. Participants with higher educational attainment, as well as those who did not receive welfare benefits, reported having higher self-esteem than their less-educated peers who received public assistance (López 2008a).

However, by far the most illuminating of all the findings was how class mitigated the overall relationship between the main variables. Specifically, as hypothesized, skin color alone did not predict self-esteem. Rather, it was the interaction between skin color and ethnic identity that predicted self-esteem.

Yet economic pressures, such as living in poverty, sometimes impeded participants' ability to partake in the cultural experiences necessary for the development of a higher ethnic identity. In particular, while an overwhelming majority of the participants had visited Puerto Rico, having the means to frequently visit Puerto Rico was associated with a higher ethnic identity and self-esteem.

Still, in retrospect, the study should have discerned if the ability to frequently visit Puerto Rico was restricted by income *or* if income was restricted because of frequent visits to Puerto Rico. Additionally, there could also have been further investigation into how psychological variables, such as ethnic and cultural identity, affected the association with income (Chen and Miller 2012; Ostrove and Cole 2003).

Finally, it could have been assessed if poverty itself was the cause of circular migration, as Puerto Ricans may seek to ameliorate their economic situation by relocating (Pérez 2004). Whatever the case, visits to Puerto Rico were an important cultural necessity that appeared intimately tied to socioeconomic status.

CONTROLLING FOR CLASS

Despite such improvements in measurement, this study still fell short because, while socioeconomic status was measured, in many respects the analysis was an afterthought that did not center on class. Indeed, a review of the psychological research notes that psychology has shifted from neglecting social class to either marginally including it (see Reimers 2007 for an excellent review) or trying to statistically control for it.

Social class is thus understood as "noise" that is distracting from "real data." Hence, many psychological researchers only gather socioeconomic information to control for it or to remove messy outliers (Liu et al. 2004a).

However, there are statistical, conceptual, and ethical concerns with this practice.

Statistically, psychologists often control for class because we wish to get unbiased estimates. We therefore often control for social class because of concerns over measurement error. However, class has its own important and independent effects on our outcome variables. Thus, while it is important not to confound the effects of class with other variables, controlling for class, in effect, isolates and removes social class from the predictive relationship.

Further, by isolating the effect of social class, we remain unable to see how different indices of class can interact with one another and differentially predict outcome. Controlling for class, conceptually, is also problematic because it fails to recognize the mutually constitutive effect that class can have on our study variables. Additionally, reducing social class to proxy measures of socioeconomic status conflates markers of poverty with class identity.

Most importantly, "controlling for class" legitimizes the erasure of people who are poor from our studies. As such, the expression "controlling for class" uses a language of force that underscores classist attitudes toward those who are poor.

In short, there is a fundamental error in viewing social class as an experience that can be controlled rather than an experience that can contribute. Instead of controlling for class, we should integrate class into our analyses. By doing so we cannot only assess its unique effects but also the additive, multiplicative, and constitutive effects of class in combination with other variables.

DIVERSIFYING OUR ASSESSMENTS AND DESIGNS

In addition to reevaluating our analyses, we need to rethink our assessments. However, progress in the field of social class research has been delayed, in part, because of the difficulties in defining and measuring social class. For example, a content analysis of close to four thousand articles in counseling journals found nearly five hundred different terms used for the overarching concept of "social class" (Liu et al. 2004a), making it very difficult for researchers to compare their findings.

Still, within this dizzying array of terms, there does appear to be a consensus that at least conceptually social class can be measured based on either an objective assessment of socioeconomic status, and/or a subjective assessment of social status (Diemer et al. 2012). Depending on the outcome in question, researchers may use one or both of these types of measurements. Diversifying our assessments, as well as our analyses, allows us to assess how these different measures may either vary from one another, converge, combine, or interact with one another to exacerbate outcomes among different populations (e.g., Miething 2013; Quon and McGrath 2014).

Objective Assessments

Most studies to date have relied on a handful of objective measures, such as measures of occupational prestige, or resources-oriented measures, such as educational attainment and income (Diemer et al. 2012; Kraus and Stephens 2012). Yet various problems have been associated with these measures. In this regard, it is worth quoting at length Rubin et al. (2014) who note:

> [O]bjective measures of social class and SES need to be benchmarked and interpreted relative to population-based standards, and these can be difficult and controversial to establish. In particular, if social class and/or SES are conceptualized as categorical variables, then decisions about how many categories to include and the cut-off points for these categories are debatable (Bourdieu, 1987, p. 2). Even after agreement is reached on such issues, the resulting standards are limited to specific time-periods and contexts. Hence, objective standards can become quickly outdated and cannot be generalized outside of the local contexts in which they were developed.

Further, participants may misreport information because of concerns over social desirability, inaccurate recall, or difficulties in understanding survey measures (Diemer et al. 2012; Godoy et al. 2008). As a result, they may overestimate, underestimate, or censor their responses to items related to financial standing (Shoemaker, Eichholz, Skewes 2002).

These inaccuracies can, therefore, affect the descriptive statistics based on the correlations of socioeconomic status with other variables. Additionally, if indicators of socioeconomic status are studied as explanatory variables, incorrect information derived from these independent variables will affect the inferences we make (Godoy et al. 2008).

Among Latinos, which has been the group that I have primarily studied, accurate and stable estimations of socioeconomic status can also be difficult to obtain because Latinos regularly spend a large portion of their income on sending remittances abroad (e.g., Pew Hispanic Research Center 2002). In fact, among immigrants in general, it is difficult to get accurate poverty estimates as migrants may send anywhere from 10% to upward of 80% of their monthly income abroad (Terry and Wilson 2005).

Thus, in my own work, I not only ask about earned income but also regularly inquire about additional expenditures, such as remittances and trips to visit family in Puerto Rico. These costs, in turn, can occur either episodically or seasonally depending on the availability and stability of employment.

Furthermore, it is important to remember that a participant's individual socioeconomic status is situated in local (e.g., school, work, neighborhood) and international contexts. These multiple contexts, in turn, can have a wide variety of effects on health, mental health, and even mortality (Dahl et al. 2006; Fone et al. 2007; McGrath, Matthews, and Brady 2006).

Understanding the importance of context has consequently affected how I do research. In particular, I have tried to focus on recruiting and studying participants not only in locations with high concentrations of Puerto Ricans but also in neighborhoods that are most representative of this group. I did this using US Census blocks based on zip codes in the continental United States (López 2008a), as well surveying Puerto Rican municipalities in Puerto Rico with the highest population density (e.g., López et al. 2009).

By obtaining representative samples, site differences could be made between Puerto Ricans residing in New York and those in San Juan. The results indicated that, despite similarly high rates of poverty in both locales, child psychopathology in New York was associated with worse outcomes, such as more stressful life events and more exposure to violence (López et al. 2009).

These site differences possibly alluded to ethnic specific factors, such as the importance of maternal warmth, which protected the children in Puerto Rico more than the children in New York. Hence, psychological processes could have ameliorated the negative effects of poverty. Indeed, other psychological factors, such as perceived competency and personal meaning, have been noted as being key in helping marginalized individuals thrive (Abelev 2009).

Subjective Assessments

Psychological experiences are, therefore, key to understanding the impact of social class. This is because objective markers of socioeconomic status cannot fully capture subjective social class. Subjective social class refers to how individuals view themselves within society with regard to markers of rank and prestige.

Determining subjective social class, therefore, entails questions beyond quantification and classification of income and education, and instead centers on issues of identity and group processes (Fiske and Markus 2012; Ostrove and Cole 2003; Ritterman et al. 2009).

Additionally, considering subjective social class allows for the assessment of variance even among groups who may show very little variability in objective economic markers. One can assess, for example, how disenfranchised groups compare to one another in terms of not only their earnings but their attributed rank.

Thus, considering subjective social class may explain why it is that even though Puerto Ricans are Americans who typically have greater access to resources than noncitizen Latinos, Puerto Ricans still consistently rank themselves as having lower prestige than other Americans (Aranda 2007). In this regard, racial and ethnic discrimination work in confluence to enforce social stratification and further serve to marginalize these communities. Considered in their totality, these factors can contribute to their sense of dislocation—despite their higher earnings and financial mobility (Aranda 2007).

Furthermore, subjective social class is important to consider as a predictive variable because it can explain a variety of outcomes above and beyond traditional measures of socioeconomic status (Adler, Epel, and Ickovics 2000; Ritterman et al. 2009). Hence, there exist many possibilities when we incorporate subjective social class into our research.

In particular, researchers can assess the degree of overlap between objective and subjective measures of class, as well as differences in the predictive utility in each measure. Additionally, as with objective economic factors, there can be a further investigation of how psychological experiences, such as discrimination, shape social exclusion based on perceived rank and power.

In my own research, I have written about how issues relevant within minority communities, such as concerns over skin color, affect not only objective life chances but also one's sense of rank, worth, and perceived beauty (López 2008b; López, Walker, and Yidliz Spinel 2015; López, Gonzalez, and Ho 2012). Indeed, my review of anxiety concerns among minority women has noted that distress over appearance is not only about gendered and racialized concerns, but is also about trying to meet beauty standards that are classed as well (López, Gonzalez, and Ho 2012).

Visual Assessments

One way that subjective social class has been assessed has been through the use of visual assessments. With these assessments researchers gain an understanding of where participants view themselves by asking them to visually mark, on a ladder, how they see themselves in relation to others.

In particular, in one of the most popular visual assessments, the MacArthur Scale, participants are shown two ladders and asked to mark an "X" for where they see themselves, in terms of their socioeconomic status and subjective social class, within the United States and their own community (Adler et al. 2000). In this way, social class is assessed in multiple contexts.

The use of visual assessments is helpful because it bypasses the need for literacy and may, therefore, be particularly useful when working with children, nonnative English speakers, and/or populations with a limited education. The participation of these samples, in turn, contributed to diversifying psychological research, because most studies to date have been based on convenience samples of undergraduate students that bear very little resemblance to the American population at large (Arnett 2008; Day, Rickett, and Woolhouse 2014).

Community Work

The use of visual assessments highlights the need to extend our methods of assessments away from traditional paper and pencil surveys. Similarly, the more we move psychology out of the lab, the more we can access populations that have been traditionally underrepresented and ignored in the field.

While community-based work may at times involve changing our recruitment techniques, and relying on nonprobability sampling such as snowballing, such efforts not only increase participation but also increase the ecological validity of our work.

Additionally, community-based participatory research requires that participants get involved in various aspects of the research to ensure that their issues are accurately represented and their needs are properly meet, which further increases the utility of our work (Foster and Stanek 2007). In fact, the ultimate goal of community-based participatory research is to ensure that the findings of studies are translated into scientifically supported interventions.

Qualitative and Mixed Methods Research Methods

Community-based projects not only alter our usual methods of recruitment, assessment, and dissemination, but they also have the capacity to alter our research designs. To date, a growing body of research has elaborated on the utility, and indeed necessity, of mixed methods as well as qualitatively oriented research. Mixed methods research, which combines qualitative and quantitative measures and analyses, allows researchers to triangulate various types of data to get a more accurate assessment of the lives of our participants.

In my own work, I have employed mixed methods research to analyze the quantitative and qualitative aspects surrounding appearance among Puerto Rican women (López, Walker, and Yildiz Spinel 2015). Quantitative results show that, despite generally high levels of ethnic identity in the sample, approximately 80% of the sample were told that they did not look Puerto Rican. Further, when queried in open-ended interviews, some reported that they were told that they did not look Puerto Rican because they did not conform to Puerto Rican stereotypes. That is, they were not "loud and rude" and did not wear "street clothes." Hence, ethnic group membership was evaluated based on hurtful and classist stereotypes.

However, despite the advantages of mixed methods research, in psychology there remains a steadfast suspicion and reluctance toward more qualitative forms of inquiry because these methods are not seen as sufficiently empirical. Yet empiricism, which refers to data gathered through experience, is not synonymous with a solely quantitative focus. Therefore, the historically exclusive reliance on positivistic measures and analyses in psychology needs to be updated in order to conduct more complex research on class.

PITFALLS AND CONCLUSIONS

In the end, my own class experiences have influenced my research. In particular, class has guided what issues I investigate, altered how I measure variables, and how I interpret and disseminate my findings. Doing class-oriented work requires that we be aware of our biases and that we process and navigate our own social class roles as researchers (Shpungin and Lyubansky 2006).

For working-class academics such as myself, this process is not always easy because our concerns, priorities, and interests are consistently undervalued (Dews and Law 1995). And while the climate can be difficult for women in academia (Tokarczyk and Fay 1993), the situation is particularly toxic for women of color (like myself) who are often presumed incompetent (Gutiérrez 2012).

Therefore, not only have my participants, and their issues, been undervalued, but my abilities as a researcher have been questioned as well. For example, my work has been dismissed because it has been viewed as too sociological, and my abilities to conduct research have also been questioned. Indeed, colleagues have suggested that my work has only been published because it is considered "novel" and "exploratory" in nature.

However, as I have progressed in my career, I have shifted from ignoring or controlling for class to prioritizing it in my work. Doing so has required learning new types of assessments, altering analyses, and rethinking my data collection and research designs. More to the point, I have realized that relying on previous ways of doing measurements, analyses, and designs have prevented those with less resources and lower rank from being involved in our research.

This, in turn, has not only led to inaccurate assessments (and hence bad science) but has created a body of research that has been based on those with the most resources. Consequently, it has produced interventions that primarily service those with the most resources. Thus, by continuing to engage in these practices, and by continuing to "control for class," we are, in effect, excluding and silencing others and engaging in classism.

Indeed, if the mission of the APA is to "to advance knowledge that benefits society and improves people's lives" (APA 2015a) then the profession needs to recommit itself to the study of social class (Lott 2014). As a

Latina, who comes from a working-class background, I know that I can no longer be silent.

NOTE

1. Even the language that we use in psychology is infused with reference to class hierarchy. For example, up until recently, individuals involved in psychological studies were referred to as "subjects" and not "participants."

Chapter Three

Class, Academia, and Ontologies of Global Selfhood

Sara Appel

He was always thinking of what else to *do* and she told him that it was rare for
her, because she had grown up not doing, but being.
—from Chimamanda Ngozi Adichie's *Americanah*

My best friend, Lauren, recently asked me to present some of my work on the
class politics of envy at "Movements and Exchanges in an Unequal World,"
a conference she had planned for the International Comparative Studies program at Duke University. Though I accepted her invitation, I was overcome
with a sense of inadequacy that I often feel when I'm asked to think about my
rather US-circumscribed American studies work as being part of a more
expansive, global project of knowledge creation and exchange.

A humanities scholar who specializes in contemporary working-class literature and popular culture, I tend to gravitate toward texts that allow me to
"think small" in analytical scale and scope. My dissertation, for example,
contained a chapter focused on a black single mother's daily battles with
poverty in Terry McMillan's novel *Mama* (1987), as well as a chapter on
Peter Sollett's film *Raising Victor Vargas* (2002), in which a young Domini-
can-American protagonist struggles to claim a bit of "privacy" for himself in
and around his Lower East Side New York housing project.

I wondered why I was concerned that my work, despite its focus on how
inequality shapes the way poor and working-class people move through the
spaces they inhabit, wouldn't fit in at a conference like this. Why such
anxiety over whether or not I was a worldly enough scholar to deserve a
voice in an explicitly transnational venue?

To frame this interrogation of such questions, some background information.

In May of 2014, Lauren and I took a two-week vacation to Mexico. This trip was the culmination of eleven years of eagerly suggested yet never fully solidified plans to get me out of the United States once and for all.

As a PhD student in the Program in Literature at Duke, where Lauren also studied anthropology, I'd grown accustomed to generally being the only person in any social situation—at a party, bar, or conference—who had never left the United States. This unique "condition" was exacerbated by the size-able cultural and geographic chasm between where I came from and where I pursued my graduate degree: between St. Helens—a northwest Oregon mill town from which an escape to the nearby Pacific coast was difficult for my family to orchestrate in the best of times—and Duke, a southeastern US stalwart of top-tier educational privilege where at least 10 percent of the undergraduate student body assume "legacy" status, and a granite wall separates the increasingly gentrified black and Latino neighborhoods surrounding East campus from the manicured grounds within.

For most of my life I've possessed what I'd refer to as an almost complete lack of cosmopolitan "libido." Put another way, I've developed little of what Mariano Siskind has called *deseo de mundo*, a "desire for the world" that, as Siskind elaborates, also implies a rejection of "nationalist cultural forma-tions" that tend to connote an at once geographic, intellectual, and ethical kind of smallness (Siskind 2014, 3).

My rural "heartland" hometown, where residents cherish their local high school sports heroes and have been known to brandish Confederate flag license plates despite being fifteen hundred miles from the nearest southern state (and therefore unable to claim the "heritage" often used to justify dis-play of the hateful symbol), could perhaps serve as a representative example of this type of cultural formation.

I often wonder if my lack of "desire for the world" has contributed to my sense of self as a small-scale scholar, generating a tendency toward my own kind of US-centric analytical nationalism. But as Lauren readily recognizes, my work is globally situated in ways that I often remain myopic to.

Taking care to emphasize that the United States remains a symbolic and material superpower whose global-capitalist reach should not be underesti-mated, Lauren nonetheless points out the importance of conceiving of the transnational as consisting of "globally scattered micro-spaces that the scale of the nation doesn't account for."

Gloria Anzaldúa similarly speaks of the concept of the "borderland," a "place where the Third World grates against the first world and bleeds" (1987, 25). This expansive, decentralized zone of psychic and geographic otherness readily includes poor black and Latina inhabitants of the United States, or anyone who lives "outside the confines of the 'normal'"—a terrain on which my work would readily find a place. Thus, it is not so much that my work isn't "worldly," or of the world. But I have difficulty seeing the world in my own work, even when my chosen texts and discursive methods are arguably transnational.

Especially in terms of class background and our personal history of global traversal, Lauren and I are very different. Her father, now retired, was a banker; she graduated from high school in Chappaqua, New York, where Bill and Hillary Clinton briefly lived following Bill's presidential tenure. She's also spent more than eight years living in Peru and various countries throughout Latin America. As an anthropologist, she studies child labor in Lima, and speaks a Spanish so fluent and particular to the Andean region that many Peruvians assume her to be a native of their country.

Yet when I think back to becoming friends a week into our first year at Duke, I remember how similar Lauren and I were in terms of the type of connection we were looking to cultivate. It was magic, sitting on the dirty tan carpet in my bedroom in a crumbling six-bedroom house in Durham, laughing and celebrating our commonalties and differences while we shared as much as we could with each other about our lives: just being there, fully present for one another, in the way that it takes to fall hopelessly in love with a friend.

For Lauren, the pursuit of a higher education went without saying. Nearly 100 percent of her graduating class went to college, with a place like Duke being a "safety school" for many. Lauren herself went to Brown as an undergrad, where a study abroad year in Chile and further intensive Spanish language training at Middlebury College were experiences readily available to her. By contrast, and as is typical of many academics from working-class backgrounds (Gardner 1993; hooks 2000; Kadi 1999), I came to view education as a means of getting the hell out of a town that I had grown to see as a dangerous caricature of "backward" white working-class tribalism.

During a visit with my family in St. Helens one Thanksgiving, Lauren was privy to an "informant's" sense of exactly what it was that I'd felt a need to escape from. Hanging out in my dad's Columbia-riverside apartment, Lauren and I watched one of his friends wave away both the suggestion of a whiskey drink and the joint being passed around.

In a voice teeming with matter-of-fact naiveté and a terror not yet fully processed, this friend explained that his doctor had told him that his heart was "basically done"; his steady abuse of alcohol and two-pack-a-day habit had made him ineligible for the heart transplant that he desperately needed.

We were, in other words, looking at a fifty-five-year-old dead man, who was born and would die in a place where dying at fifty-five was treated as a reason to pour another one for the dearly departed rather than cause for much concern. Speaking of her own beloved family members, southern writer Dorothy Allison beautifully echoes my exasperation with such normalized situational apathy: "death," as she has put it, "was the seed and the fruit of that numb and numbing attitude" (2002, 96).

Though I was fortunate that my mother operated like a life raft in a storm despite her own daily struggles to fend off such fatalism, I watched this seed of death lodge itself in my father and his various "cronies" (as my mother often referred to his friends), with the twin fruits of postindustrial hopelessness and hypermasculine self-delusion growing more rotten by the day. Moreover, when I look at Facebook status updates from friends who never left the St. Helens area, I continue to see so much death being mentioned, so much more than in the updates of those I went to graduate school with.

So if pursing higher education was a strategy employed to escape the specter of fatalism that poverty and "small" life perspectives signified to me, then why put on the brakes at the edge of the continent? How does one reconcile a desperate desire to "get away" from fear of an immobilized life with an equally palpable lack of desire to move too far, or with too much momentum? What causes a person to cultivate or embrace a sense of self as a "global subject" rather than as one contained within the boundaries of nation, class, or any other positionality that condescends to set a limit on one's ability to move, on either horizontal (geographic) or vertical (socioeconomic) axes? And in what ways does the relationship between the desire to move (or not move) and global subjectivity matter to poor and working-class people the world over who have little control over whether and how they migrate?

Elevating the image of Lauren and me laughing on some dirty Durham carpet as a tableau of present and *presence*-centered movement, this essay argues for the value of a form of global subjectivity grounded in situated relational intimacies rather than a "desire for the world" that posits productivity, profit, or even this nebulous thing called "experience" as its source of attraction. Or, to draw further ammunition from my epigraph: Chimamanda Ngozi Adichie's lower-middle-class black Nigerian protagonist's way of *being* in the world, rather than her wealthy white American boyfriend's emphasis on *doing* things in the world, is positioned at the forefront of thinking about how we want to imagine and live community in a global sense.

As Michael Hardt and Antonio Negri have put it, the conditions of possibility of global subjectivity could function as a means for us to "discover the commonality that enables us to communicate and act together" (2004). In Adichie's protagonist's thought, this commonality is, at least in part, about class. Poor and working-class people must *be*, because they rarely possess the resources to *do*.

One must take care, however, not to romanticize such ways of being; the hometown scene described above, with its whiskey and weed and glasses raised to the dead by the dying, represents a troubling form of antidoing, more a state of denial and disconnect in a context of relative socioeconomic powerlessness than a generative mode of togetherness.

But where *being* with others is figured as a way of moving within intimacy rather than a state of stagnation, located (if not *localized*) "means of encounter" contain the potential to open toward forms of global collaboration and solidarity. This way of being could offer a subversive alternative to discourses of transnational desire and "experience" that facilitate a deeper entrenchment of the prerogatives of global capitalism (Hardt and Negri 2004).

"SO ALL OF THIS REALLY DOES EXIST!"

In Adichie's *Americanah*, behind protagonist Ifemelu's observation that she grew up *being* rather than *doing* lies an assumption of relationality. Her "being" is understood to have been solidified with and through others, rendering her very sense of ontological certainty dependent on maintaining global "circuits of connectivity"—an issue that becomes central to the novel's narrative unfolding as Ifemelu migrates from Nigeria to the United States for college, only to return again to Nigeria more than ten years later to reconnect with her first love, Obinze, the one with whom she could always just *be.*

As both a terrestrial plane and object of desire, the "world" as Ifemelu, Lauren, and I understand it mediates a series of "complex, unfinished paths between local and global attachments" (Clifford 1998). The complexity of these attachments and the intersection of pathways depend on the particulars of one's situatedness as a global subject—where factors like race, gender, and national belonging underlie the ever-precarious nature of lines of connection and flight.

However, to more thoroughly investigate the emergence of a global-libidinal lack such as mine, it is worth considering some of Sigmund Freud's thoughts on how the relationship between class and the developing sense of self can influence whether and in what ways one internalizes a "desire for the world."

In "A Disturbance of Memory on the Acropolis," a seventieth-birthday letter-present written by the analyst for French author Romain Rolland, Freud turns his clinical gaze on an incident from his younger days to help explain his theory of derealization, or a state in which one finds herself doubting or refusing to fully believe in a "piece of reality" that she nonetheless *knows* to be true in her rational mind (1936).

Standing in front of the Greek Acropolis with his younger brother, Freud recalls how "a surprising thought suddenly entered my mind: 'So all of this really does exist, just as we learnt at school!'" Digging into the psychology behind this moment, Freud relates his thought back to the "gloom" and negativity with which he and his brother responded to a friend's suggestion that they skip their initial vacation plan to visit the island of Corfu, and see the Acropolis instead:

> We discussed the plan that had been proposed, agreed that it was quite imprac-
> ticable and saw nothing but difficulties in the way of carrying it out. . . . We
> spent hours . . . wandering about [the town of Trieste] in a discontented and
> irresolute frame of mind. But when it came the time, we went up to the counter
> and booked our passages for Athens as though it were a matter of course,
> without bothering in the least about the supposed difficulties.

Freud attributes a psychological link between these incidents— his "depres-
sion at Trieste," and his disbelief upon beholding the Acropolis for the first
time—to experiences with childhood poverty that disabled his conviction
that seeing a place like the Acropolis would ever be within his grasp. He
ascribes his "too good to be true" reaction at the Acropolis to a class-based
fatalism grounded in the feeling that one is ultimately not "worthy" of the
experience being denied. If he were truly worthy of seeing the Acropolis,
Freud's logic goes, Fate would have granted him that privilege;[1] so this
derealization, or projection of disbelief, "[serves] the purpose of defence," of
keeping a desire for something that seems like it is not within reach from
penetrating the ego as one's sense of self develops.

In her essay "The Parrot or the Pit Bull: Trying to Explain Working Class
Life," Mary Childers makes a further critical connection between this dis-
avowal of desire and a poor person's attempt to assert agency—or at least
something that *feels* like agency—in the face of the powerlessness of wanting what remains mockingly out of reach (2002). Quoting a woman named
Maggie Anderson, whose story she includes as one among several in her
discussion of the effects of "cumulative" everyday trauma in the lives of
women in higher education from poor and working-class backgrounds,
Childers shares:

> When I was about to turn six, [my mother] asked me if there was anything
> special I wanted for my birthday. Since I had been learning the wonders of
> elaborate birthday parties from my wealthy friends at school, I told her I would
> like to have a party. She turned suddenly somber, or maybe angry. . . . I
> remember that my mother took me by the shoulders and her voice echoes still
> with the resonance of instructions from the dead: "I don't care what you do
> with your life, but I *don't* want you to want a party." . . . A class-based lesson
> for the second generation: "This is not a good, or even a possible, thing to
> want." (207)

Somewhere in my early grade school years, my "desire for the world"
died a little death. This death may have had something to do with how I went
to school with very mixed-class peers—some of my classmates had lived in
cars, others, in sprawling Columbia-riverside estates—and was frequently

exposed to eleven-year-old white girls returning from the Bahamas with effortless tans and beaded braids, or middle-class kids relaying their spring break Disney World adventures to an envious group of those left behind (like me).

I know there was a time when I thought to myself, "It's not fair! Why don't I get to go?" But considering how easily US Americans internalize the discourse of class in terms of deserving/underserving status in the way that Freud intuits, the answer to the question "Why don't I get to go?" quickly lodges itself in one's consciousness as a lack of worth: I don't get to go, because my family cannot produce the capital necessary to turn a "desire for the world" into proof of our right to want such a thing.

For the poor and working classes, killing the desire itself—"this is not a good, or even possible, thing to want"— can function as a powerful weapon in the battle against a shame that threatens psychic, as well as geographic, immobilization.

"YOU REALLY HAVEN'T LIVED . . ."

I do have poor and working-class friends and colleagues whose "desire for the world" appears to have remained intact or grown stronger over time. Indeed, the drive to "get out" of or away from poverty can resonate in a more geographically expansive way than my experience can account for.

Moreover, there are many factors besides class that would impact the development of one's sense of self as a global subject; ethnicity and diasporic family connections, as I will momentarily discuss in more detail regarding Lauren's personal history, would certainly be among the most obvious correlates. But my three younger sisters, only one of whom has been out of the United States, share my global-libidinal lack.

In an essay that she wrote as part of her teacher-training program, my youngest sister, also named Maggie, takes her lack of "desire for the world" from the psychological to the political in a way that deserves critical attention.

In the darkly ironic tone for which she is notorious, Maggie describes her experiences as a "world traveler" trekking across the exciting world of Columbia Blvd., the working-class street that she and her friends grew up on (and on which our mother still resides). After sharing several of her more notable adventures with the reader—scaling a "massive, towering mountain of gravel"; the "culture shock" of smelling the "pet-stain odor" of her childhood best friend's home; how "you really haven't lived" until you've tried "this chicken . . . that you put into a bag full of salty crumbs and shake it. And THEN you bake it"—Maggie takes a moment to articulate the critique behind the satire:

I have nothing against people who've seen more of the geographical world
than I have. . . . I do, however, have something against people who have told
me how important it is that I "travel and see the world." . . . As if my character
will be lacking in something if I don't. As if they've got advice to offer about
"experience" because they stood in the middle of an open-air market in a pair
of cargo shorts, looking around at all the people who will probably never travel
themselves.

This tableau of a person standing in an "open-air market in a pair of cargo
shorts" is evocative of a white, likely male, first-world class-privileged subject whose "desire for the world," expressed in his gaze upon the likely black
or brown inhabitants of Maggie's market, resonates as distinctly colonialist.
In a keyword entry titled "Cosmopolitanism," postcolonial scholar Pheng
Cheah defends the concept of cosmopolitanism—what he defines, from the
word's Greek origin, as an ethos of being "nowhere a stranger," or feeling
oneself to be a "citizen of the universe"—while acknowledging an important
critique of cosmopolitanism that rises to the surface when one considers the
types of people who are and are not able to partake of this feeling of "universal" global (or perhaps even transglobal) belonging (2006).

Cheah wants to uphold the value contained in Kant's idealistic sense of
cosmopolitan feeling as a force that, if benevolence can be assumed, could
call forth a universal "sense of belonging to humanity" that could both help
people the world over begin to see themselves as part of a "global public
sphere" and counter the kind of "particularistic and blindly given ties to
kinship and country" that made me want to run from my hometown. But in
practice this cosmopolitan feeling remains largely "a form of consciousness
without a mass base," or the province of wearers of cargo shorts.

This does not mean, however, that members of this "mass base," who
perhaps cannot partake of this universal feeling of belonging, do not move.
Complicating Maggie's vision of those *laboring* in the market—the brown or
black people who "will probably never travel themselves"—we know that
third-world poor and working-class people do traverse the globe with fre-
quency.

The issue is the degree of agency such subjects have over whether they
get to remain in communities or nations of choice; where they wind up, if
socioeconomic or political conditions necessitate their movement; and, every
bit as crucially, their reception in the communities and nations to which they
migrate. Thus, for third-world diasporic peoples, the sense of feeling oneself
to be "nowhere a stranger" that privileged philosophers and cargo-short
wearers may enjoy with aplomb—the feeling of one whose "experience"
need not be affected regardless of whether the black and brown people in the
market actually welcome him or her—is more likely to register as a feeling
of being *everywhere* a stranger.

This feeling is, in many respects, what Gloria Anzaldúa is naming when she speaks of those who reside in the borderland, a "vague and undetermined place created by the emotional residue of an unnatural boundary" (25). The borderland is a space both psychic and geographic, with the "unnaturalness" of this boundary also signifying a homeland returned to—but one where the violence of the cosmopolitan imagination, with white "global citizenship" interpreted as an entitled right to conquer and subdue, has rendered this home an "alien" zone for its brown and black returnees.

An example from Adichie's novel contains further poignancy when considering how the privilege to envision oneself as "nowhere a stranger" can influence one's sense of global selfhood. When Ifemelu's wealthy, white American boyfriend spontaneously suggests a trip to Paris, Ifemelu's reaction is affectively similar to Freud and his brother's when initially presented with the idea for the Acropolis trip. "I just can't get up and go to Paris," she immediately replies. "I need to apply for a visa, with bank statements and health insurance and all sorts of proof that I won't stay and become a burden to Europe" (2013, 242). But unlike the Freud brothers, who simply book their trip "as a matter of course" despite their grumblings, Ifemelu's concerns are very real in light of the racist history of French discrimination against immigrants and visitors from North African countries.[2]

Moreover, Ifemelu's reasons for migrating to the Unites States, or becoming a "worldly" subject, are not the same reasons that her boyfriend wants to go to Paris. In the context of teacher strikes against a corrupt Nigerian military regime that continually threaten her burgeoning university education— "Campuses were emptied, classrooms drained of life," Adichie cryptically writes—Ifemelu's diasporic movement is motivated by the realization that *not* moving would in all likelihood immobilize her economically and psychically (120).

Having a tandem experience of diasporic flight in the UK, Ifemelu's first love, Obinze, describes this force for movement as "the need to escape from the oppressive lethargy of choicelessness" (341). By contrast, Ifemelu's white boyfriend's desire for Paris is motivated by nothing *but* choice, or the privilege of having your choices match your urge to *do*, to go, to be fully satiated in consummating one's longing for a destination.

In Anzaldúa's sense, Ifemelu and Obinze's migration puts them in a borderland where their "desire for the world" may never be satiated because it's not essentially a desire, but more urgently a *need*. It's a choice to flee relative choicelessness; a compromise between parts of one's sense of self, and one's sense of place.

Ifemelu struggles to both inhabit a US American sense of self and resist Americanization. She recognizes that even if she *wanted* to fully "belong," she would be forever thwarted in this desire by her status as black, as finance-poor, as woman, as foreign in a place where race, class, gender, and citizenship privilege underlie the upbeat contentment that she finds both "admirable and repulsive" in her wealthy white boyfriend (242). She can never fully *do* in the "trouble-free" way that he does (243).

Ifemelu's global subjectivity has been shaped less by the "exciting" traversal of continents and seas, and more by the struggle to simply (or not so simply) *be*, to inhabit her borderland life in a way that allows her to exist in and with an ambivalence (admiration *and* repulsion) that may never cede its grip.

BECOMING LATINA

I also find myself residing in a border zone where a tangled distinction between need and desire may never completely sort itself out. I've felt a need to escape the "oppressive lethargy of choicelessness" that Obinze describes by fleeing poverty's stark limitations, while also feeling ever the impostor among an upper-class educated elite who seem to move through the world with ease.

But I want to stress an important distinction between the type of "trouble-free" movement that Ifemelu observes in her white boyfriend, and the way that Lauren has internalized her own form of borderland global subjectivity. Though she enjoys the class privilege that I lack, and her relationship to the world as an "object of desire" has taken shape differently as a result, the particulars of our lives have nonetheless generated the kind of similarly complex pathways between "local and global attachments" that render the process of "worlding," as Gayatri Spivak has called it, a form of movement situated in the vulnerability of struggling to be rather than a directional mode that posits entitled experience as its end goal (Robbins 1998).

My trip to Mexico with my best friend consisted of three days spent in Mexico City visiting Lauren's uncle and other family and friends; four days enjoying the food and sights around Oaxaca City; and a week at a hippie bungalow in Mazunte, a beachside town a few hours west of Oaxaca City.

I marveled at Lauren's confidence as she orchestrated our movement between destinations with a level of "street smarts" that clearly distinguished her from your average gringa tourist (like me).

On our way from a small airport in Huatulco, Oaxaca, to Mazunte, Lauren knew how to get us onto a bus taken by locals and, for the final leg of our drive into Mazunte, a *camioneta*, or a pickup truck with wooden benches nailed into the bed for laborers and others coming and going to pile onto.

That Lauren knew we had these options, and knew to ignore the pleas of the taxi drivers who periodically pulled up to offer us overpriced rides as we waited for the bus, is reflective of how thoroughly she can embody a Latina sense of global subjectivity—a part of her identity that, despite being half

Cuban and having a father who "[has always been] so, so proud to be Latin American," she hadn't really internalized until Peru.

Born in Brazil, Lauren spent the first two years of her life in Latin America. Though she didn't begin learning to speak Spanish until high school, the various opportunities she was introduced to from that point forward—a summer in Costa Rica, an undergrad study abroad year in Chile, an additional summer spent in intensive language immersion at Middlebury College—allowed her to work toward second language fluency. But living in Peru, she says, "is what made me Latin American."

The particulars of Lauren's family history are essential to understanding how the "residue of an unnatural boundary" has influenced her ever-changing global sense of self. Today, Lauren is an ardent critic of US imperialist interventions into Latin America and has a complex sense of the relationship between communism and the US embargo of Cuba. But as a child, according to a family member, she "wanted to get rid of Castro so that I could see my family."

Her father—whom all of Lauren's close friends refer to simply as "Papi"— has long been ambivalent about the conditions of his own exile from Cuba. Never a member of the anti-Castro right wing—Lauren tells me that he has generally been supportive of Castro's politics—he nonetheless left Cuba for the US when the revolution came, a move that severed him from his parents and other beloved family members for decades.

In *Americanah*, Ifemelu's first diasporic encounter with the United States is largely motivated by the "lethargy of choicelessness" that Obinze describes above. Papi's class privilege in Cuba, by contrast, allowed him to spend time in the US prerevolution. He'd attended some high school in the states, so when the revolution came, his decision to exile himself to the United States on a more permanent basis revealed a complicated mix of the practical and political. He'd in many respects already laid the groundwork for the level of assimilation necessary to "make it" in the US in a way that immigrants with less class privilege would have a harder time doing.

After moving to New York, Lauren's father didn't see his parents until twenty-five years later, when a work commitment that took him to London along with Lauren, her mother, and younger sister opened the door for an emotional reunion. Thus, as a certain kind of diasporic though also class- and nationality-privileged subject—Lauren says she still "very much understood myself as American" despite her childhood of movement between Brazil, London, and the US—Lauren's developing sense of self as Latina was contextualized by an undercurrent of familial loss and longing refracted as much through her father's desire for reconnection as her own ambivalence about her multifaceted identity (she's also half Jewish-American). "My father's heavy accent but ambiguous national identity made things confusing for me," she recalls. English was the language spoken at home; assimilation to US white upper-class cultural norms was a prerequisite for living in a place like Chappaqua. But "when it was time to learn a language in middle school I had no choice but to take Spanish."

Here, the confluence of capital and normative heteropatriarchal authority exerted a notable influence in Lauren's life. Lauren's father is one of the most generous, loving men I've ever known but also very much a patriarch. He was able to use the capital he possessed to help mobilize Lauren in ways that, though they may have felt a bit "forced" upon her initially, did facilitate her becoming a global conduit for sustaining and further deepening connections that mean a great deal to both of them.

There's something healing for Papi, I'd argue, in the way that Lauren is able to move through the world. How she's used her impeccable Spanish skills to get to know his younger brother, Carlos, the one we stayed with in Mexico City, who has lived there in exile since the mid-1990s; how she can communicate with Carlos's oldest son, Manuel, and his family, who speak little English and live six people in a 600-square-foot stucco house in West Palm Beach, Florida. When Lauren took me to visit Manuel's family, class was very much on my mind as we drove into Palm Beach, past Donald Trump's oceanside mansion. I've yet to visit another place in the United States where the class stratification between adjacent cities is so damningly evident.

HALFWAY HOME

One key feature of the ontology of global selfhood that I'm calling "being" rather than "doing" is a certain relational circularity that is in no sense politically neutral. Working-class people who are privileged enough to experience mobility on both the vertical "economic" and horizontal "geographic" axes often feel, as Sandra Cisneros has put it, a sense of commitment to coming back for "the ones who cannot out" (1984, 110). The going away is itself motivated by a commitment to return, which casts mobility in an entirely different light than for those who are motivated by a desire to "experience" the world as something to be consumed or owned as the rightful spoils of individualist striving.

I've never felt a desire to relate to the world as a thing to be consumed, or as an experience whose coming-to-pass would itself prove whether I was "deserving," from the perspective of capital accumulation, of the right to be somewhere new, exciting, perhaps even sublime. Furthermore, one of the most memorable episodes from my Mexico vacation alerted me to the potential value in not just returning for those who "cannot out," but in perhaps bringing something of the localized, conscripted world that I associated with stagnation and even death along with me—claiming, and even loving, the "smallness" of that world as fundamental to the way that I experience my sense of self as a global subject.

Enjoying a drink in a mezcal bar in Oaxaca City, I squealed with delight when I realized that the game being televised featured the Portland Trailblazers. This is the local NBA team that I'd grown up following while my dad, who was generally unemployed, sat in front of our TV at home, escaping into a fantasy where a heroic last-second buzzer shot could make everything okay in the world.

As much as I disdained his presence, or the "black cloud" that his fatherly ineptitude and negligence cast over our family, there were nonetheless times when my dad and I would meet each other halfway, where a moment of mutually experienced joy would shine through the gray. I'd walk by the TV right at that critical instant, the team down 98–96 and 0.9 seconds left in the game, and we'd suddenly just be a daughter and her dad cheering for the team. So while the bemused men lining the *mezcalería* grinned at my over-the-top gringa enthusiasm, my dad was with me again, briefly, as Damian Lillard sank a three-point buzzer shot, ensuring that the Blazers would advance to the second round of the Western Conference NBA finals for the first time in fourteen years.

To have found a joyful aspect of the home from which I fled in a bar in Mexico, while also being there with Lauren—someone with whose path between local and global attachments had also made a particularly bleak stop in my father's own living room—is testament to the power of what can be accomplished when the ability to simply be with a friend or loved one opens an intimate "circuit of connectivity" to the world. Because ultimately, this mode of being is about knowledge—about recognizing and validating difference from a place where what's universal, or the same, is a shared commitment to openness itself.

NOTES

1. Freud's deployment of the concept of "fate" is remarkably similar, in terms of its classed implications, to the idea of Calvinist predestination that Max Weber explores in *The Protestant Ethic and the Spirit of Capitalism*.

2. Including Nigeria, though the bulk of African immigrants to France come from Algeria, Morocco, and Tunisia. As reflected in *Americanah*, the majority of Nigerian immigrants to Europe move to the UK, unsurprising considering Nigeria's history as an English colony and current status as a member of the British Commonwealth. See "In France, All Immigrants Are Not Equal," by Michael Cosgrove, http://www.theguardian.com/commentisfree/2010/apr/23/france-immigrants-discrimination; and "Nigerian Immigrants Struggle with British Identity," by Victor Obasaju, http://www.huffingtonpost.com/indiana-university/nigerian-immigrants-strug_b_5265055.html.

Chapter Four

Survival Strategies for Working-Class Women as Junior Faculty Members

Lynn Arner

As a graduate student in English, I eagerly thumbed through feminist theory anthologies, chronically searching for theorizations of gender and class in academe. I never found those articles. Instead, I found Donna Langston's "Tired of Playing Monopoly?" a smart piece, but I never understood why Langston relentlessly performed the autobiographical at the expense of the theoretical, when the writings of Pierre Bourdieu clearly structured her essay; seemingly, the theoretical had to be hidden or the piece would somehow be elitist and insufficiently working class, a participant in what Langston calls "academic jargon [used] to justify and rationalize classism" (Langston 2000, 399). I found such logic disturbing, as if working-class scholars were too feeble-minded to comprehend and mobilize complex theories for their own purposes.

I vowed to someday write a theorized article on gender and class in academe that would be heavily anthologized in women's studies textbooks. I realize now the naïveté and arrogance of that vow. However, I never stopped looking for those theoretical pieces on gender and class in academe and have found little.

Now tenured, I have started crafting my own pieces on working-class woman in academe, with my analyses unapologetically thought through contemporary theory, and this chapter represents one such piece. This chapter traces some of the web of disadvantages that routinely envelop working-class women who are junior faculty members at American colleges and universities (that grant a minimum of a BA), disadvantages that make the playing field more arduous for these women than for their male counterparts and for their middle-class colleagues of either gender. This chapter also outlines strategies for negotiating this terrain.

I focus primarily on the discipline of English not only because I am an English professor, but because English is conventionally considered the central pillar of the humanities and because the importance of social class is heightened in a discipline whose central mission is curating a rich cultural legacy for its inheritors.

THE DEMOGRAPHICS OF THE PROFESSORIATE

What proportion of the American professoriate is from working-class backgrounds? Analyzing the data elicited from thousands of faculty members by the Carnegie Commission on Higher Education in 1969 and collected in their subsequent survey in 1975, Seymour Martin Lipset and Everett C. Ladd Jr. determined that approximately one-quarter of faculty members across the disciplines at American universities and colleges come from working-class backgrounds, origins considerably more common among older faculty members. As a pool of laborers, female faculty derive from somewhat higher socioeconomic backgrounds than their male colleagues: in the 1975 survey, for example, 21% of female faculty had parents in blue-collar occupations, compared to 27% of the male faculty, a disparity echoing previous studies (Lipset and Ladd 1979, 320–24 and 332).[1]

Melinda A. Zeder detected similar patterns in a 1994 survey conducted by the Society for American Archaeology of its members: the majority of respondents reported being from the middle classes (56% of the men, 54% of the women): fewer men than women (20% vs. 27%) reported being from the upper classes; and more men than women (24% vs. 19%) reported coming from the lower classes (Zeder 1997, 14).[2]

According to the 2013 Survey of Earned Doctorates (SED), advanced degrees were held by 39.6% of the fathers and 29.9% of the mothers of new PhD recipients who were either US citizens or permanent residents. Irrespective of nationality, 43.2% of the fathers and 32.5% of the mothers of new PhD recipients in the humanities held advanced degrees, rates higher than in any other academic division, just as a smaller percentage of these parents (21% of fathers and 24.4% of mothers) than any other academic division had completed only high school (National Science Foundation 2014). Such statistics indicate that the middle and upper classes are strongly represented among PhD recipients, especially in the humanities.

Class is a large determinant not only of who joins the ranks of the professoriate but also of *how* one joins. Lipset and Ladd demonstrated that class background has a strong bearing on where a PhD holder will teach. Prestigious, research-based universities draw their professors disproportionately from the higher social strata, with faculty members' children typically being the best placed, followed by the progeny of those in big business and professionals. By contrast, the children of the working classes and from farm backgrounds most commonly teach in the lower-status colleges (Lipset and Ladd 1979, 323–24). Other studies, such as the work of Diana Crane as well as Kenneth Oldfield and Richard F. Conant, have likewise demonstrated correlations between familial socioeconomic status and the prestige of a university into which a permanent faculty member is hired (Crane 1969, 1; Oldfield and Conant 2001).

The most important determinant of the jobs that candidates will be offered is pedigree. As Dorothy E. Finnegan explains in her examination of segmentation in the American academic labor market, "For graduate students who aspire to top-tiered positions, securing entry into the professorial system means relying on sources of prestige external to themselves; the prestige of their institutions, graduate departments, and mentors plays a combined ascriptive role in securing the first academic position" (Finnegan 1993, 621). Studies by Robert McGinnis and J. Scott Long and by Michael J. Shott likewise conclude that pedigree has a considerably stronger effect than scholarly productivity on where a new PhD holder will be hired (McGinnis and Long 1997; Shott 2006). Similarly, Aaron Clauset, Samuel Arbesman, and Daniel B. Larremore, analyzing the placement data of nearly nineteen thousand faculty members, found that the prestige of a doctoral institution is of monumental importance in where a doctoral recipient is hired and that "faculty hiring follows a common and steeply hierarchical structure that reflects profound social inequality" (Clauset et al. 2015).

In the discipline of English specifically, David Colander has demonstrated the profound influence of pedigree on tracking patterns in PhD placements. Based on rankings from the *U.S. News & World Report*, Colander divided the over 130 American graduate programs in English into four tiers: the first tier, consisting of programs ranked 1–6; the second tier, ranked 7–28; the third tier, ranked 29–62; and the fourth tier, ranked 63 and below. Colander explains that while students in the top programs have reasonable chances of garnering tenure-track jobs at a "national research university or national research liberal arts colleges, the chances for such placements are essentially nil for students graduating from lower-ranked programs." The top six English programs derive nearly 60% of their tenure-track professors from the other top six programs; over 90% from programs in the top two tiers; and 0% from the fourth tier. A PhD holder from English programs in the fourth tier has a less than 5% chance of garnering a tenured or tenure-track post at either second- or third-tier universities and a less than 7% chance of getting a tenured or tenure-track position at the liberal arts colleges ranked 1–28. Most fourth-tier PhD holders who find tenure-track jobs end up at fourth-tier research universities, at local liberal arts colleges, or at community colleges.

Those with third-tier PhDs fare marginally better, holding 4.6% of the ten-ured and tenure-track posts in first-tier PhD programs and 7.07% of such posts in second-tier schools (Colander 2015, 139–43; see also Wu 2005).

Regarding part-time labor, in his study of history placements, Robert B. Townsend found that in the top-tier programs, lesser ranked PhD-granting institutions are much more readily found among part-time than full-time instructors. In departments that do not confer PhDs, significantly more full-time faculty received their PhDs from a top-tier institution than from lesser ranked PhD-granting institutions, although in the part-time labor pool, most instructors earned their degrees outside the top tier (Townsend 2005a). Such studies imply that PhD holders from less prestigious humanities programs are overrepresented in part-time posts.

Who earns degrees from the most celebrated schools? Not surprisingly, students from affluent backgrounds are dramatically overrepresented at both the undergraduate and the graduate levels in these institutions. In *Degrees of Inequality: Culture, Class, and Gender in American Higher Education*, Ann L. Mullen argues that socioeconomic background has become less of an indicator of college attendance than for the *type* of college or university a student attends. Elite colleges and universities graduate overwhelmingly the children of privilege, in terms of class and race, while the lowest-ranked universities disproportionately educate students of color and of lower social origins (Mullen 2010, 5–9; see also Bourdieu and Passeron 1979, 7). Antho-ny P. Carnevale and Stephen J. Rose explain that 74% of students at the 146 top colleges are from families in the highest quartile of the socioeconomic status scale, compared to only 10% from the bottom half (2004, 106).[3]

One benefit of top-tier colleges is that they provide greater access to graduate studies (Carnevale and Rose 2004, 109). Accordingly, in his study of the undergraduate origins of history PhDs, Townsend found that the doors to graduate studies at elite private American universities are largely closed to students who received their previous degrees in public institutions, with the exception of a few universities with top-tier PhD programs (Townsend 2005b). As Diana Crane explains, even when lower-class students do obtain PhDs from major universities, they are less likely than their middle-class counterparts to subsequently acquire positions in major universities (Crane 1969, 1).

The gendered distribution throughout the professoriate has been well doc-umented. The National Center for Education Statistics (NCES) determined that in 2013, full-time male faculty outnumbered full-time female faculty (436,456 vs. 354,935) in American degree-granting institutions. The number of male full professors was more than double that of female full professors (125,836 vs. 55,694). Men also outnumbered women at the associate level (87,420 vs. 67,675), although there was near gender parity among assistant professors (82,331 men vs. 83,714 women). Outside the tenure stream, men were outnumbered by women in full-time posts, both as lecturers (16,588 vs. 20,140) and as instructors (42,877 vs. 56,427) (NCES 2014). In 2011, the NCES indicates that at public and private universities that grant the minimum of a BA, men constituted the majority of full-time faculty, while at two-year colleges, women formed the majority of full-time faculty (NCES 2012).[4] Likewise, at all types of doctoral, master's, and baccalaureate institutions, men outnumber women as full and associate professors, while as lecturers and instructors at all these types of institutions, women outnumber men, with the sole exception of parity in the number of lecturers at private master's-level institutions (Benedict and Benedict 2014, Table 12).

Regarding English departments specifically, "Women in the Profession, 2000," a report issued by the MLA Committee on the Status of Women in the Profession, explains that, according to a 1995 study by the National Endowment for the Humanities, the largest group of white male faculty members were full professors; the largest group of men of color were associate professors; the largest group of women of color were assistant professors; and the largest group of white women were instructors, adjuncts, or of comparable ranks (McCaskill et al. 2000, 201). Gendered discrepancies in the volume of degrees conferred cannot account for such employment inequities, since, according to the NCES, women have earned more PhDs in English than men each year since 1980–1981 (NCES 2013).

In short, as the distribution of working-class academics and female academics across the professoriate indicates, working-class women are the least likely group to make it into the professoriate. When these women do enter the professoriate, they are the least likely group to hold tenured and tenure-track posts and are disproportionately relegated to the contingent labor pool. When they do obtain tenured and tenure-track posts, working-class women are the most heavily represented in the low-status colleges and universities.

Given this state of affairs, what is the best way to negotiate being a working-class female junior faculty member? I am not suggesting that working-class women should attempt to bourgeois-ify themselves, as if such outcomes were achievable (or desirable). Instead, my goal is to help working-class women identify some difficult spots in an uneven terrain that frequently cause them to stumble as junior faculty members and, where possible (sometimes it is not), to offer strategies designed to help them better navigate this terrain, while maintaining their integrity—and, if they wish, their pro-working-class politics and identifications.

SURVIVAL STRATEGIES ON THE JOB MARKET

The most important rule of thumb is that, as a general modus operandi, because of the dramatically uneven playing field, working-class women need to resist internalizing setbacks in the profession. In practice, such resistance means, for example, that when working-class women are beaten out by Princeton, Yale, and Berkeley PhD holders for tenure-track posts in the more esteemed PhD-granting English programs or in top-ranked liberal arts colleges, it is important to recognize that hiring committees' decisions have less to do with the performances of individual job candidates and more to do with the pedigree and the prestige of the successful competitor's educational history and with an elaborate network of class- and gender-based dynamics enveloping such interviews (Arner 2014). Working-class female scholars should avoid chastising themselves for not being finalists for such posts and should not automatically assume that they performed poorly during the preliminary interviews, holding themselves culpable for forces largely beyond their control.

As the post-PhD years pass, it is crucial to keep privilege and its rewards in mind: because of the advantages accrued to those with prestigious degrees and teaching posts, the claim that graduate students and faculty at well-pedigreed institutions possess more promise and talent than those at lower-ranked universities becomes a self-fulfilling prophecy. Better faculty posts typically garner more research time, more research grants, more effective professional networks, better publication records, and more influence in the discipline (Clauset et al. 2015). In short, working-class women should not blame themselves when they fall short of their aspirations: the unequal playing field disadvantages such women in myriad ways while overadvantaging their better-heeled competitors and male colleagues.

Despite the intense class-based and gendered tracking patterns in hiring, working-class women with recent doctorates should not abandon their hopes of obtaining desirable tenure-track posts. However, working-class women who long for jobs in the top-tier PhD schools may need to think more expansively about their options for good permanent posts. Since tenure-track jobs in the first three tiers are beyond the grasp of most working-class women, except for those rare women who received their PhDs from top-tier programs, working-class women who attended third- or fourth-tier programs should not squander their precious immediate post-PhD years in contingent posts at top research universities or at the most celebrated liberal arts colleges working hard to please these departments, naïvely thinking that if their publication records and teaching stats are stellar, they will be hired into tenure-track lines at these institutions. Rather, these young scholars need to invest sufficient energy in their research and publications to secure good tenure-track jobs at the institutions more likely to commit to them long-term, such as fourth-tier research universities, liberal arts colleges that are slightly less celebrated, and comprehensive universities.

Simultaneously, new PhD holders should keep in mind the Modern Language Association's (MLA) statistics regarding how many years post-PhD one could reasonably expect to be hired into a tenure-track line: within the first year of PhD conferral, a job candidate has the greatest chances of being hired into the tenure track, and these chances decline with each passing year (Hutcheon et al. 2002, 206; MLA 2010, fig. 12). This decreasing window does not mean that a candidate should leap into the first tenure-track job offered, if the teaching load, location, and other factors are thoroughly unappealing. Instead, these statistics convey the importance of working hard to generate well-placed publications during the first several years of the post-PhD career.

While waiting for a desirable tenure-track job, it is strategic to maintain as light a teaching load as possible. Colander explains that PhD recipients from the most celebrated English programs are more likely to go into research-based postdocs than students from lower-ranked programs (Colander 2015, 140). PhD recipients from lower-tiered programs are more likely to be offered postdocs and other temporary posts with heavy teaching components, with little time or funding for research. Obtaining a research postdoc typically propels a young academic dramatically ahead in her publication trajectory.

Keeping this advantage in mind, rather than assuming heavy teaching loads in the immediate post-PhD years as contingent faculty, if at all possible financially, it is strategic to maintain a light load to invest time in publications. Most working-class female graduate English students teach numerous courses during their PhD studies, in part because of limited familial support and in part because they do not usually attend the top programs. As Marc Bousquet points out, although in the wealthier private research universities English PhD students may teach one or two courses in only two or three years of their fellowship, English graduate students elsewhere frequently deliver as much as five to seven years of full-time teaching before completing their doctorates (Bousquet 2008, 23–25). Consequently, most working-class women with newly minted PhDs in English have sufficient teaching experience to satisfy hiring committees.

SURVIVAL STRATEGIES ON THE TENURE TRACK

Another wish fantasy I had as a graduate student was to coauthor a book with Pierre Bourdieu on class and gender in academe. Sadly, Bourdieu died before I had a chance to approach him with my scholarly proposition. Nevertheless, his work on class can be mated with feminist theories to analyze the terrain for working-class female scholars. Just as Bourdieu demonstrates how thoroughly class infuses education (Bourdieu and Passeron 1979; and Bourdieu 1996), the nexus of socioeconomic class and gender subtends everything from the jobs a scholar will be offered to the quotidian interactions with students, colleagues, and administrators.

In the humanities, feminist theorists have produced sophisticated analyses of the ways in which gender structures careers in American academe (e.g., Wiegman 1999; Messer-Davidow 2002), while critical race theorists (often also theorists of gender) have generated sophisticated analyses of the ways in which race structures academic careers (e.g., Wallace 1990; Bramen 2000). There is not an equally rich body of comparable humanities scholarship theorizing the effects of class.

This dearth of such theoretical analyses is overdetermined: this gap is produced by the obliviousness to class among most of the current professoriate; this scarcity results from commonplace, impoverished understandings that foreground economic class at the expense of social class, although the latter is more insidious in academe; this shortage results from the lack of agreement regarding how to categorize socioeconomic positions in contemporary America; and this dearth results from the seemingly self-evident nature of gender and race but not of class (for example, most people assume they can identify a person's gender and typically race, but socioeconomic position seems more elusive). Furthermore, this dearth is encouraged by the entrenched convention of discussing class in sustained autobiographical modes, as in Langston's essay, an approach that feminist theorists have critiqued as highly problematic and have largely discarded (e.g., Alcoff 1995; Callaghan 1995; Sawhney 1995; Elam 1995).

Praxes surrounding socioeconomic class in the professoriate need to be thought akin to the complex ways in which feminist theorists and critical race theorists have learned to think their careers through gender and race, as an elaborate, complicated network of practices with effects that are typically heavily mediated and subtle: it is enormously helpful to borrow preexisting theoretical models, including concepts and methodological formulations, from other subfields (not only feminist and critical race theory but also queer and postcolonial theory) to guide our understandings of this complicated web of disadvantage. While we wait for—or help to propel—the intellectual conversation about class in academe to become as theoretically sophisticated as the analyses offered by these other subfields in the humanities, individual scholars can deploy their theoretical training in gender and race to think, by way of analogy, through the mediated effects of socioeconomic class in their lives in academe.

As Pierre Bourdieu and Jean-Claude Passeron explain, the arts in academe promote bourgeois aesthetics and understandings of the world (Bourdieu and Passeron 1979, 17–27, 67–76; see also Bourdieu 1984, part I). Practitioners of the humanities are expected to embrace and perpetuate such bourgeois aesthetics and politics. Consequently, a working-class scholar should proceed with caution when discussing class with other academics; class in the professoriate is not a topic that typically endears a scholar to her colleagues.

As part of their enculturation, many, if not most, working-class academics sever identifications with, and political commitments to, their original communities, especially since, as Claudia Leeb argues, an abjection of the working classes, especially working-class women, generally subtends academe (Leeb 2004, 112–30). Because working-class scholars are heavily encouraged to identify with, and support, bourgeois interests, a large proportion of working-class academics attempt to assimilate with their middle-class colleagues, either consciously or unconsciously and to varying degrees. Such assimilationists can be unenthused when pro-working-class colleagues discuss their socioeconomic positions, since recruited members of the subaltern classes might not wish to be reminded of their backgrounds, for sundry reasons, including feeling shame about their backgrounds. Such recruits may resent being outed and may grow impatient, or annoyed, when a pro-working-class colleague attempts to engage in conversation about their respective class backgrounds.

Similarly, when working-class faculty members discuss their socioeconomic positions with middle-class colleagues, the latter can become defensive, since few people enjoy examinations of their privilege as a topic of conversation. Because tenure-track jobs, and resources more generally, are so scarce in the humanities, a middle-class scholar might resent any implication that she or he has an easier terrain to traverse than a working-class scholar; with publication demands currently so inflated, most middle-class scholars work hard to succeed and therefore can demonstrate incredulity at any suggestion that they enjoyed unearned advantages. Because socioeconomic position is rarely recognized as a legitimate rubric through which to conceptualize structural inequities in academe, working-class academics who discuss their socioeconomic status can be perceived as whining, as having a chip on the shoulder, or as claiming victimhood, irrespective of their intentions, and thereby risk alienating colleagues from various socioeconomic strata.

It is equally important to proceed cautiously when discussing socioeconomic class with students. When an instructor comes out in the classroom as working class, she risks undermining her credibility. Students can resort to an essentialist identity politics whenever the instructor subsequently offers class-based analyses: students can assume that she has an ax to grind, rather than viewing her analyses as a legitimate intellectual endeavor.

At more exclusive colleges or universities, some affluent students may consider an instructor's class-based disclosure an invitation to treat her disrespectfully, since she shares a similar class position as the domestic workers, groundskeepers, skilled tradesmen, and massage therapists that the families of these students often hire, a likelihood exacerbated if the faculty member is a woman of color. Even if an instructor does not out herself, affluent students frequently detect class-based disparities between themselves and the instructor and can use this knowledge to their personal advantage, such as, for example, having their hefty-tuition-paying parents phone a dean or departmental chair to force the instructor to cater to a wealthy student's personal schedule, including granting individualized midterms and exams to facilitate a student's vacations.

In an instructor's office, on a need-to-know basis, it is sometimes helpful to come out to poor and working-class students, since such disclosures convey that earning graduate degrees and joining professions are realistic goals for young scholars from these socioeconomic strata. It is usually strategic to save such disclosures until the end of a semester, to decrease the possibility of such revelations becoming common knowledge throughout the classroom and of unleashing unintended consequences. When considering the possible consequences of disclosure, it is helpful to think of such coming out of the closet as, in many ways, not unlike coming out as gay or lesbian: the reception of such a disclosure in the classroom can produce a web of complicated consequences.

The cues through which students and colleagues alike may detect a faculty member's socioeconomic background are bound up with her bodily hexis. Bourdieu employs the term "bodily hexis" to describe the embodiment of class in one's physical being and social bearing, including the class-based ways in which bodies walk, move through space, gesture, and appear. The body—a social product—is commonly perceived as an expression of a person's innermost nature. Bourdieu writes, "There are no merely 'physical' facial signs: the colour and thickness of lipstick, or expressions, as well as the shape of the face or the mouth, are immediately read as indices of a 'moral' physiognomy, socially characterized, i.e., of a 'vulgar' or 'distinguished' mind" (Bourdieu 1984, 192–93, 207; see also Bourdieu 1991, 81–89).

The hexes of working-class bodies typically undermine their performances as academics. It is not simply sartorial selections that betray backgrounds but, more importantly, the *ways* in which working-class women wear garments, makeup, and hair styles that can mark them as out of place: more affluent academics can detect a certain "je ne sais quoi" about working-class academics that is off-putting, a sense that these scholars do not belong and are incompatible with the rest of a department or with other scholarly organizations.

Academics are rarely sufficiently well-versed—on a conscious level—to recognize what they are reading as class codes but more routinely interpret these codes as evidence of personal characteristics. Hence, because of their bodily hexes, working-class female professors are positioned to be read as less worthy and less competent than their colleagues. In short, working-class academics, especially women, risk having their corporal signifiers stripped of socioeconomic significations and replaced by meanings that construe these signifiers as evidence of other traits, especially, as possessing common, not distinguished, minds.

Bodily hexis is bound up with the ability to convey authority. In the humanities, much of this authority is incarnated as cultural authority, a sense that the practitioner is a member of a group akin to what Bourdieu and Passeron identify as "the elect," the chosen cultural inheritors who stand out against the grayness of the unenlightened multitude (Bourdieu and Passeron 1979, 1–27; Bourdieu 1984, 30–32). The ability to guarantee cultural authority is particularly important for faculty members in the humanities. Literature professors (and various other types of humanities professors, such as art historians) are expected to be the guardians of rich cultural legacies that they, in turn, are conventionally understood to curate and to entrust to a select few disciples. This cultural authority is bound up not only with the intellect and with "superior" taste but is embedded in the physicality of practitioners, a sense that the members of the elect exude authority at multiple bodily sites: for example, through elegant mannerisms, an elegant carriage, and a commanding presence.

The ways in which working-class bodies emote, gesture, and inhabit space do not bespeak cultural authority or refinement, nor do these bodies exude distinction. Instead of being rarified, such bodies are commonplace. Consequently, the bodily hexes of working-class women typically undermine their performances as professors. These women do not stand out against the grayness of the multitude for their physical comportment generally makes them blend in with the multitude. In contemporary America, working-class women have been hegemonically deemed inappropriate guardians of rarified cultural heritages. Hence, the bodily hexis of a working-class female professor undermines her authority.

A greater awareness of the semiotics of class, whereby academics recognized class codes as such, would greatly benefit working-class women. Middle- and upper-class academics who understand these codes as a class-based semiotics are better equipped to resist reading such markers as evidence of an individual's personal characteristics and are able to assess less affluent colleagues in more legitimate terms; for example, informed colleagues would be less apt to judge their working-class colleagues on such bases, for example, as the latter's unauthoritative physical presence.

Because class codes are deeply ingrained in the foundational ways that bodies move through, and conduct themselves in, the world, it is naïve to think that a working-class woman can thoroughly adopt, or even mimic, the physical presence and bearing of middle-class women, despite the exemplum that is Eliza Doolittle. With acclimatization over a long period of time, however, working-class women in the professoriate have adopted at least some middle-class behaviors, or else they would have been deemed unfit for the profession. Their physical class codes are to varying degrees hybrid or inconsistent, an admixture both from their earlier communities and from their adopted communities.

Greater understandings of corporal signifiers could help working-class women deploy at least some of these signifiers more strategically. A strategic manipulation of those codes over which she has some agency can grant her greater purchase at important moments. For instance, a working-class woman who can self-fashion her physical appearance and posture to a greater degree to accord with the dictates of academe can improve her chances of success in meetings with administrators because she will seem more "professional," thereby encouraging administrators to spend less time registering her physical bearing and greater time listening to the content of her speech. Admittedly, though, because of the ingrained nature of bodily hexes, such passing is limited. Also, such masquerades may raise ethical dilemmas about the extent to which a working-class person actually wishes to appear more middle class, since not all working-class professionals aspire to do so.

Speech is another site of embodiment (at least in part) at which working-class female academics are typically disadvantaged. Bourdieu and Passeron argue that bourgeois speech patterns are heavily valorized and rewarded in education. Such speech patterns are characterized by a sense of ease, casualness, mannered elegance, and assurance and are generally marked as authoritative. This speech typically features a steady tone and a slow, casual diction, asserting an awareness of the speaker's right to take his time—and the time of others. By contrast, members of the working classes generally lack a sense of entitlement to verbal space; consequently, they tend to speak hastily and plainspokenly (Bourdieu and Passeron 1979, 15, 20; Bourdieu 1984, 174, 176–77, 194, and 218).

For working-class women, a lack of entitlement to airtime is exacerbated by gender, since, other demographic variables being equal, women in academic settings usually occupy less verbal space than their male counterparts.[5] The implications of such disparities in the occupation of verbal space are profound. For example, working-class women who race through their ideas can appear, in the presence of hiring committees or senior colleagues, intellectually unsophisticated when they provide skeletal ideas instead of full-blown, nuanced formulations, or they can seem to be poor pedagogues, irrespective of how they perform in the classroom.

An increased awareness of such gendered and class-based patterns of behavior and comportment is helpful for a working-class female academic, although, admittedly, speech patterns are extraordinarily difficult to alter, especially in an environment where she must compete with both male privilege and class privilege for airtime. Once fully aware of such speech patterns, a working-class woman can start to exercise more control over her speech, such as moderating her verbal velocity at faculty meetings, thereby sounding more authoritative and confident than if she speeds through comments.

After she accepts that her better-heeled colleagues, especially the men, have acquired their oratory skills through acculturation rather than giftedness, a working-class woman is less likely to chastise herself for her own perceived verbal shortcomings and is more likely to accept that, over the years, she too could become an impressive orator, once she insists on her fair share of airtime and once she is further acclimatized to academe.

When a junior faculty member persists in her commitments to a visibly pro-working-class politics, articulates working-class worldviews, or engages with art through working-class sensibilities, illegibility can surround her scholarship. Working-class academics frequently pursue different issues than—or different approaches to the same issues as—their better-heeled colleagues. Consequently, colleagues, reviewers, and editors alike can have difficulty recognizing the legitimacy of such scholarship and may dismiss it as idiosyncratic or as insufficiently informed by discussions in the field. Working-class academics who have not given themselves over to the bourgeois aesthetics that (as Bourdieu and Passeron explain) structure the arts in education are susceptible to being condemned as poorly trained, ungifted, and incapable of truly appreciating art. [6]

Rather than capitulating to bourgeois politics and aesthetics, a working-class scholar can fortify her writing against potential challenges, including by choosing prose extremely carefully and by deploying sufficient endnotes. More importantly, such an author can adopt an explicitly oppositional stance, demonstrating that she is conversant with the hegemonic arguments in the field but finds these approaches inadequate, that she is deliberately deviating from these understandings rather than being incompetent, and that there are important reasons to introduce a nonhegemonic perspective into discussions of a particular topic.

When submitting a journal article—the publication venue with the heaviest gatekeeping—an author can sometimes guide the selection of reviewers by briefly explaining in a cover letter how the article is politically dissonant in the field and which groups likely constitute sympathetic readers. Fortunately, monographs with nonhegemonic politics and points of view are often easier to publish than journal articles, in part because an author participates in the selection of reviewers and in part because a monograph provides space to explain how a perspective that counters reigning assumptions makes an important contribution.

Anthologies often provide more latitude than journal articles for incorporating nonhegemonic politics, but rather than issuing formal calls for papers, most editors solicit contributions from acquaintances. With generally poorer networks than male and middle-class scholars of either gender, working-class women are not the ones who typically receive personal invitations to contribute to anthologies, especially to those central in their fields.

Given these publication difficulties, it may be some consolation that many undergraduates are more receptive than colleagues to pro-working-class politics, subjectivities, and understandings of the world. Undergraduates have rarely been sufficiently disciplined by their respective disciplines to possess a good grasp of the hegemonic assumptions structuring their fields. These students are rarely immersed in their fields to such a degree that they are able to detect when an instructor is teaching texts or offering analyses that deviate from dominant paradigms. Also, except at prestigious universities and colleges, a substantial number of undergraduates are themselves working class.

Working-class female academics should be cautious about the amount of service they undertake. As several feminist scholars have argued, including Michelle Massé and Katie J. Hogan, female academics typically bear a disproportionate amount of service work compared to their male colleagues.[7] Working-class women as a body of laborers likely perform unusually high levels of service because of both their gender and their class. Heavy volumes of service could be expected partially as a result of others' perceptions and partially because of their self-perceptions. Because working-class female professors share the same gender and comparable socioeconomic backgrounds as most of the domestic workers, spa employees, restaurant employees, salesclerks, and other service-related personnel that routinely wait on middle-class Americans, working-class female faculty are the group most likely to be perceived as particularly well-suited to undertake service, even more so if they are also women of color.

Regarding self-perceptions, working-class women rarely possess a sense of entitlement in academe. Hence, compared to more affluent colleagues, working-class women as junior faculty members may feel a greater need to help with departmental housework and to please colleagues. Working-class women need to protect their research time and avoid being cast as departmental serving wenches, a role facilitated by male privilege but also not infrequently facilitated by a stronger sense of entitlement among middle-class colleagues of either gender.

Working-class female faculty members can strain relations with senior colleagues and administrators over class-based issues involving students. The attitudes of some better-heeled colleagues can be trying, if these colleagues assume that working-class students do not require substantive educations because such students have low career expectations or are ill-equipped for intellectualism. Working-class junior faculty members can encounter dissonance with colleagues over the distribution of student awards, since criteria such as efficient timelines through programs are typically rewarded, although efficiency, as Bourdieu and Passeron explain, is routinely facilitated by familial wealth, rather than being a legitimate index of talent (Bourdieu and Passeron 1979, 2, 9–14; see also 70–71). It is often possible to convince fellow adjudicators to support a competitive working-class student by pointing to evidence of her economic disadvantage, such as engagement in substantial paid employment during the semester.

A working-class female faculty member would do well to resist overidentifying with working-class students and investing inordinate amounts of time trying to assist them in much more labor-intensive ways. Because working-class academics know the pitfalls that commonly ensnare working-class students, the former can be tempted to go to Herculean lengths to aid the latter, such as, for example, offering free one-on-one tutoring in writing to those who write poorly. Doing so may jeopardize precious research time in an early career. As airlines warn, put on your own mask first and then assist others. In the long run, more working-class students will benefit if a working-class faculty member produces sufficient research to secure tenure.

UNEARTHING CLASSISM IN ACADEME

The web of classism is so thick and subtends academe in such foundational ways that it is hard to know how to effectively take on this behemoth. Yet because working-class faculty members represent one-quarter of the current American professoriate, and even more of the student body, the working classes possess the ability to become a vast army of theorists, ethnographers, and survey-designers collaborating on multiple fronts to ferret out the complicated and nuanced mechanisms and logic by which classism thrives in academe, the classism that produces such commonplace outcomes as the funneling of disproportionate numbers of talented working-class students and PhD holders out of academe, the generation of contempt for the masses, and the general reproduction of the socioeconomic order.

When considering how cultural theorists can grapple with this hydra, I believe that, in addition to borrowing insights from Marxist theory and especially British cultural studies, the last thirty years of feminist theory is a good place to look: although too much feminist theory has underestimated the importance of class, and in many cases replicated classism, feminist theory is an intellectual goldmine that offers a plethora of tools, methodologies, and insights to mobilize and alter, to analyze the complexity of class in academe.

I am inspired by Eve Kosofky Sedgwick who, in her *Epistemology of the Closet* in 1990, lamenting the impoverished understandings of sexuality compared to the complexity of analyses of gender, drew on her extensive training in feminist theory and set out in her brilliant book to propel changes in conversations about sexuality (Sedgwick 1990). A quarter century later, in part thanks to Sedgwick, discussions of sexuality are incredibly rich and complex. I would like for us cultural theorists who care about class to emulate Sedgwick's model; and, a quarter century from now, I hope that a field of what I'll for now call "class theory"—class being another closet that needs analyses of its epistemology—will be as intellectually rich and as vibrant as feminist theory and queer theory are now.

NOTES

1. On the higher socioeconomic backgrounds of women, see also Finnegan, 635–36, 641, and 647.

2. Regarding academics specifically, 21% self-identified as lower class and 24% as upper class (cited as personal communication in Shott 2006, 231).

3. Socioeconomic status here is measured by combining family income and the educations and occupations of parents.

4. Statistics on this topic for 2013 are not posted and do not appear to have been collected.

5. On conventional gendered speech patterns in American classrooms, see, for example, Martin 2000, 88–90.

6. On this logic, see Bourdieu and Passeron 1979, 14–27, 67–76.

7. On service by female professors in literature and language programs, see, for example, Massé and Hogan 2010, esp. Hogan 2010.

Part Two

Teaching

Chapter Five

Boundary Crossing

Social Class and Race in the Classroom

Andrea D. Lewis

My father was so embarrassed. One hot summer day we went to visit my great-aunt who lived in a metropolitan high-rise apartment building for seniors. I remember seeing box fans turning rapidly in the window. In my six-year-old inquisitive voice, I asked, "Why don't you have central air?" This was my first lesson in social class.

As demonstrated by research and real life, social class in the United States is a political construct that defines one's position in society. Researched in depth by Karl Marx and Max Weber, social class is characteristically dependent on an individual's level of wealth, power, and prestige.

There are wide variations in wealth, material possessions, power and authority, and prestige in American society. Social class affects our life experiences, professional work, and intellectual understanding of inequalities.

Traditionalists recognize three categories of social class in America: low, middle, and upper. However, in light of the nation's fluctuating economy in the last decade, new categories have been added to reflect changes in society: low, working, lower middle, upper middle, and upper. The lower class differs from the working class in that lower-class Americans live below the poverty level, while working-class individuals have low-paying, but often consistent employment such as factory and restaurant workers and nursing home staff.

The distinction between the lower middle class and the upper middle class is often the attainment of higher education. The differences in an individual's education, healthcare, social affiliations, and leisure activities are typically based on their social status in America.

According to deMarrais and LeCompte (1999, 169), "social scientists define social classes as groups of people who share certain characteristics of prestige, patterns of taste and language, income, occupational status (though not necessarily the same jobs), educational level, aspirations, behavior, and beliefs." In addition to determining where one lives, social class includes peoples' manner of talking and acting, moving, dressing, socializing, tastes in clothing, likes and dislikes, competencies, and literary and artistic forms of knowledge (Bourdieu 2001).

Additionally, social class is defined by one's occupation and income, as well as how a person relates to a process by which goods, services, and culture are produced (Anyon 1980). Pattillo-McCoy (1999) define social class as a vague concept based on socioeconomic factors and normative judgments.

The social class that is most valued is possessed by the dominant culture, which, in the United States, consists of middle-class whites (deMarrais and LeCompte 1999; Wilson 1978).

BOUNDARY CROSSING: REFLECTIONS ON RACE AND CLASS

I was raised in a predominately white middle- and upper-class community in Southern New Jersey. My parents afforded me the opportunity to live in a three-story home with decks, garden, and pool in the backyard. This was their "American Dream" in a post–civil rights movement era.

For context, I was born six years after Dr. Martin Luther King Jr.'s untimely assassination. Our neighbors included the local school superintendent, fire chief, lawyers, doctors, and prominent business owners. Although we were not rich, my parents were able to provide me with supplemental academic activities, enrichment camps at prestigious institutions, membership in highly regarded organizations, and summer vacations that provided experiential learning.

My father, the town's first black elected official, was a member of the school board. I attended the local public schools, which were known to be on a par with neighboring private schools. Our school facilities were equipped with the latest resources for optimal learning.

Though the resources were bountiful, the personal and cultural connections were not. In my education from birth through high school graduation, I had a black teacher for twenty-two days during a middle school industrial arts rotation. It was a challenging experience to have to prove myself, to be twice as smart as the white children in order to receive a hint of recognition, to serve as the representative for my race in class, and not to have a familiar face at the front of the classroom. Because of this void, my desire was to return home after college to serve as a role model and point of connection for the few black students and to break the ever-present color barrier.

Research by Bourdieu and Wacquant (1992) addressed how and why individuals tend to interact within familiar settings. Habitus is here defined as a system of dispositions and perceptions that are constructed over time and shape how individuals make sense of and act on a particular field. Habitus merges the structure of a field with an individual's preferences and everyday choices of activities. It organizes the way individuals perceive objects, events, and actions; it systematizes the social world for individuals; and it guides how individuals act in their world.

It is important to note that the habitus is not unitary or fixed and that individuals can interact in multiple social contexts. Experiences across various social spaces influence one's habitus, changing the habitus over time or being expressed in different ways as we move between varieties of contexts. Consequently, one person may be socially proximal to spaces that are relatively distant from each other. The habitus is somewhat long lasting because it reinforces itself by moving toward similar experiences and away from dissimilar ones, which gives more credence to early experiences and contexts (Bourdieu 2001).

The habitus is practiced in education through the process in which teachers make career decisions. Cannata (2010) studied teacher applicants' actions and attitudes during their initial job searches. Since habitus is controlled by individuals' social position, Cannata (2010) found that teacher applicants from different cultural and social backgrounds behave differently because their habitus has opposing principles.

Teacher applicants were more likely to desire schools that were socially proximal to their own social and cultural position. When individuals with similar habitus were brought together, they felt a bond with each other that was connected to having comparable social experiences and conditionings.

I did not receive a response the first year I applied to my home school system during my senior year of college. The second year I applied, my father ensured I had an interview. On the day of the interview, I was not necessarily nervous. The interview was held at the middle school I attended, the potential job was at an elementary school in the community, and I knew the interview panelists. At the outset of the meeting, the lead panelist made it clear that I was only interviewing for a part-time kindergarten teacher position with no benefits.

Although at times class may be more salient than race, I always believed that I was not hired by my home school district because of my skin color. I was raised in the neighborhood where the school superintendent resided. I knew the individuals who interviewed me through their children, neighborhood, religious, or organizational affiliation. I attended private school in the community for preschool and kindergarten. I was educated in their school systems from first grade through twelfth grade. I was in Girl Scouts, orchestra, sports, and church groups with their sons and daughters. I played in their homes. I graduated summa cum laude from college and was attending an Ivy League university for my master's degree. I had teaching certifications in two states and had passed both a state and national teaching assessment. But in the end, I was not good enough to educate the children of their community.

Especially in the United States, social class significantly affects the experiences of women and people of color. Social class is often correlated to ethnicity, race, and gender; therefore, it is challenging to have a discussion about one topic without referencing the other (Cole and Omari, 2003).

In the United States, social class is another mechanism used to create further divisions in the community structure. Our interactions with each other do not have to be limited by one's access to and completion of higher education, neighborhood, place of employment, or choice of clothing; however, our country's history and political nature divide us by these classifications.

Social class is an ideology of and by America that has defined our interactions, placed value on our economic status, and created a labeling system in academic institutions and everyday life. As our nation experienced economic turmoil in the 2000s, the realities of social class became more pronounced and uneven (deMarrais and LeCompte 1999).

TEACHING IN POVERTY THROUGH A MIDDLE-CLASS LENS

In my naïveté, I thought all children had access to the same textbooks, qualified teachers, and updated resources that I had as a child. When I participated in field experiences and student teaching as a child development major in college, I began to notice that the children did not have the same resources as I remembered in elementary school.

The schools, located in a large urban southern metropolis, had fewer computers in the class, and those that existed were not in working order. There were more children in the class. I grew up with about twenty classmates. These students had approximately thirty classmates. I grew up in a home in a quiet subdivision. These students resided in fast-paced housing projects.

My married parents attended college, my father had a terminal degree, and both worked professional jobs. The students I worked with in college mostly lived in single-parent homes supported by public assistance. Both of my grandmothers were senior citizens. These students had thirty-year-old grandparents.

I entered a different world each time I walked through the doors of the school. In my mind the experience would be short-lived because I was returning to my hometown to teach. I empathized with the students, but my life's work would be back home. When reality set in, and I was denied the opportunity to work in my hometown, I accepted a teaching job at the school where I had completed my student teaching.

During the preplanning and teacher orientation days, I was faced with four empty walls and no school budget for setting up my room. My mother, a veteran teacher, traveled to assist me in setting up my classroom. She inquired about my classroom decorations, school supplies, and resource materials.

In her school system, all supplies, including stickers and incentives, were covered by her school system. She and I made multiple trips to the school supply store to set up my new classroom. In a sad twist of fate, a young teacher had passed away a few years prior and her belongings were stored in a teacher workroom. The teachers on my grade level suggested that it would be an honor for me, another enthusiastic young teacher, to claim her belongings for my classroom. So with my mother's assistance and supplies from a deceased teacher, I began my teaching career.

On the first day of school I was met with bright-eyed students who looked to me for the answers to their academic questions and personal dilemmas. They did not have freshly sharpened pencils, a new back-to-school wardrobe and shoes, and an abundance of school supplies overflowing from their new book bags as I had envisioned.

Instead I purchased clothes, underwear, socks, shoes, coats, school supplies, backpacks, public transportation tokens, food, and whatever else my students needed to be successful in the classroom. When their parents did not answer notes and phone calls home, I knocked on doors.

My young students often challenged me and said I was too afraid to come to their community, and truly I was, but I did it. I went knocking and met some of the nicest and most genuine individuals I have ever met. I visited my students on the weekends, took them to run errands or back to my house. I kept students after school for tutorials and took them to sporting events. My students and their families taught me the true meaning of how to be a teacher. I learned early in my first year that teachers cannot teach a subject. They must teach individual children who have varying needs and ability levels.

Those parents knew that I was a caring teacher and for that they were eternally grateful. They fussed and cussed, but they always knew that I had their child's best interest at heart. While other teachers had their cars vandalized and stolen, mine was never touched. Most likely it was because my silver sports car was a familiar sight to the community members.

Akkerman and Bakker (2011) discussed the terminology *boundary crossing,* which symbolizes how professionals enter into work environments in which they are unfamiliar, often unqualified, and negotiate components from different contexts to achieve hybrid situations. For the author, this manifested in learning to become comfortable teaching in an unfamiliar environment.

Within the realms of today's classrooms, discussions of social class are typically combined with conversations about race because race, poverty, and low rates of educational achievement are highly correlated. Students who reside in low-income communities are often given less encouragement, have less interaction with the teacher, receive less rigorous class work, and have lower expectations for success from teachers (Akkerman and Bakker 2011). Studies focused on risk and resilience demonstrate that family income is highly correlated to a child's academic success during preschool, kindergarten, and the primary years (Jensen 2009).

Research by deMarrais and LeCompte (1999) has demonstrated that teachers favor children who share their personal values, despite the student's academic ability. Since many teachers were either born into or acquired cultural capital through their own educational advancement, and have the habits and aspirations of the middle class, many find it difficult to interact with students who are not middle class.

Studies of the school curriculum, hidden curriculum, social organization of the classroom, and authoritative relationship between teachers and students suggest ways schools contribute to social reproduction and maintaining middle-class values in the schools (Lareau 1987). Bourdieu (1977) proposed that schools draw disproportionately on social and cultural resources of the mainstream society, including linguistic structures, curriculum, and patterns of authority.

The cultural experiences of a child's home life dictate his or her success in a school environment. Lareau (1987) found that class provided social and cultural resources, but the resources must be utilized to manifest into cultural capital.

TEACHING WITHIN AN UNEQUAL SYSTEM: THE COLLISION OF RACE AND CLASS

Now back at the urban school eight hundred miles and light years away from home, I was again faced with the dilemma of my social class versus the social class of my students. It was compounded by my race.

Why couldn't these little black children receive the same quality of education as me? Why didn't they have access to more technology? Why did the schools in the northern part of town that educated the white children, which were part of the same school system, have better resources, school lunches, more computers, and supplemental programs? Why couldn't I connect with the parents of my students? My social class and racial identity collided, as I learned the careful negotiation of boundary crossing.

Kunjufu (2002) was inspired to write *Black Students, Middle Class Teachers* after a principal experienced difficulty in social class and value conflict between middle-class black teachers and poor black students. Kunju-fu (2002) detailed middle-class school scenarios, including assumptions made by practitioners who discount classism among black teachers and students.

There are often assumptions that racial connections are automatic between teachers and students of the same skin color, but when the teacher is unfamiliar with a student's culture capital, a boundary-crossing experience will have to occur for the teacher to experience success. It is not unusual for this to occur when a teacher raised in a middle- or upper-class community begins teaching in an urban metropolis.

An important question becomes: who is willing to teach in today's urban schools, which are typically located in low-income communities? In the past, black teachers valued jobs in urban schools because it afforded them a stable middle-class income (Hunter-Boykin 1992). With the increase in the black middle-class community and a decrease in the number of black teachers, black teachers are no longer confined to teaching in low-income communities (Rist 1970).

The percentage of black teachers in the United States is the lowest it has been since the early 1970s, which is credited to the era of desegregation (Hunter-Boykin 1992). A 2012 publication from the National Center for Education Statistics states that only 7% of full-time teachers are black.

Data from a 2014 Center for American Progress report echoes the finding that over the past fifty years, teaching has become a predominately white profession. Eighty-two percent of public school teachers are white, but America's students have become increasingly diverse, and as early as 2043, people of color will make up more than half of the American population.

Currently, students of color make up nearly half of the nation's public school population. In 2011, 52% of the fifty million students enrolled in public elementary and secondary schools were white. Additionally, in high-poverty urban schools, 40% to 50% of the teachers transfer within their first five years of teaching for other professions or schools in higher socioeconomic communities according to the Center for American Progress.

Within high-poverty schools, those that are almost 100% minority are often taught by a majority-white teaching force, depending on the region of the United States (Kunjufu 2002). These alarming gaps and rates detail the critical need for highly skilled and qualified black teachers.

Traditionally, the largest percentage of black teachers received their teacher preparation at Historically Black Colleges and Universities (HBCUs), which have been enhanced through legal decisions and federal initiatives. In 1977, *Adams v. Richardson* ordered states to strengthen and enhance HBCUs to become full partners in providing educational services and called for a commitment from individual states to ensure HBCUs had the same resources as predominately white colleges and universities (Hunter-

Boykin 1992). More recently, efforts by President Barack Obama have promoted excellence, innovation, and sustainability through the White House Initiative on Historically Black Colleges and Universities.

Though enrollment and interest in HBCUs is steady, there are varied reasons for the decrease in the number of black college students entering the teaching profession. While the older generation of blacks regarded teaching as a long-term commitment, many of today's college students view teaching as a stepping-stone toward a more lucrative career. Additionally, many were encouraged by their educator parents not to enter the teaching profession because of the lack of discipline in schools (Kunjufu 2002).

TEACHING PRESERVICE TEACHERS TO TEACH WITHIN AN UNEQUAL SYSTEM

It did not take long after my transition from elementary school to higher education to see my reflection in the mirror. My reflection came in the form of my college students who mostly had the same economic upbringing as me. These future teachers were being presented with similar challenges in their field experiences and clinical experiences as they prepared for careers in education.

For example, students expressed uncertainty in their ability to connect with parents of children in low-income communities who may perceive them to be snobbish because of their upbringing. Additionally, I heard student conversations around wanting to return home to teach because home is what felt familiar, as opposed to the urban schools where they were completing field and clinical experiences.

Studies by deMarrais and LeCompte (1999) confirmed that teachers favor children who share their personal values, despite the students' academic ability. Teacher education programs must find ways to prepare preservice teachers to successfully negotiate boundary-crossing experiences within coursework and field experiences. This process will look different because teacher education programs vary by racial, geographical, gender, and social class demographics across the country.

Additionally, cultural identity and familiarity are paramount to a teacher's success in the classroom. Although their research focused on black teachers in desegregated suburban schools, Mabokela and Madsen (2003) found that cultural identity among teachers affects the way they are socialized and embraced into an organization. Included in their research, cultural identity acknowledges one's sense of self as a cultural being and having manners in which the culture is reflected within the norms and values of the group. A consequence of intergroup tensions includes being pressured to act unnaturally and having a split identity at work and at home.

Boundary heightening occurs when an individual from a different environment enters an organization. The heightened awareness of differences that exist between the majority and minority brings frustration, overreliance on stereotypes, and culture shock. While their study pertains to black teachers in predominately white suburban schools, the same notions of difference can be found with black middle-class teachers in high-poverty schools. In both situations, there is a level of unfamiliarity that includes social class (Mabokela and Madsen 2003).

The same boundary heightening that exists in research by Mabokela and Madsen (2003) was also conceptualized by Barth (1969) who analyzed how ethnic groups negotiated social boundaries amongst themselves. He found that identities are socially constructed through a group's interaction with each other and that group identity does not emerge from a group's isolation from other cultures, but from ongoing contact with other cultural groups. This phenomenon relates to this chapter as the black middle- and upper-class preservice teachers negotiate their feelings toward teaching and learning in high-poverty urban schools.

In relation to education, social class is possibly one of the most significant sources of inequality in public and private schools and was one of the first factors, after intelligence, researched by scholars as a source of difference in academic achievement. Schoolchildren are often judged on how closely their social class mirrors the values of white middle-class citizens (deMarrais and LeCompte 1999). Teachers may perceive children who do not meet those standards as less capable of academic achievement than their peers who have a better command of the proper dialect, style of communication, and manners (1999).

Teachers, who play a pivotal role in nurturing and educating youth, are often the crucial link in advancing children from poor communities (Rist 1970). Teacher quality, longevity, and intentions can make or break a child's zeal to learn. A teacher's expectation of a student's academic performance has a strong influence on the student's actual performance. As Hilliard (2001) stated in a Kentucky Educational Television teacher workshop,

> The critical lesson to learn is that the power is in the teacher to make a difference in students' lives. No special equipment, reform, or technology is needed. The good news is that the solutions to the problem have been found. The only questions left are how will this information be disseminated and do we have the will to implement the solutions? There are four things teachers can do to be successful with all students: set high goals, be problem solvers and collaborate to figure out strategies, use feedback daily to plan instruction, and acquire deep content knowledge.

As a professor, I tell my students frequently that it is important for them to find their niche or purpose in the teaching profession. Just as each child is different, each teacher has her own strengths and weaknesses. It is just as important for effective teachers to know their limitations as well as their strengths.

When preservice teachers enroll in traditional teacher education programs, coursework and field experiences consisting of an assigned number of hours observing in public or private school classrooms are mandatory components of their preparation. Questions have been raised regarding the effectiveness of these practices in relation to teachers' preparation for culturally diverse classrooms (Ladson-Billings 2001).

The criticism of teacher education programs engaged in institutional practices, such as field placements, suggests that critical reflection and questioning surrounding issues of access, equity, and social justice are lacking, and that conservative ideologies emphasize assimilation and perpetuation of the status quo (Nieto 2006).

Traditional observations are often disliked by preservice teachers because they involve occasional observations, lack analytical self-reflections, and feature discussions on a broad range of topics. Additionally, teachers in training may experience a disconnect between their cognitive ability, ideals, and willingness to teach in diverse settings.

There is also the notion that teachers cling to prior knowledge and beliefs about others with tenacity, and it is often difficult for them to release preconceived notions regarding diversity and social class. These beliefs lead teachers to reject theories of white privilege and diminish the effects of past and present discrimination of others (Wiggins, Follo, and Eberly 2007).

Negative stereotypes tend to be perpetuated during traditional field experience observations, but when teachers are able to immerse themselves in placements they gain a more concrete understanding of the cultural life of the school and cultural norms of the children (Ladson-Billings 1995; Wiggins, Follo, and Eberly 2007). Immersion programs—or those in which preservice teachers spend increased hours in classrooms, have college courses in school buildings, and attend faculty and PTA meetings—are one answer to teacher educators' call for program transformation. Another response is changing the lens by which teachers are prepared.

Studies involving teacher preparation programs have shed light on the need for multicultural education and giving practitioners and faculty members concrete examples to provide a much needed paradigm shift.

In addition to truly integrating diversity practices into current teacher education programs, additional frameworks of teaching are beneficial to assisting both preservice and inservice in changing preconceived notions and learning best practices to work in diverse communities. Experiential learning, critical analysis of clinical experiences, and service learning are examples of instructional models that could be enhanced or added to teacher education programs.

CONCLUDING THOUGHTS

Whether or not preservice teachers complete their teaching careers in high-poverty urban schools, a contrasting community, or one in between, the critical component is that they do what is right for the children they serve. Given the need for more excellent teachers in high-poverty urban schools, teacher preparation programs must incorporate more effective boundary-crossing experiences for middle- and upper-class preservice teachers.

Race and class are highly complicated and personal constructs that need to be acknowledged in teacher education. As referenced in this chapter, race and class have been inexorably linked in the United States for generations and the lack of dialogue surrounding these intersections leads to difficulty in locating a framework to discuss one construct without the other. This is especially difficult for preservice and inservice teachers who must engage in boundary crossing in order to effectively teach and reach the diverse children in their classrooms.

Soto (2008, 12) compared the intersection of race and class as "watching a bird fly without looking at the sky: it's possible, but it misses the larger context." In education, this profound intersection can be the catalyst that changes a teacher's pedagogical lens to identifying the various socioeconomic and racial differences that may impact and hinder student interaction and learning.

Chapter Six

Lessons Learned

How I Unintentionally Reproduce Class Inequality

Jessi Streib

Educators not only distribute knowledge, but also opportunities. Without intent, many educators allocate more opportunities to students born with more class privilege (Bourdieu and Passeron 1977; Lareau 1989, 2003; Kusserow 2004; Rist 1970; Streib 2011). Despite actively trying to create equal opportunities for all students, I find myself complicit in the process.

In this chapter, I use vignettes to highlight examples of my teaching, draw upon social science research to show how each incident may have furthered class reproduction, and then discuss strategies I now use to avoid the mistakes I once made. By exposing my mistakes I hope to help others avoid the unintentional reproduction of social class inequality.

THERE IS NO SUCH THING AS AN INNOCENT QUESTION

It was the first time I taught my own course and the first time I wrote my own midterm. As I handed the University of Michigan students their graded midterms, one bright student, "Carolyn," reluctantly took her exam, looked at it, and sighed. Under her breath, she muttered that she couldn't remember the title of the books the essay question asked her to compare. With a blank memory, she did not write a word. She received zero points for the essay.

I froze when I heard her. I knew that what just happened was an example of class reproduction. And it was not any example of class reproduction—it was the kind I study. Despite my own awareness of how class inequality is reproduced and my dedication to undermining these processes, I had instead been complicit in reproducing the inequalities I tried to alleviate.

Let me explain. I was teaching a summer class with only nineteen students and had gotten to know them well. I knew Carolyn was a first-generation college student from a working-class background. I also knew that her classmate "Beth" was raised with far more class privilege.

As I handed out the midterm, I instructed the students to raise their hands if they had questions. After several minutes, Beth raised her hand. An essay question asked her to compare the explanations for urban inequality given by two sets of authors—how William Julius Wilson's argument compared to the argument given by Douglas Massey and Nancy Denton. Beth asked if I could remind her of the titles of the books we read by those authors.

I paused for a moment and realized that it was in graduate school that I learned to use authors' names as a shorthand for their work—likely a result of the fact that the authors were among us, at our conferences, in our circles. For the undergraduates, they were just names. I told Beth the titles of the books and returned to my seat. I assumed if others had the same question they would ask.

My assumption was wrong. Beth went on to write a strong essay. The comment Carolyn made as I handed back her graded test revealed that she had the same question but did not ask it. Carolyn's intelligent comments in class discussions led me to believe she had a strong grasp of the books she was asked to compare. Yet, by not asking her question, she could not respond to the essay prompt. Carolyn received a zero while Beth earned an A. The student with more privilege earned a much higher grade, not because she knew more, but because she asked a question.

Social class is often thought about in dry categorical terms—as an indicator of income, occupation, or education. These simple categories, however, produce profound differences in how individuals navigate the social world. Working-class parents, for example, keep their jobs, in part, by following authority figures' demands and not asking too many questions.

Wanting to prepare their children for the world they will enter, many teach their children to also be quiet around authority figures (Calarco 2011, 2014; Kohn 1969; Lareau 2003). By the time they are four years old, working-class children tend to avoid asking authority figures many questions, approaching them, or taking up too much of their time (Streib 2011).

Middle-class workers, in contrast, spend less time following orders and more time giving them. As authority figures themselves, they treat other authority figures as equals (Kohn 1969; Lareau 2003). To prepare their children for their lives, middle-class parents tend to teach their children to do the same. They coach their children to ask authority figures questions, request individualized treatment, and approach authority figures with confidence and ease (Calarco 2014; Kohn 1969; Lareau 2003). By the time they are four years old, many middle-class children have internalized these tendencies (Streib 2011).

These practiced tendencies mean that by age twenty, Beth had a decade and a half of experience asking teachers for help. Carolyn had a decade and a half of experience treating teachers as distant and unapproachable authority figures who should not be publicly questioned. Knowing their class backgrounds, it is not surprising that Beth raised her hand to ask for clarification while Carolyn did not.

Beth's A then partly reflects the socialization she received growing up in the middle class. Carolyn's zero reflects her working-class socialization. Both students knew the material. Their grades reflect class inequality, not knowledge, merit, or skill. If each applies to graduate school, Beth will appear to be the better student. In fact, she was just the more privileged one.

Lessons learned: Writing answers to students' questions on the board allows all students access to the same information. This applies to contexts outside of exams as well. When appropriate, publicly announcing answers to questions students ask over e-mail, after class, and in office hours allows all students to gain the same knowledge, regardless of whether they feel comfortable approaching professors.

EQUALITY REQUIRES INSTRUCTIONS

The following year I taught my second class. I asked my students to write a short essay. I gave them a prompt that tested their ability to understand the material and use it to make an argument. I reviewed guidelines about citations, format, and length. I did not offer specific instructions about how to organize their papers. I considered it, but concluded that many options were possible. I did not want to stifle their creativity.

I wanted to be fair. I created a rubric to ensure that I give the same weight to each component of each student's paper. I assumed I would grade based on the merit of each essay.

As soon as I began grading, my assumptions of merit and fairness were shattered.

Many of the students from privileged class backgrounds—backgrounds like mine—organized their papers in a way that made sense to me, a way that I expected, a way that I considered appropriate and clear. Many of the students from less privileged class backgrounds did not. Their theses were not at the beginning or end of the first paragraph, or the first page. The introductions did not include the information I thought was necessary. The flow of the papers was not what I expected. Information I considered irrelevant took center stage.

The box on the rubric where I was meant to write a grade for "organization" stared at me.

Was the privileged students' writing style really better—more meritorious—or was it simply the one I grew up with and shared? Did the less privileged students' essays seem organized to them, and I was just unable to see it?

What was fair? Was it fair to penalize working-class students' organizational styles for taking an approach I did not recognize? Was it fair to penalize students for being born into class conditions where a different communication style made sense, or for attending schools that did not teach middle-class writing styles? I could "correct" working-class students' essays without penalizing them, but would doing so communicate that they did not fit the mold of a smart college student?

At the same time, was it fair to not attend to the students' writing styles? If I did not correct their writing, would employers pass them over? Would graduate school admissions committees deem them unsuitable due to their writing?

Whatever I did, could I avoid privileging the class privileged and disadvantaging the disadvantaged?

Language styles are never neutral (Bourdieu 1991). Though many language styles are effective—providing consistent standards by which speakers can understand each other—not all are equally valued. The privileged tend to define their language style not as one among many equally valued styles, but as the one that is right. "Proper" grammar and "proper" organizational styles are the styles used by the middle classes (Bourdieu 1991; Delpit 2006).

Linguistic styles follow from different ways of growing up. Working-class children tend to grow up around a smaller group of people (Bernstein 1971; Lareau 2003). Since everyone knows the context, working-class children learn that they do not need to comment on it. Everyone may also know the main point of the story, as more people were around to experience it for themselves. The "thesis" of the story may need less emphasis (Bernstein 1971).

Middle-class children are more likely to grow up around more people. Their parents drop them off at extracurricular activities and take them on more trips. Middle-class children meet more adults and learn they need to explain information that is not apparent to others (Bernstein 1971; Lareau 2003). They practice communicating to new audiences.

Parents of different classes also talk to their children in different ways. Compared to working-class parents, middle-class parents are more likely to ask their children to summarize their days. They ask their children more questions and encourage them to emphasize particular details. They tend to give fewer orders than working-class parents, and instead encourage their children to make arguments for what they want (Lareau 2003).

Middle-class parents also tend to encourage creativity and originality (Kusserow 2004), while also asking their children to translate emotional arguments into intellectual ones (Walkerdine, Lucey, and Melody 2001). The result of asking children to summarize, give details, craft arguments, negotiate, make original points, and intellectualize claims is that middle-class children are routinely socialized to make the types of arguments that schools reward.

It is not easy for working-class students to learn the norms that colleges expect (Armstrong and Hamilton 2013). They have years of experience answering questions with fewer words, following instructions more than presenting arguments, and speaking to a well-known audience (Hart and Risley 1995; Lareau 2003; Kusserow 2004). In school, many working-class students then have to change to earn the highest grades. Middle-class students, by contrast, can earn high grades by expressing themselves as they always have.

There are consequences of different styles of organizing one's thoughts. Many educators do not think about how middle-class linguistic styles result from their own experiences. Rather, they see them as natural and correct. Likewise, they see working-class styles as unnatural and inferior—as something to be corrected or criticized (Delpit 2006).

Such sentiments can facilitate class reproduction. Working-class students may receive lower grades, as they express themselves in ways that make less sense to middle-class educators. They may also notice that they are corrected more than their middle-class peers, and internalize a sense that they are less smart than their more privileged counterparts. They may learn school is not for them (Bourdieu and Passeron 1977).

Even for those who make it to and through college, working-class linguistic styles can be a liability. Employers also do not think of linguistic styles as equally valid products of growing up in different classes. Rather, they use linguistic styles as a signal of competency and merit (Jackson, Goldthorpe, and Mills 2005). Getting hired can depend on talking and writing like a middle-class person (Rivera 2015).

This puts professors in a conundrum. "Correcting" working-class students' writing may make students feel that they are less smart than their peers. Not correcting their writing can make it harder for them to learn the linguistic styles that can help them find middle-class jobs. Both options unintentionally contribute to class reproduction.

Lessons learned: Clarify expectations about how papers should be organized before grading begins. Teach about theses, arguments, evidence, and flow. For the first paper assignment, include an outline of what type of information is expected in each paragraph.

SILENCES ARE UNEQUAL

"Kate," a first-generation college student from a small rural town, sat in the back of the small classroom. She obviously listened but never spoke.

For weeks I idly wondered why she did not participate, and hoped as time went by she would join the class discussion. Meanwhile, each day she did not speak I gave her a low participation grade. Participation was worth 20% of the students' grades; her silence was costly.

Finally, I took Kate aside and asked her why she rarely spoke in class. "I'm too intimidated," she said. "The other students use such big words and are so articulate. I wouldn't sound so smart."

As she said it I realized I had done it again—I had unintentionally reproduced class inequality.

By the time they are four years old, upper-middle-class children have heard over thirty million more words than poor children (Hart and Risley 1995). By the same age, upper-middle-class children have *said* more words than poor children have *heard* (1995). The vocabulary gap does not close over time. By the time they graduate from college, first-generation college students still struggle with words more than their more privileged counterparts (Arum and Roska 2014).

Styles of talking also differ by class. Upper-middle-class parents teach their children to intellectualize arguments. Working-class and poor parents more often accept and encourage emotional arguments (Walkerdine, Lucey, and Melody 2001). Educators ask students to back emotional arguments with evidence, but less often ask students who produce intellectual arguments to add more emotion.

Styles of debate also differ by class. Privileged students debate to show off knowledge and win an argument. Working-class students more often want to build consensus (Dews and Law 1995; Stephens et al. 2012).

College students from more privileged class backgrounds dominate college classrooms at selective schools (Astin and Oseguera 2004). Professors also tend to be from privileged class backgrounds (Dews and Law 1995). Their speaking styles become the norm.

Participation policies that treat everyone equally give students with class privilege an advantage. Students born into privilege know the norms and how to succeed in them. They find it easier to speak in class and are given high grades for it. Those from less privileged backgrounds find speaking in class harder, and may be penalized for doing it less. Rules that treat all students equally, regardless of their good intent, can create unequal outcomes.

Lessons learned: Set a norm of talking and try to cultivate comfort with speaking in class by including low-stakes, but required, ways for all students to talk. In small classes, this could include going around the room to say one thing each student found interesting about the readings.

EQUAL TREATMENT YIELDS UNEQUAL OUTCOMES

I was a teaching assistant in a class that required students to have a doctor's note or a death in the family to have their absence excused. Feeling aware of class differences, I also told the students that I would excuse their absence if they brought in a note from a boss that explained they were needed at work.

I had not received a doctor's note, boss's note, or notice of a death in the family from "Greg." He had missed many classes. Eventually, I asked him why. He had to take care of his grandmother who did not have health insurance. His mother worked, his father was unavailable, and he was the oldest child. It was his obligation to care for her.

I asked Greg why he hadn't let me know. His reply: "It wasn't on the list of excused absences. I didn't think it would be excused."

First-generation, poor, and working-class college students often have obligations that multiple-generation, middle-class, and upper-class students do not. The former are more likely to work for pay (Walpole 2003). They are also more likely to financially and socially support the generations above and below them, which can also draw them away from academic classes (Vallejo 2012). Their families are also more likely to experience poor health and afford fewer healthcare services (Adler et al. 1994).

In addition, poor and working-class students contend with crises that more privileged students can mitigate with additional resources. When a roommate suddenly disappears, a poor student may not be able to pay the rent and may be evicted. When a boss cuts their hours, they may need to search for a second job. Working-class and poor students are more likely to live at home than their more privileged peers (Mulder and Clark 2002). When gas prices go up, regular trips from their parents' home to college can become harder to justify. More privileged students also deal with these events, but are more likely to have the resources to pay an extra month's rent or drive extra miles. These events do not lead to their absences.

Rules that assume that everyone can attend class unless they are ill or mourning do not take into account students' different life circumstances. Accommodations for less privileged students are unlikely to be made, as the very students who need them are those least likely to ask (Calarco 2011; Streib 2011). Though unintended, absence policies that do not acknowledge students' different circumstances can reproduce social class inequality.

Lessons learned: Write flexible absence policies or verbally announce the types of absences that may be excused.

TIMING IS EVERYTHING

The students' final papers involved several steps. They were to conduct interviews, transcribe them, analyze them, and write a paper about the findings.

I warned the students that the project would take time. "People need some notice to do an interview, and the first people you ask may turn you down," I advised. "Transcribing is time-consuming. Assume it will take four times as long as the interview. Coding sounds simple, but I expect it to take you about twenty hours to complete."

A day before the paper was due, I received a panicked e-mail from "Jake." He wanted extra time to write the paper. Securing interviewees took longer than he expected, and transcribing the interviews was taking longer than he planned too.

I had reminded the students to plan their time carefully several times. I gave mock deadlines of when I thought they should have completed each stage of the project. As a result, I felt justified telling Jake that he could not have an extension. It was unfair to the students who had better managed their time.

Only later did I realize that it was also unfair to Jake, whose class background did not prepare him to do so much planning.

Planning is useful for people who have a predictable life and the power and resources to enact their will. Planning is more likely to be futile for people who have unpredictable lives, little power, and few resources. For them, unexpected events, others' orders, and a lack of money and authority make going with the flow a smarter strategy (Burton and Tucker 2009; Streib 2015).

Even after decades in the middle class, those born into poverty and the working class can find it harder to plan than their counterparts born into the middle class (Streib 2015). In addition, middle-class people's efforts to turn working-class-origin people into planners often fail (2015). Instructors who briefly remind students to plan are then unlikely to be effective. They also must contend with another fact—that their working-class students' lives are likely to still be more unpredictable than their middle-class peers (Armstrong and Hamilton 2013).

Grades that are based upon students' ability to plan are grades that may inadvertently reproduce inequality.

Lessons learned: Divide big projects into smaller steps and create mandatory, not suggested, deadlines.

EXPLAINING HIDDEN RULES STILL LEAVES A LOT HIDDEN

To stem class reproduction, I reserved a day of class to talk about cultural capital—knowledge and strategies that allow students to navigate institutions in ways that garner rewards. I explained that colleges tend to be filled with middle-class people, and that middle-class people tend to reward the type of cultural capital they gained from growing up in their class. Poor and working-class people tend to grow up with a different set of cultural capital—a set that is useful in navigating their environment but that can be penalized when navigating middle-class institutions.

I offered a few examples. One was about how to write e-mails to professors. I stressed that e-mails called for formal speech. Students should call professors by their title and exclude phrases like "What up?" or "lol." I explained that professors might mistake informality as a sign of disrespect rather than just not knowing the norms.

A few days later, I passed a student in the hall. I was lost in my own thoughts and in a rush, so when "Jennifer" said hi I barely noticed her. I muttered a belated and unenthusiastic "hi," and did not think much of the interaction.

That evening, I received an e-mail from Jennifer profusely apologizing for saying "hi" instead of "Hello, Professor Streib." Rather than teaching Jennifer the cultural capital needed to succeed, I left her unsure of the norms and fearful that she had violated them. I worried that I made it more difficult for her to talk to professors as she became hyperaware of saying the wrong thing.

Individuals who grow up in the middle class repeatedly engage in middle-class institutions and gain an intuitive sense of how to do so. Individuals who grow up in poverty or the working class tend to find middle-class institutions more perplexing. Not having grown up as an insider, the norms are foreign and the rules are unclear (Bourdieu 1984; Dews and Law 1995; Lubrano 2004; Streib 2015).

The process of adapting to middle-class institutions is not straightforward. It takes a long time to learn the subtleties of new institutions—why saying "hi" to a professor in person is appropriate but starting an e-mail with "hey" is inappropriate. Students who are new to middle-class norms are likely to make more mistakes. It can take decades to internalize them, and many do not fully internalize them at all (Lubrano 2004; Streib 2015).

Telling students about norms is not enough to undermine class reproduction, as norms are complex and rarely communicated fully. At times telling students about middle-class norms may help them. At other times it may make students feel even more self-conscious and out of place.

Even when intending to undermine class reproduction, it is easy to fail.

Lessons learned: Communicate norms explicitly and repeatedly, without critique and without assuming that the lesson was internalized the first time. Remember that norms are subtle and take repeated practice to internalize. Assure students that you understand that mistakes are likely and will not cause offense. Keep lines of communication open. Keep trying.

KNOWLEDGE ISN'T ALWAYS POWER; SOMETIMES COMFORT IS POWER

"If you think you should have received a higher grade, you can challenge it," I told my students during a lesson on cultural capital. The students from privileged backgrounds nodded knowingly. The working-class students, instead, responded with shock: "People do that!?"

One working-class student piped up: "The professor knows so much more than we do. Who are we to challenge it?"

"I don't appreciate that students challenge their grades because I also think that professors know more than students," I responded. "But if some students challenge their grades they have more opportunities to receive a higher grade than students who do not."

To emphasize my point, I let them in on a secret: "Some professors don't want to deal with students' challenges, so they raise the student's grade simply because they asked."

"Here's how you challenge your grade as to not offend your professor," I continued, thinking I was leveling the playing field by giving working-class students the same access to the hidden strategies that their middle-class peers already possessed. "Go to your professor's office hours. Say that you are confused by your grade, and want to learn how you can do better in the future. In the process, nicely ask why you got points off for things that you think you got right. It may be that the professor realizes she made a mistake."

"No way!" said one of my working-class students. "I could never do that!" The other students nodded and chimed in: "I can't believe students do that!"

There is a huge difference between access to strategies and feeling comfortable using them. Students tend to feel comfortable enacting strategies that are similar to ones they have used in the past. They tend to feel uncomfortable using strategies that challenge their ideas of who they are (Bourdieu 1984).

Middle-class students tend to grow up with a sense of entitlement (Lareau 2003). They have practice asking adults to accommodate their needs or reconsider their evaluations. Working-class children tend to grow up learning to conform to institutional requirements (Lareau 2003).

Senses of entitlement and conformity are deeply internalized (Bourdieu 1984). Like many internalized strategies, they are not easily changed (Streib 2015).

Information is not always power. Simple lessons on middle-class strategies are not powerful enough to allow working-class students to feel comfortable using them.

Lessons learned: Imparting knowledge of norms is useful, but not enough. Comfort matters too. Have students practice challenging their grades to gain comfort with the idea that they can do this. Keep sharing middle-class strategies, because it gives working-class students the opportunity to try a practice after they get used to the idea. Remind middle-class students that their strategies are not universally used. When changing a grade, find ways to change the grades of all students who made the same point on their exams, whether or not they asked for their grade to be revised.

GOOD INTENTIONS CAN BACKFIRE

Feeling like a failure for allowing class reproduction to happen in my classroom, I offered all students an opportunity to complete an extra-credit assignment. Though this strategy could not level the playing field, at least, I reasoned, it could give those whose grades suffered a chance to bring their grades up.

I did not expect the extra-credit assignment to increase inequality, but it did.

More students from privileged class backgrounds completed the extra-credit assignment—a book report—than students from disadvantaged class background. Many privileged students' grades rose; many less privileged students' grades remained the same.

Extra-credit assignments take time, and students with class privilege tend to have more time. They spend fewer hours working for pay (Walpole 2003). They are more likely to have parents who take care of routine tasks for them, less likely to need to care for others, and less likely to worry about meeting their basic needs (Armstrong and Hamilton 2013; Lareau 2011; Vallejo 2012). They have more time to complete unexpected assignments.

Attempts to level the playing field can backfire. However, they also provide valuable insights about how to teach in ways that mitigate class privilege.

Lessons learned: Make extra-credit points available from in-class activities. Activities such as an extra-credit pop quiz may better level the playing field.

PRACTICE DOES NOT MAKE PERFECT
BUT IT DOES LEAD TO IMPROVEMENTS

As I prepare for another semester of teaching, I have little confidence that the playing field in my classroom will be completely level. The lessons I have learned, however, give me confidence that my classrooms are less tilted than when I began teaching. I can partially equalize knowledge, if not immediately also familiarity and ease. I can make my classroom rules less biased, allowing all students equal chances to succeed. I can keep my eyes open for new ways in which I might unintentionally reproduce social class inequality, knowing that equality is not achieved by good intentions alone. With constant vigilance, I hope that as each year passes my classrooms become places where all students have equal opportunities to succeed.

Chapter Seven

Making Class Salient in the Sociology Classroom

Melissa Quintela

Students from different class backgrounds experience the college setting and academic material differently (Roscigno and Ainsworth-Darnell 1999; Paulsen and St. John 2002; Goldrick-Rab 2006). And while there is information on working-class professors' graduate school experiences and their trajectory through the academy (Ryan and Sackrey 1995; Mar 1995; Muzzatti and Samarco 2006), little is known about how class background affects the *academic* work of faculty members. This is particularly true in the case of pedagogical techniques used to reach students, but true also in terms of mentoring and service areas.

This chapter will focus on the intersecting social class, pedagogy, and service work of a working-class member of the college faculty. It begins with a critically reflexive personal description of the ways class is salient in situating oneself in the classroom and in the academy. It then describes how class works in terms of practices.

In contrast to class as an unconscious internalization (Bourdieu 1990), this description outlines how class operates as a very conscious reflection developed in praxis (Freire 1970). The chapter includes a discussion of how the working-class social location of the teaching professional affects mentoring techniques and service work, and ends with a critical reflection of the effect of social class on one's own knowledge of self.

A CRITICAL REFLECTION ON CLASS

As the daughter of former janitors turned HVAC technician and police officer, social class is salient to me. I'm reminded of it daily when contrasting my own experiences to the students I teach at private liberal arts universities, where the tuition for one academic year is more than both my parents' yearly incomes combined.

I'm reminded of it every pay period when I think of the massive student loan debt with which I am burdened, because my parents did not attend college and had no access to forms of equity into which I could tap. I'm reminded of it when I struggle with the decision to continue taking part-time, low-paying teaching work (that I love so but which gives no economic stabil-ity), when I also foresee a future in which I may need to care for my aging parents because, as members of the working class, they did not have access to large pension plans and at some jobs were not even allowed to pay into Social Security until 1984 (Nelson 1985).

I am especially reminded of it during class lectures, when I realize that the less privileged on whom I seek to shed light are a population that most of my students have never encountered. This awareness of difference and the ways in which I understand access to economic privileges leads me to focus on class and knowledge about class as an ontological difference. It leads me to focus on pedagogical techniques that target epistemological differences. It is the description of these techniques to which I now turn.

PEDAGOGICAL TECHNIQUES

The social class of a faculty member affects what is taught and how it is taught. Intellectual understandings of the social order lead working-class faculty to understand the "norm" in different ways than others (Sleeter 1992). Critical awareness of this ontological difference supports teaching techniques that allow knowledge to be constructed and not merely discovered (Freire 1970; Guba and Lincoln 1994).

As any "construction" of knowledge entails, each course has to begin with an examination of *what* knowledge students hold and from where it comes (Freire 1970). Four techniques for doing this are outlined below, in the form of a process that begins with an awareness of held knowledge, continues with an integration of social class into the curricula (through both subtle and explicit means), and includes a description of how the personal experiences of the professor are utilized.

These four techniques are some of many techniques used to assist stu-dents in developing the sociological imagination. Students use a sociological imagination to question the status quo and situate oneself within larger soci-ety and history (Mills 1959). This basic foundational exercise prompts stu-dents to begin thinking about different social locations, including social class.

Of the four techniques described here, "Questioning Knowledge" should occur first; however, the other techniques do not typically happen in the same order in which they are described here. When the instructor chooses to use a technique is affected by the order of the subject matter, the number of students in the class, the level of rapport with students, and when rapport is developed.

TECHNIQUES IN THE CONSTRUCTION OF KNOWLEDGE

There is a specific set of techniques the faculty member uses to discuss the sources of knowledge and how people use knowledge. The process usually begins with the Questioning Knowledge technique: a discussion of ontology and epistemology. This technique is used first, regardless of the subject matter, in order to set up the idea that everyone has different experiences and social locations that inform their view of reality.

Usually, with every class, after learning about the students, their names, interests, and what they did over the summer, I announce that I want to tell them a story about the end of my summer. This brings full attention from the class because everyone loves a good story.

The story (fictitious) begins with a description of me attending a fancy reception at the university president's house in order to welcome all faculty back to campus (this did occur once). I describe a delicious hors d'oeuvre at the reception and mention that, after about eating eight of them (this did not occur), I ask one of the wait staff for the ingredients.

Much to my and the students' horror, he describes them as earthworms, deep-fried (nor did this occur). After the gasps and gags have died down, we launch into a discussion of why eating worms is "gross."

I then present the students with information on the actual nutritional content of earthworms, citing them as a source of iron, magnesium, potassium, phosphorus, and copper, and point out that the protein gained from them is the same as when eggs or cow's milk is consumed (Gordon 1998). I then show various slides of earthworm sushi or stew, from various cultures of the world.

This story and the presentation of information alternative to the students' worldview lead to a discussion of how realities are constructed and how they vary between groups and cultures (Guba and Lincoln 1994; Cunliffe 2004). The paradigms students operate within are discussed as ontological realities, which themselves are pointed out as an ongoing accomplishment of social actors. This discussion inevitably leads to the understanding that everyone has different experiences that inform their reality and that reality shapes our understanding of the social world.

This process leads to the Integrating Class technique, in which the understanding of different experiences developed in the first technique is capitalized upon throughout the course. Because it can be a significant aspect of a working-class faculty member's experience, the topic of social class emerges as an intersection for many topics in praxis.

By integrating examples that show how class shapes an understanding of the social world, the professor points out ways in which social class can filter what people see. This helps to make class differences salient for those who may not think of them at all (Cunliffe 2004; Pearce 2012).

In the Integrating Class technique, social class is integrated throughout a course that is not centrally focused on stratification or social class. As an example of how this is done, I offer a vignette from the Sociology of Children and Youth:

This class begins with several premises basic to understanding children in the social world: all processes in life involve contact with people, we learn how to function from others, and finally, we, as humans, need contact with others in order to define ourselves and our place in the world (Corsaro 2015).

The basic principles lead to several discussions throughout the course of the class, such as the rights of children to participate in their own social processes, their own views of their life, and their strong desire for social interaction with others. Inevitably, discussions regarding children's desired social interaction with others and differences in desire at particular ages turn to young children's fears of sleeping alone at night.

It is here that I take the opportunity to integrate some of my favorite teaching materials (Pixar movies) by showing a clip from *Monsters, Inc.* (2001), a movie in which children sleeping alone in their rooms conjure fantastical stories about what lurks in their rooms, particularly in their closets, when lights go out and it is time for sleep. Students enjoy the break from theory and have a lively discussion about their own childhood fears, reasons for them, and how they overcame them.

If it doesn't happen organically, then toward the end of the discussion, I take care to point out that, as just evidenced in our discussion, not everyone has the same experiences. I ask them to also think about the fact that social class structures the very experiences they just reviewed, for not every child has access to his or her own room or the thought that monsters may exist in their closet, because they may have to share a room with siblings or sleep in a nonbedroom without a closet. I pull up one of several popular photo essays in which children's bedrooms from all over the world are photographed and we discuss social class and cross-cultural difference in childhood.

This presentation of information with an explicit critique of a middle-class to upper-class bias broadens students' understanding of social experiences. This technique can be used in a variety of courses.

For instance, in the Sociology of Immigration class, assumptions inevitably arise that peg immigrants as poor and uneducated. When that occurs, the professor points out that immigrants are usually of higher socioeconomic status than the ones who stay behind and that, by necessity, they have to be in order to afford the journey economically. Or in Sociology of Race and Ethnicity, or Race and Ethnic Relations courses, the professor links past racial discrimination to current home equity inequality and the lack of wealth among minority families and individuals (Krivo and Kaufman 2004).

In the third technique, Focusing on Class, social class is explicitly focused upon, in that it becomes a pivotal social location on which to build knowledge. Each course (regardless of subject) contains a section that specifically considers social class. For instance, in Introduction to Sociology, one week is devoted to the study of social class. The course begins with a general understanding of the concept of stratification. It then moves to an active construction of knowledge regarding what stratification actually means and how people in particular social situations have to make decisions.

The interactive online activity Spent (McKinnney.com 2011) is played and the class becomes quite lively in deciding how to survive as a single parent who has lost a job and home. Usually, I ask for a student volunteer to run the game and joke that the student will need to act as a ref and "break up fights" as there will be several points within the game when classmates may disagree on the course of action.

I first preface the game by explaining that the character in the game has access to $1,000 in his or her checking account and has a child and a pet. Students proceed to play the game, at every turn making cost-cutting decisions on housing, commuting, grocery shopping, extracurricular events for their child, healthcare, decisions about their pet, and helping out other friends and family. As the game proceeds, disagreement becomes louder; one student wants to buy all ramen noodles and is arguing with another over the nutritional value of the expensive apples.

Students began to look over at me and wail that "it is impossible" and that it is "too hard to live like this." I simply respond by encouraging them to finish the game as best they can and encourage the "ref" to take a vote when there is disagreement. Sometimes, the class will end the game with a few dollars left in their account and big sighs of relief, to which I point out that rent is due on the first of the month again and they must figure out a way to keep going.

Other times, students lose their job halfway through the game or meet an emergency situation that completely wipes out their savings and the game ends prematurely. Discussions after the game involve understanding the decisions with which people in lower SES brackets struggle and how easy it can be to fall into poverty when very little is had to begin with. The students then conduct a wealth audit (Seiter 2003) to discover the assets to which they actually have access that prevent them from getting into a situation such as the scenario in Spent.

While one of the goals for this technique in the preceding example is to engender an experiential understanding of the constraints under which the poor work when making decisions, the point is also made, through the wealth audit, that most will not ever be in a situation in which they will need to face similar conditions. The combination of ontological theory and active building of knowledge leads to a stable understanding of social class and its impact; fully 75% to 80% of students in my classes score 75% or higher on exam questions that ask about the impact of social class on social life.

The fourth technique in the construction of knowledge, Faculty Self Disclosure, involves the working-class faculty member sharing personal examples to give depth, dimension, and connection to social class concepts. Within the academy, professors are usually discouraged from revealing personal experiences, and instead, the transmission of objective knowledge is encouraged (Ferfolja, Jones-Diaz, and Ullman 2015).

However, explicitly acknowledging the personal, classed trajectory facilitates students' understanding of class in that they can connect concepts to a real person, especially when the instructor ties personal experiences to theories and concepts from the course (Downs, Javidi, and Nussbaum 1988).

While not only working-class instructors are able to utilize personal experiences as learning tools, a working-class faculty member's lived experiences within socioeconomic constraints provides students with a real-time example of how constraints may play out and a point of connection if questions remain. The Focusing on Class technique described above can be illustrated in Introduction to Sociology by the professor's own "rock and a hard place" experience.

Usually, discussion after the game of Spent turns to how easy it is for one to fall into poverty after a seemingly stable existence (with a house, job, and car). We talk about the difference between the working poor and those in absolute poverty. Of course, I cite McDonald's and Walmart employees as some of the largest groups that receive public assistance despite working full-time or almost full-time.

Depending on rapport with students, while simultaneously passing around my Medicaid card, I explain that, despite my education, I am a member of the working poor, receive public assistance at various times of the year, never buy my son or myself new items of clothing, and am on an income-based repayment plan for my student loans.

I then connect this experience to experiences of single parenthood (as in the game Spent), lack of wealth and access to resources to build wealth (as in the wealth audit), and the restrictions of academia and its effect on part-time faculty (Jacobs, Perry, and MacGillvary 2015). After a particular class session like this, several students usually stay after class to thank me for sharing my experience.

The personal experiences become a point of connection both with students who may have never had experience with someone poor and also with poor and working-class students (although there are few of these at private, liberal arts universities) who may not otherwise hear experiences similar to their own (Downs et al. 1988; Pearce 2012).

Two processes occur within this point of connection. First, when personal experiences are shared, students' level of comfort in class is usually increased and therefore students' participation and engagement in class is increased (Downs et. al 1988).

While the sharing of personal experience could also vex some students, the tying of these experiences to larger social forces empirically illustrates the sociological imagination, which, via its goal to question the status quo, can itself be a disquieting process (Mills 1959). This pattern of allegorical connection occurs for students from all backgrounds; however, students with a similar social class to the professor have their particular "situation in the world" reflected (Freire 1970, 85), which can lead to increased engagement.

Within this process, students have come to the instructor in dialogue, seeking out the faculty member as a source of support, sharing their own experiences of hardship, or wanting to learn more about the faculty member's life path.

Second, a faculty member with a similar class background to students is more likely to notice nuances in students' performance, such as evidence that they are struggling with deadlines or time management. The faculty member may be able to let first-generation students know about tutoring services, learning centers, and writing centers on campus. Because many working-class students are also first-generation college attendees, students may have little or no knowledge of such campus services because they have no direct experience with academic services and neither do their families (Stanton-Salazar and Dornbusch 1995).

The pedagogical techniques described lead to student understandings of social class in ways which may be different if taught by professors of different class backgrounds. Particular nuances of the way class operates at both micro and macro levels are made salient to the student, by virtue of the professor not only having experiences with them, but communicating these experiences through teaching and examples.

CLASS INTERSECTIONS WITH SERVICE WORK

In addition to social class serving as a point of pedagogical connection with students, faculty members' class location may affect their service work. As mentioned above, because of classroom experiences, students may seek out a faculty member for social support. Instead of seeing conditions as oppressive or limiting, a critical awareness of social class can inspire instructors to focus on situations that can be transformed (Freire 1970; Pearce 2012).

Through dialogue with students of similar class backgrounds, the faculty member can encourage students to reflect on the reasons for limits and alternative paths available. However, this is not conducted in the spirit of a "knower" transmitting knowledge to another. Rather, much like the construction of knowledge in the classroom, the dialogue encourages student consciousness and development of efficacy. The goal in this method is to move a student to be "the owner of one's own labor" in finding effective solutions (Freire 1970, 185). An example of how this process occurs at a state university follows:

Each semester while in graduate school, my dissertation advisor would invite me into her class to guest lecture on my experiences working with immigrant and low-socioeconomic-status youth in the community. Rather than a standard lecture, I would have the students participate in several theater-like exercises, such as a "privilege line" in which students physically moved their bodies according to social conditions within their lives.

I used this activity to make salient the different experiences each person brings to the college table. After each class, students would later contact me with questions about the college process, scholarship funding, mentorship, and the like.

In particular, three first-generation college, undocumented-immigrant students contacted me. They were struggling with the out-of-state tuition they were required to pay at the university (even though they had graduated from a local high school) because their status did not qualify them as residents. I, along with another graduate student in education, began to have conversations with them about the obstacles they faced, such as financial resources and a visible platform from which to let others know about their issue.

I offered the knowledge I had previously gained as a working-class student on issues such as financial aid, university structure (including rules on how to form university student groups), and laws affecting immigrant status (such as the DREAM Act). I also used my status as an instructor to reserve meeting rooms for the students, even during times at which I could not attend.

The group grew to over fifteen students. The students decided to apply to be a university student group and asked me to be a faculty advisor. I filed the paperwork and DREAM U (a pseudonym) became official. The group began to hold workshops and give lectures on immigrant student status, rights, and hardships. They gained visibility throughout the university and larger community. They requested and were granted office hours with the university president, who was sympathetic to their plight.

After about a year and a half of self-advocacy, the state university, in defiance of state regulations, granted in-state tuition to undocumented students. In the same time period, the students from this group were active at the state level, gaining an audience from several senators. Eventually, the state as a whole moved to granting undocumented immigrants in-state tuition if they graduated from a local high school.

In this case, even though the faculty member was not an immigrant, the experiences of being working class and having to navigate similar situations to the students' affected the methods used to serve students. Personal knowledge of the difficulties of financing an education with little to no financial resources led the faculty member to be sensitive to this cause. And because the "path of no funds" had been walked by the faculty member before, the faculty member was able to guide students to unexplored and unknown avenues of funding.

In addition, the faculty member's social capital regarding the requirements of university, state, and federal financial aid systems shortened the time period students themselves had to spend understanding how to qualify for certain programs. This freed their time to gain more knowledge about residency requirements and their particular situation of documentation. The faculty member then utilized this existing interest and energy to encourage self-advocacy.

COMING FULL CIRCLE:
A CRITICAL REFLECTION ON SOCIAL CLASS SALIENCY

In the classroom exercise described above, students physically moved their bodies in relation to others in the room. However, depending on the social class makeup of students, some expressed feelings of marginalization as they ended up in the back of the room.

While both Freire (1970) and Mills (1959) encourage uncomfortable experiences as a means to transformation and student development, in most college settings the "privilege line" exercise should be handled with some caution because, by virtue of structural and historical conditions (Krivo and Kaufman 2004), there will be less of the working-class populace than not and their experience may be uncomfortably juxtaposed to the majority of their classmates.

In line with the idea of knowledge being "restless, impatient and continuing," (Freire 1970, 58), the critical reflection of both social class background and the effect it has on teaching should itself evolve in praxis, such as reflected in the critical evaluation below.

Currently, while I may still use the "privilege line" in local community organizing, in the classroom I practice this technique in varied ways:

1. I will give students a sheet with all "privileged statements" written and have them add and subtract points if the condition applies to them, similar to the wealth audit. We then discuss differences in broad terms.

2. I still conduct the exercise with physical movement, but turn the exercise on its head and have students move forward when they DO NOT experience privilege, which results in the "least privileged" students being in front.

Then, similar to Freire (1970), I point out how access to a variety of social experiences such as theirs is useful in that it gives crucial insights into societal conditions and reasons for them, for which others may not have a clear understanding. These contradictions about reality may lead to transformation, both in terms of knowledge and personal development.

In the pedagogical practice and reflection above, the instructor's working-class status itself also morphed in depth and dimension, even while serving as a source of university cultural capital for others (Stanton-Salazar and Dornbusch 1995; Cunliffe 2004).

CONCLUSION

This chapter begins and ends with a critical description of the ways social class is salient in situating oneself in the classroom and in the academy. Through a reflectively conscious process, the ontological understanding of social class and economic privileges leads to discoveries of "existential experience" and transformation (Freire 1970, 61), both for faculty and students.

This analysis discussed four pedagogical techniques that allow social class differences to become salient and support transformation, but it has also shown how the particular social location of the teaching professional nuances this process.

The effect of social class on the pedagogical techniques and service work of working-class members of the college faculty may, of course, play out differently than described here, depending on the particular experiences of the faculty member. However, it is of utmost importance to acknowledge that class background *does* affect academic work in many ways, from pedagogical techniques to service work with students of similar class backgrounds.

Chapter Eight

Witnessing Social Class in the Academy

Dwight Lang

Witness so that people may find love and fellowship. (1 John: 3–4)

Our interests and efforts can be traced back in time—even before memory. The "mysterious quality" of the present is often understood by exploring the "deep past"—often invisible, yet profoundly significant (Lemert 2012).

I grew up in Rio Linda, California (north of Sacramento), with working-class parents who felt everyone should have a fair chance to develop their talents. A thorough Catholic education—grade school through three years of college, 1960–1970, reinforced the idea that all human beings deserve respect.

I attended a Roman Catholic seminary for nearly six years (1964–1969) where we were encouraged to improve lives of the disenfranchised. Concerns with social injustice remained strong even after leaving the seminary and I eventually completed a bachelor's degree in social welfare. During a counseling internship I observed the daily struggles of those affected by poverty and unemployment. I witnessed desperation in the eyes of middle school students and their parents.

WITNESSING

The dictionary tells us that a witness has personal knowledge of something: to witness is to know by direct understanding. Even though I no longer consider myself a Christian believer I still think about the Bible's important message of witnessing as a way to support one another and build community solidarity.

"Conduct yourself with wisdom toward outsiders, making the most of the opportunity. Let your speech always be with grace . . . so that you may know how you should respond to each person" (Colossians 4: 5–6). The Apostle John testified to the healing component of being present with others, of witnessing "so that people may find love and fellowship."

As a sociologist I have always been concerned with those on the margins of society—especially the poor and working class who feel invisible. I advocate for policy initiatives that help achieve justice for those left behind in powerful globalization processes of twenty-first-century capitalism. Of course, this is related to where I was born in our social class structure, but it is also a part of my teaching, research, and writing interests over the years (Lang 1987; 1995; 2012; Lang and Lang 2013).

FIRST-GENERATION COLLEGE STUDENTS@MICHIGAN

At this stage of my career, since 2008, I have had the opportunity to act as faculty advisor to the University of Michigan's Sociology Department–sponsored undergraduate organization: First-Generation College Students@Michigan (First-Gens@Michigan). This role is a natural extension of my teaching about social class difference. Students seem to appreciate the presence of a person who has firsthand experience as a first-generation college student and can offer advice from a deep working-class past.

While I explore the "upstream" causes of structured inequality in courses I teach (e.g., how capitalism functions to maintain social class difference; lack of jobs; how culture and politics justify suffering associated with class inequality), I witness firsthand the difficult "downstream" outcomes (Grusky 2014) of social class stratification in a university setting where approximately 3,400 undergraduates (13% of the undergraduate population) are first in their families to attend and/or graduate from college (first-gens). Most of these students are low income and nearly 1,200 first-gens have grown up in poverty. Michigan seeks to be a campus where working- and lower-class students feel connected: thriving and not merely surviving.

FIRST-GENERATION EXPERIENCES ON COLLEGE CAMPUSES

Low-income first-gens are often invisible on campuses where continuing-generation students (continuing-gens—students whose parents graduated from college) are in the majority. First-gens can feel out of place and overwhelmed (Hertel 2002), less integrated into campus culture, and have less interaction with peers outside the classroom. They find their own way on campuses where continuing-gen values and experiences represent the norm (Lightweis 2014; Pascarella et al. 2004; Reay et al. 2009; Stuber 2015).

Middle-class staff, faculty, and students can view first-gens as miracles—individuals somehow wanting to escape flawed family and community settings, seeking to develop preferred middle-class identities and position, as Hurst and Warnock (2015) have described. Upwardly mobile first-gens also confront feelings of self-doubt (Engle et al. 2006), being outsiders, imposters, "straddlers" between two worlds, or not being authentic (Dews and Law 1995; Lubrano 2004; Hurst 2010).

Social class "downstream" outcomes are usually invisible on campuses where first-gens find it hard to openly talk about integration into campus culture. But at First-Gens@Michigan activities and during office hours I hear powerful stories of struggle and persistence. I witness the difficult sides of starting new lives. This can be hard for eighteen- and nineteen-year-olds experiencing college as a portal to the middle class. I admire the risk-taking and boundary-crossing strengths of today's first-gens who quietly take chances in a place that feels like a foreign culture. I am reminded of my own complicated journey.

These largely invisible "downstream" outcomes include the following experiences shared in first-gen group meetings and individual conversations:

- Realizing the dorm you move into for your first year of college is better than the home you have lived in for the past eighteen years
- Dealing with parents who are unsure that going to college is a good idea
- Hearing sympathetic, more affluent students ask what it was like to "grow up in nothing"
- Work-study hours that take away from needed study time
- Being unable to take unpaid summer internships, because summer wages must pay for books and tuition
- Having no money to travel with overseas educational programs
- Hearing rude comments about trailer trash and ghetto inhabitants
- Interacting with large numbers of more affluent peers and adults for the first time in one's life
- Hearing continuing-gen peers question with wonder how anyone could possibly overcome insurmountable odds
- Feeling self-conscious and exotic on a campus dominated by privileged students, faculty, and staff

SOLUTIONS TO CAMPUS ISOLATION

An unrelenting sense of isolation and difference is not easy to overcome in the early weeks and months first-gens step foot on continuing-gen majority campuses. Desperate feelings of marginality can be successfully addressed by colleges actively seeking to improve first-gen adjustment and engagement. Participation in extracurricular activities (Pascarella et al. 2004; Tinto 1999) and opportunities to connect with first-gen peers contribute to adjustment, academic success, and persistence (Lehmann 2013; Woosley and Shepler 2011).

Involvement with a college's social and peer networks can have positive effects on a variety of college outcomes, including a sense of control over academic and degree planning. "Extracurricular and peer involvement during college may be a particularly useful way for first-generation students to acquire the additional cultural capital that helps them succeed academically" and feel more closely connected to a wider campus culture (Pascarella et al. 2004, 278). First-gens benefit from colleges that proactively encourage student/faculty interactions outside the classroom (Inkelas et al. 2007; Stuber 2011).

I support students and reflect with them as they negotiate difficult experiences—sometimes recalling my earlier career plans to work in low-income communities. When a first-gen student hears that his roommate's father is a doctor and his mother is a trial attorney, should he disclose that his parents did not graduate from high school? When fellow students talk about growing up in exclusive suburbs, should another first-gen disclose how she was raised in a trailer park?

How do you tell fellow students that for much of your childhood there was not enough food on the table? And how does one react to students in Anthropology 101 who casually refer to multiple family trips to South America, Europe, or Asia before high school graduation?

These and other stories are honestly shared, but other concerns are explored as well—especially related to family.

EVER-PRESENT FAMILY CONCERNS

Besides social adjustments on campus, first-gens struggle with their working-class roots and allegiances—sometimes complicating relationships with parents and childhood friends (Lehmann 2013). First-gens do not receive as much support from parents to attend college, when compared with continuing-gens (Pascarella et al. 2004; Saenz and Barrera 2007).

Parents lack knowledge of college life and as a result their children often have difficulty communicating college experiences and stressors (Lightweis 2014). First-gens also have less parental support regarding fitting into campus life (Bradbury and Mather 2009) and often experience difficulties moving between two cultures, while meeting academic, family, and social demands (Dews and Law 1995; Hsiao1992; Hurst 2012; Lubrano 2004; Pascarella et al. 2004).

Upward mobility can be costly in personal and social terms. Lehmann (2013, 2) summarizes Pierre Bourdieu's reflections on problematic student experiences thus: "Our dispositions are shaped in significant ways by our social milieu; in turn, leaving a social environment in which we are comfortable to enter a new field has the potential to cause confusion, conflict and struggle."

By choosing a different path many first-gens invariably judge parents and communities where they grew up. Some feel that family members and friends back home are "wasting" their lives (Lehmann 2013). Not surprisingly this generates considerable conflict. Hurst (2010) created a typology that contrasts "Renegades" (middle-class-identified first-generation college students) and "Loyalists" (working-class-identified first-generation students).

In a later piece, she and Warnock demonstrate how Renegades stress a newfound individualism and achievement of the American Dream through hard work far from home (Hurst and Warnock 2015). With a strong sense of agency these first-gens actively seek something better, regularly creating boundaries between developing middle-class selves and working-class pasts.

As these students embrace new worldviews and related cultural capital, they ironically retain a simultaneous, conflicting sense of being on the outside, not really knowing the subtle rules of the higher education, middle-class game (Lehman 2009b). These mobility uncertainties, reflecting conflicts between the past and present, are often resolved by some first-gens who embrace the university mission of successful social uplift—the future (Hurst and Warnock 2015).

Common first-gen efforts to actively seek separation from the past lay the foundation for another "hidden injury of class" (Sennett and Cobb 1972). Still not feeling comfortable with developing identities, many first-gens eventually regret social and cultural breaks with family members who raised them and others with whom they formed childhood memories (Lehmann 2013). Upward mobility is no easy task and there are painful blunders along the way.

Not all first-gens seek separation. Some maintain strong connections and commitments to their working-class roots, while keeping their distance from a strong sense of middle-class individualism. These "Loyalists" (Hurst 2010) seek upward mobility and a solid career, do not see their families and communities as flawed, and are often alienated from university narratives framing working-class life as less than or defective. Other first-gens comfortably move between working- and middle-class cultures. "Double Agents" (Hurst 2010) are more at ease negotiating boundaries—comfortably remaining connected to home, enjoying powerful personal transformations while in college, and embracing a future filled with new possibilities.

Over the years I have observed many of the first-gen experiences we read about in the extensive literature describing working-class student transitions and experiences. First-gen students I advise enter the University of Michigan with strong academic records, but feel contradictory pulls and pushes from family and community.

In a variety of ways all first-gens negotiate various mobility processes and family dynamics—paths experienced differently by continuing-gens. Some first-gens have uncomfortable and complicated experiences (especially the Loyalists and Renegades), while others (Double Agents) accomplish social and cultural transitions with much more ease and grace. Parental support, attitudes, and feedback make all the difference.

Michigan first-gen students I have known are a combination of Loyalists and Double Agents. They are generally comfortable with most elements of middle-class culture, but are trying to maintain complex connections with family and community. They devote considerable effort to these adjustments, keep up with life on the home front, and share campus experiences with family.

I suspect that Michigan Renegades feel little need to participate in First-Gens@Michigan as they move down a new path perceived as significantly different or even better than their working-class roots. At this point they really do not want to talk about their pasts. I would predict, however, that current efforts to separate will change after college when these first-gens have time and energy to think about and integrate old and new identities.

I have witnessed a variety of concrete circumstances and family-related questions that students meet head-on every year. For example, will a first-gen's parents understand her desire to major in anthropology, with minors in American studies and international relations? Will they appreciate that she wants to stay in college after the bachelor's degree, attend a PhD program in anthropology, learn Hindi, do fieldwork in India, and finish graduate school in her early thirties? How will they react when they hear she has no intention of marrying anytime soon and if she does marry she will not give them grandchildren until after she has job security? Can they understand a future partner's or spouse's upper-middle-class background and be able to easily communicate with his parents?

How will her cross-class marriage work out? Will she be able to comfortably love and collaborate with a partner raised in very different social and economic circumstances? (Streib 2015). Will she understand her own children being raised in the upper middle class with values very different from the working-class values of her upbringing? Surely she will not promote that dreaded middle-class entitlement or respond to a son's request for a new car after his sophomore year of high school with: "In my day . . ."

Whatever the career goals of first-gen students I have known, nearly all find themselves in that liminal space between working- or lower-class positions and expectations—their very own deep past—and final locations in the odd world of economic privilege. Most first-gens wrestle with the inevitable guilt of leaving behind struggling family and community members.

How will they keep up reasonable contact with parents, siblings, and high school friends when they move to the other side of the country to pursue dreams and careers? By the time a first-gen student completes his senior year he may be contemplating how a veiled working-class self can comfortably merge with a new middle-class identity. This process is not part of a continuing-gen's senior year as she more or less replicates the social class trajectories of her parents.

UPWARD MOBILITY ON COLLEGE CAMPUSES

"When you have people together who believe in something very strongly—whether it's religion or politics or unions—things happen. . . . The end of all education/knowledge should surely be service to others" (Cesar Chavez, president of United Farm Workers, quoted in Hammerback and Jensen 2003, 27).

While upward mobility is widely celebrated in American culture, I hear most first-gens hesitantly talking about this process. I witness predictable degrees of uncertainty and fear. As I think about America's social class structure I know there will always be an unending supply of low-income students at Michigan dealing with first-gen issues. I hope they can endure the inevitable "performance fatigue" and not be worn down by those "first generation Blues" (Lang 2015). Knowing that others on campus are interested in first-gen struggles is enormously helpful for students I advise.

For example, one student who actively seeks to make the university more first-gen friendly effectively speaks at staff and faculty meetings. People are surprised to hear that it is not as easy as it appears. Shouldn't students be happy about moving on up? And isn't college a great place to do this? What they hear are hidden sides of first-gen lives. They listen to heart-filled honesty as this student hopes her sister can someday attend the University of Michigan and learn without fear.

First-gens certainly talk with one another and others, but I also encourage them to write about their experiences. This helps to publicly recognize first-gens and raise awareness of first-gen campus issues. Some have posted short essays on our first-gen website. Others have written to me and described complicated aspects, including being looked down on by more affluent college peers, feeling the need to do everything with little or no help, or encountering anxiety about being successful in a new world (Boshers et al. 2013). I give students a lot of credit for their honesty and willingness to inspire and inform others with their openness.

First-Generation College Students@Michigan provides a needed and friendly place for students to gather, seek advice, and explore possibilities with others who intuitively understand. On a campus where many believe social class does not matter I encourage and hear first-gen students participating in lively conversations about social stratification in a country where all women and men from various social classes are not created equal. As students take challenging courses, negotiate social class terrains, and encounter inequality debates in their post-Michigan years, I hope they continue to ask: What about class?

I am honored to witness and support first-gens during their four-year stay at the University of Michigan. In a sense, this is a sacred act of affirmation.

Chapter Nine

The Classroom Crucible

*Preparing Teachers from Privilege
for Students of Poverty*

Michael Svec and P. L. Thomas

P. L. THOMAS: I AM A SECOND

If you're afraid they might discover your redneck past There are a hundred
ways to cover your redneck past.
—"Your Redneck Past," Ben Folds Five

My maternal grandfather's given name was Harold, but he went by "Slick."
As his first grandchild, however, I christened him "Tu-Daddy"—a child's
twisting of "two," as in my second father. But "two" also captures the two
enduring images I have of him: (1) Harold/Slick lost his little finger on his
left hand in the machinery of the yarn-dyeing mill where he worked in the
hills of North Carolina, and (2) virtually every time I saw him, Harold/Slick
was barefoot—typically, sitting outside in nothing except a pair of cut-off
jeans, silent and alone.

My name is also connected with "two" because I am a second, named
after my paternal grandfather, Paul Lee Thomas, who people in my second
hometown of Woodruff, South Carolina, knew only as Tommy. And I was in
second grade when my teacher, Mrs. Townsend, sent me into the hallway for
arguing with her about my name.

When she took the first attendance (everyone in Woodruff knew everyone), Mrs. Townsend informed me that I was a junior, named after my father
she stated with the assurance of a teacher, but I explained, "No, ma'am, I am
named after my grandfather. I am a second." As was the case in my home, in
school, children did not argue or correct adults so to the hall I went—

although I was right, and she was wrong.

I was already petrified of Mrs. Townsend, a small woman, because I knew her husband, Corporal Townsend, a highway patrolman, whom I had met at my grandfather's gas station that sat in the middle of town—the sign prominently stating, "Tommy's 76." The yarn mills in the hills of North Carolina to the mill villages of upstate South Carolina, then, are the fertile soil of my redneck past—working-class families sometimes disrupted by alcoholism on one side and mostly living their lives with little or minimal formal education. In these formative years, I was enculturated to respect authority in the two most important worlds: my home (ruled by my father) and my school.

I have watched as the world has pulled away from my working-class family. The poor, the working poor, and the working class have become sources of derision (not the friendly laughing at ourselves of my high school classes)—for their financial poverty, for their so-called poverty of language.

Like the two worlds of the golf course and the basketball court of my youth, two worlds have materialized around me as I have buried myself in books as a great escape from my redneck past. And in the end, I am still that second grader, banished to the hall, embarrassed and frustrated because even when I am right, I feel inadequate, powerless—nearly daily as I walk among my mostly class-privileged university students and meticulously groomed university grounds.

I am the second, I think in a whisper. *I am the second*.

THE TENSIONS OF CLASS IN TEACHER EDUCATION

The university classroom becomes the crucible in which both the student and the teacher are thrown into cognitive dissonance. Within the classroom, university students and potential teachers confront their unexamined beliefs and expectations about learning, teaching, race, language, and socioeconomic class.

Since a teacher's beliefs play a significant role in how they respond to the children in their classroom, it is critical that future teachers engage in a critical analysis and reflection upon those beliefs and the implications. For many, critical self-reflection is an uncomfortable and difficult process.

As teacher educators from working-class backgrounds who teach at a selective university with students mostly from the upper middle class, ours is a complex and difficult task. How do you encourage future teachers to recognize their privilege, resulting in more inclusive K–12 classrooms? How do you engage future teachers to recognize the myths that deform us? Finally, how do you help the future teachers rise above the obstacles created by class privilege and those myths in order to recognize the unavoidable political nature of teaching?

We are challenged to develop within future teachers an awareness of the daily lives of children who have different experiences than their own. Teachers-in-training need to develop supportive relationships with diverse children to enable both children and teacher to thrive and succeed.

For the classroom to function as a crucible, education professors must subject to intense scrutiny two ideas student teachers may hold: the deficit perspective and role of political power in education. Paul Gorski (2008a, 522) argues for

> shifts of consciousness that, I propose, are fundamental to preparing a larger shift from a colonizing to a decolonizing intercultural education. Many of these shifts, in the most basic terms, refer to *seeing what we are socialized not to see* [emphasis added] and pushing back against hegemony; against its diversions from dominance and our complicity with it.

Those shifts include the following: recognizing that "cultural awareness is not enough"; promoting "justice first, then conflict resolution"; recognizing and "rejecting deficit theory"; "transcending the dialogic surface" and "acknowledg[ing] the power in-balances"; "acknowledging sociopolitical context"; claiming "'neutrality' [maintains the] status quo"; and "accepting a loss of likeability" as a consequence of "speak[ing] truth to power" (Gorski 2008a, 522–23).

Deficit thinking is tantamount to "blaming the victim" and provides both the classroom teacher as well as the larger educational and political institutions a means to shift the responsibility from themselves onto the students and their families. Valencia (2010) described six characteristics of deficit thinking: blaming the victims, oppression, pseudoscience, temporal changes, educability, and heterodoxy. Within this chapter we discuss deconstructing the deficit thinking of individuals who will be classroom teachers as well as recognizing the larger institutional and political influences that encourage deficit thinking.

In addition, there is the necessity for students to wrestle with the political forces that may have benefited them as individuals and likely will inhibit them as teachers. Our students are middle- and upper-middle- class students; many are second- or third-generation college graduates. Raised with a middle-class/affluent sense of entitlement, how do they also come to understand that their success often comes at the expense of others and is built more on their privilege than their merit?

RECOGNIZING CLASS PRIVILEGE

Michael Svec: Professor's Dissonance

I am a first-generation college graduate from a large urban city in the North teaching at an elite, selective, private college in the suburban South. Both of my parents worked, with my father transitioning from a blue-collar-manufacturing to a white-collar-management career after the plant closed and the family struggled for almost a year.

Today my father's lack of a college degree would keep him from the management position in which he succeeded. My parents nurtured my interest in science through family trips to museums, PBS, and an encyclopedia. The management position provided the financial means for me to attend a Catholic grammar and high school followed by a public university.

My awareness of class and education began in high school when I moved from the college prep program filled with students from my working-class neighborhood, to the honors program, populated with middle-class students from more affluent western suburbs. Academics were fine, but I never fit in socially with the other honors students. That promotion to the honors program was possible because a teacher advocated on my behalf. This was one of many times when the support and encouragement of individual teachers allowed me to violate my initial school placements.

During my teaching career I am reminded of the differences between my experiences and expectations and those of my students. Some of those experiences are generational but many are socioeconomic. Increasingly I am aware of the need to listen to the students to better understand their perceptions.

A graduate from our teacher education program in a master's-level course completed an assignment that asked her to identify an artifact that was used in a classroom to give students a sense of belonging and connection to the larger classroom community. Lacking a current classroom, she wrote a paper analyzing artifacts from her educational experience as a college student. Not being from the South, she reflected on what she had to do in order to "fit in" at the Southern university, and it required money.

The focus was on the cultural significance of Jack Roger sandals. As a first-year student, she quickly learned the importance of brands, especially when one of her neighbors displayed a collection of twenty pairs. At our small school she observed and participated in the homogenization of the students.

So common, important, and visible was this specific brand that even community teachers in field placement came to identify the university with these hundred-dollars-a-pair sandals. Her conclusions were that being a small tight-knit community encouraged homogeneity over time and that image and status required money. When she saw those shoes it evoked fond memories of beach weekends and sorority events and generated a sense of belonging to the community.

Her paper initially left me very conflicted. Over the years I have observed many fashion trends but never fully appreciating the key role they played in creating for the student a sense of belonging. Unfortunately the student never critically evaluated her experience at a homogenous privileged university and applied that analysis to the diverse classrooms in which she will teach.

My goal was to take students from privilege and prepare them to teach in situations where they will be the outsider teaching in situations and creating relationships that will likely be unfamiliar, awkward, and challenging. Yet the larger university culture exerts a strong force upon the teacher candidates that only reinforces middle-class values that, when expressed in the public school, only serve to reproduce the existing class structure.

The teacher education candidates at our university are overwhelmingly homogeneous with approximately 95% of the students in upper-level education and graduate courses being white and female.

According to university admissions, 5% of the university population is first generation with neither parent graduating from college. About 80% of the students are from the geographic South of the United States—with 40% from South Carolina specifically. Economic status is more difficult to ascertain, but it is estimated that fewer than 60% of the education majors have no financial need. Sorority participation is typically about 50% among education majors. Our population bears little resemblance to the larger state that is 65% white with 27% of the children living in poverty.

In order to explore the impact of class privilege and cultural capital on children and parents, several courses reference Lareau's (2011) study *Unequal Childhoods*. Informed by the work of Pierre Bourdieu, Lareau assumed that children grow within a stratified social system that influences how families and social institutions such as schools interact. Middle-class parents engage in concerted cultivation child rearing, in which children have multiple activities orchestrated by adults, are encouraged to negotiate with adults, and have parents who intervene with institutions on behalf of the child.

Children often developed a sense of entitlement, which is masked by how those experiences work as invisible connections to the norms of school and society. Working- and poverty-class families used more directive discipline with the children, had more unstructured time, enjoyed time with the extended family, assumed an attitude of deference to institutions such as schools, and often felt a sense of powerlessness, frustration, and constraint when engaging with schools (Lareau 2011).

Many of the characteristics described by Lareau's (2011) concerted cultivation are consistent with our university students' beliefs and practices. Our students maintain full calendars, and activities such as a sorority function or team practice take priority over academics. Students engage and expect negotiations with professors over course due dates, grades, and attendance. Some parents do insert themselves into the student's preparation, including one example of a parent who challenged a field placement in a Title I school.

Consistent with Gorski's first shift to address the tensions of class that "cultural awareness is not enough," and following the examples, strategies, and approaches detailed in his work *Reaching and Teaching Students in Poverty* (Gorski 2013), students complete assignments throughout the teacher preparation program that help the instructors better understand the university students and to begin to engage them in their own critical self-awareness.

Introductory courses have field placements in Title I schools and students compare that experience with their education, expectations, and media portrayal. The senior practicum engages the candidates in a multicultural inquiry project and an analysis of student learning based on demographic categories. Graduate students complete an educational autobiography and a cultural inquiry project (Svec 2013).

In the vignette that opens this section, the student's paper on Jack Roger sandals revealed an uncritical reflection on the role of appearance on the sense of belonging within the community. The paper became an affirmation of the role of money in gaining status, illustrating Valencia's (2010) characteristic of heterodoxy. Bourdieu's (1988) concept of *doxa* was maintained and the heterodox goals of the assignment were unrealized. It was positive that she recognized the powerful effect of belonging, but she failed to recognize that it was the result of spending money, a complex proxy of social class.

The student was never able to connect her experience with shoes to how a teacher in a public school could create a sense of belonging for students without financial means. The student's cultural practices within the university institution reinforced middle-class/affluent values that she will then bring into the public K–12 schools and reproduce the existing class structure.

As professors with roots in both the working and middle class, we have the unique opportunity to share personal narratives that often differ and challenge the students' experiences and expectations. By doing so, there is the potential to help challenge students' deficit perspective built on their uninvestigated privileged assumptions. It is also an opportunity to model authentic critical reflection.

The classroom culture and environment must be constructed in a manner that is safe, and one way to accomplish that is for the professor to use the capital that comes with our *acquired* (and at least for uncritical students, *earned*) status of middle class in the classroom context. A safe classroom environment emerges over the semester and involves many subtle actions on the part of the professor, including eliciting and acknowledging the experiences of the students, resisting judgment of student ideas, fostering mutual respect, and working through the emotions and feelings associated with the discussions.

Carefully selected school field experiences, course readings, statistics, and class discussions create many opportunities to challenge popular student beliefs and assumptions. Being challenged and having the invisible benefits of privilege exposed often results in a cognitive dissonance. This dissonance for students can create feelings of discomfort and that response may further entrench the students' commitment to their deficit beliefs. The working-class-turned-middle-class professors are now the guides helping the students resolve the dissonance.

Pierre Bourdieu's (1988) work provides the professors a means for examining and modeling for the students the impact of class position within teacher education since his models draw attention to conflict, change, and systematic inequality. Individuals of different social locations are socialized differently, and that socialization provides a person with a sense of what is comfortable or natural, for Bourdieu, *habitus*.

The background experiences are also shaped by the amount and forms of resources provided them as children (cultural capital). Individuals draw upon both *capital* and *habitus* as they confront various *fields* or institutions such as schools. Lareau's (2011) study demonstrates this point for the practicing teachers in the graduate program.

The vignette above is consistent with Bourdieu's assertion that *habitus*, in this case taste in shoes and specific brands of clothes, influences students' interactions with the institution. This student's parents had capital that allowed her to maintain her social standing through assimilation. It captures a moment of cultural transmission and social reproduction specific to that university.

Recognizing one's cultural capital and habitus is the first step in exploring teachers' personal beliefs about children with different socioeconomic statuses. Assumptions and instructional practices based on a privileged teacher's lived experience do not necessarily translate into successful practices in different school settings. To be a successful teacher necessitates the teacher come to know and accept the students' habitus and cultural capital.

As teacher educators, we do have authority and power in determining who becomes classroom teachers, which can work either to maintain social strata, or dismantle the hierarchy of class (or Bourdieu's *field*). Yet this authority is under threat and shaped by many outside sources—bureaucratic processes and traditional structures that often are as privilege-bound as the students with whom we are working and hoping to help move beyond their class assumptions. With the power comes the necessity to be aware of the consequences of our action on children as well as to argue for and defend our authority (Freire's *authoritative*, and not *authoritarian*), resisting political forces with hidden agendas.

In our roles as critical teacher educators, we offer opportunities for students to confront their own privilege, but that confrontation is one part of a much larger process that moves beyond the individual and requires a similar unpacking of social norms and myths. One of the most pervasive and *deforming* narratives that must be challenged is the myth of meritocracy.

"MYTHS THAT DEFORM US": THE BELIEF IN MERITOCRACY

P. L. Thomas: My Redneck Past

My mother finished one year of college (after attending seven high schools because her family constantly moved), and my father graduated junior college (by then already with a full set of false teeth, having lost all his in high school). My father as an adult worked in machine shops, quality control, most of my childhood, and often came home with black grease under his fingernails and in the lines of his hands. Even after retiring, my father worked in a machine shop part-time, under the weight of manual labor that taxed his arthritic shoulders (he depended on the kindness of his coworkers, who often lifted parts for him).

We lived for six or seven years in Enoree, South Carolina (nothing more than a crossroads at the edge of the Enoree River), and then in Woodruff just to the north (a mill town with a wide main street that if you stood on one end, you could see the other and the two stoplights along the way). My working-class childhood, however, was one of gender (male) and race (white) privilege.

My parents worked relentlessly to provide for my sister and me far above our working-class means. The fruits of that work ethic in the 1960s and 1970s included a greater degree of racial privilege in the South that working-class and working-poor families in the twenty-first century do not experience—primarily because of the shifts in racial demographics in how class has evolved in my lifetime.

Even though I eventually earned a series of college degrees resulting in a doctorate (all from state schools), I am still extremely uncomfortable with affluence. My discomfort is in part driven by my Southern drawl that many people continue to hold against me.

I am frequently accused of being ungrammatical when I talk (when I have not been), and I have even had university students say directly to my face that I don't sound smart—even though they know I am smart. When students enter my university office, typically their first comment is—after scanning the entire wall of shelved books that loom over the small space—"Have you read all those books?"

This persistent response from most students entering my office exposes their lack of a critical lens, their inability to consider ways of negotiating the world (my use of academics and scholarship to shed my redneck past) unlike their own.

You are damned right—I do not say—I have read all these books. Instead, I smile, explaining, "Of course, and there are this many more in my library at home."

Formality, dressing up, fine dining, ceremony—all the trappings of upper-middle- and upper-class normality make me incredibly anxious, still—despite all my formal and informal education. I am the embodiment of a powerful lesson about life: you can leave your redneck past behind, but you cannot erase your redneck past, including the complex myths inculcated by your family, your community, your region, and your nation.

A foundation of our situation as working-class academics is the meritocracy myth that is dominant in the United States: if you work hard enough, you will succeed. Our parents from the mid-twentieth century and then our own formative years in the 1970s and 1980s certainly contributed to both our belief in meritocracy (and the importance of education in that promise) and even our ability to apparently embody (and thus prove as *true*) that myth—recognizing that our race (white) and gender (male) privilege likely shielded us from the more corrosive consequences of this ideology.

Increasingly, the myth is not supported by evidence because upward social mobility has deteriorated in the United States while gender, race, and class inequity have remained robust (Thomas 2014). Having succeeded in the education system, our presence may well strengthen the appearance of a meritocracy.

Kurt Vonnegut's *Cat's Cradle* (1963) introduces readers to Bokononism, a religion with a central concept called *foma*: "Live by the *foma* that make you brave and kind and healthy and happy," read The Books of Bokonon I: 5. *Foma* are "harmless truths," and for our working-class success, the meritocracy myth worked as *foma*, again with our belief in this promise significantly impacted by the mostly invisible advantages of race and gender privilege that may have and could continue to delude us into reading our privilege as merit.

As scholars and educators, however, we had also to shield ourselves against the corrosive influence of privilege through a critical lens, one expressed by Freire (2005, 41):

> I also understand that as we put into practice an education that critically provokes the learner's consciousness, we are necessarily working against the myths that deform us. As we confront such myths, we also face the dominant power because those myths are nothing but the expression of this power, of its ideology.

Michael Svec and P. L. Thomas

If we had remained trapped in the arrogance of confusing our privilege with merit, the meritocracy myth would have manifested itself as one of the "myths that deform us" instead of serving us as mostly positive *foma*.

Yet, the critical lens that grounds us as scholars and teachers places us in conflict with the mostly privileged students we teach—ones convinced of their merit, often blind to their privilege, impassioned with the paternalism of "missionary zeal," and trapped in a deficit perspective (Dudley-Marling 2007) of social class.

For our students, middle- and upper-class people exhibit qualities everyone should aspire to and then the impoverished, working-poor, and working-class are defined by how they *lack* those preferred qualities. As Lareau (2011) details, however, social classes may be different in the qualities each class exhibits, but every class has strengths and weaknesses—although the privileged class(es) qualities are rendered invisible through the norms of any culture.

As noted earlier, confronting privilege and then investigating deforming cultural myths is a process—one that may take many years and, for a student, many classes. Some of the strategies we incorporate range from simply introducing students to critical theory and texts (Michel Foucault, Paulo Freire, bell hooks, Paul Gorski, Annette Lareau)—even in introductory courses—to activities that require teachers-to-be to apply the theory and newly acquired lenses of themselves and the world.

For example, in several classes, students are asked to examine a children's picture book, *Click, Clack, Moo* by Doreen Cronin and Betsy Lewin, through a feminist and Marxist perspective to deconstruct the inequities along gender and worker/owner divisions. Since the children's book is easily read, teachers-to-be are allowed the necessary space to manage the dissonance of the critical perspectives that are both new and disturbing.

While Gorski's (2008a) shifts and framework noted earlier speak to and inform our work as working-class professors confronting privilege in our teacher candidates, Gorski's work also creates more tensions. Below, in conclusion, we investigate some of these shifts in the context of the discussion above.

RISING ABOVE CLASS PRIVILEGE AND THE "MYTHS THAT DEFORM US"

Svec and the Deficit View of Single Parents

Connecting to and building relationships with students often requires finding common ground, yet economic status, background, and even differences in ages and life experiences often hide the commonalities. I am also a divorced single parent who has been raising my youngest son since sixth grade. He finished high school this year, and our conversations about what is next have not lived up to the expectations of what most people would assume about the child of a middle-class college professor.

While internally wrestling with parenting, I came across two senior elementary education students presenting a poster on single parenting as part of a required diversity class. Their placement was at a Title I school and the focus was on approximately a dozen children with poor single mothers. The students were identified because of behavior problems.

The poster focused on observations of those behaviors and proposed solutions yet lacked interaction with the actual parent or community to explain the causes for the behavior challenges. The operating assumptions were that two parents were necessary to provide structure and that a father was needed only to be a role model of proper controlled behavior. Having a single parent results in bad behavior.

I spent most of my time listening to the poster presentation clenching my teeth and heavily editing my responses trying to remove or hide the emotional edge. These were students I had taught and I knew they were well-intentioned. Most of the problems they observed in their classrooms focused on behavior, and to them and their placement teachers, the children of single mothers in a poor community were the most challenging.

The solutions, echoing the comments of their cooperating teachers, centered on blaming the parent for not providing structure at home or a male role model. The interpretation of the children's behavior and proposed solutions were steeped in the deficit perspective and in the children's economic status. Children and parents were talked about but not talked with.

I recognized that many of their assumptions were based on the economic status of the mother and stereotypical gender roles. As a middle-class parent no teacher ever suggested my child's unfinished homework was due to my parenting. No teacher ever suggested that my son needed more discipline; it was assumed as a male I was providing that. No teacher suggested my son needed a female role model because his behavior, not his emotional state, was the focus. Structure and role models don't compensate for the trauma of losing a parent in a divorce yet schools seem unable to acknowledge that emotional struggle.

During the student's presentation, I did not share my personal experience but tried to frame questions based upon my experience to get them to see how their assumptions were incomplete. Professionally we are trained to be objective and dispassionate, which makes personal experience irrelevant.

In addition, there was a feeling that sharing this kind of personal information marked me as different from my student, opening myself up to rejection, or at least, not being seen as relevant to their personal goals. As a teacher educator and a parent, it is difficult to compartmentalize the professional and personal.

The teachers' habit of blaming the parent or family for a student's behavior is a typical deficit perspective response (Valencia 2010; Gorski 2013). It ignored the socioeconomic status of the family and permitted a sidestepping of the school's role in meeting the child's needs. Gorski (2013) illustrated the dangers of the "culture of poverty" deficit perspective that assumes that people in poverty share a consistent culture and that culture results in their poverty.

The hidden goal of the deficit perspective is that the existing economic system is left unchallenged, "In our determination to 'fix' the mythical culture of poor students, we ignore the ways in which our society cheats them out of opportunities that their wealthier peers take for granted" (Gorksi 2008b, 33).

Just as class designations are not simple, the journey to rising above one's own class-, race-, or gender-based assumptions about the world is not simple or predictable. For educators and teacher educators, however, the need to confront and investigate class-, race-, and gender-biases is not a frill but a necessity. Below we touch on further the struggle of overcoming deficit perspectives and then explore tensions created by acknowledging the politics of education in the classroom and assuming a critical theorist perspective in both teaching and scholarship.

Although the authors of this chapter were able to climb the social ladder, we ultimately recognized the political links in our lived experience as children and educators. Individual teachers impacted our ability to succeed as well as inspired us into a career in education more so than the educational institutions themselves.

The critical shift for us, and one we teach to our students, required us to recognize and embrace the essential political nature of teaching.

> Thus, proponents of critical pedagogy understand that every dimension of schooling and every form of educational practice are politically contested spaces. Shaped by history and challenged by a wide range of interest groups, educational practice is a fuzzy concept as it takes place in numerous settings, is shaped by a plethora of often-invisible forces, and can operate even in the name of democracy and justice to be totalitarian and oppressive. (Kincheloe 2005, 2)

The critical "political" is not the partisan "political" students tend to recognize, however.

After helping students navigate their popular and skewed understanding of "political," we must help them move to situating themselves within a more nuanced appreciation for teaching as political act. To be critical is to be political *as an act against indoctrination*, the primary mechanism of perpetuating privilege and inequity, and to dismantle the status quo.

Recognition of these educational politics suggests that teachers take a position and make it understandable to their students. *They do not, however, have the right to impose these positions on their students* [emphasis in original]. . . . In this context it is not the advocates of critical pedagogy who are most often guilty of impositional teaching but many of the mainstream critics themselves.

When mainstream opponents of critical pedagogy promote the notion that all language and political behavior that oppose the dominant ideology are forms of indoctrination, they forget how experience is shaped by unequal forms of power. To refuse to name the forces that produce human suffering and exploitation is to take a position that supports oppression and powers that perpetuate it.

The argument that any position opposing the actions of dominant power wielders is problematic. It is tantamount to saying that one who admits her oppositional political sentiments and makes them known to students is guilty of indoctrination, while one who hides her consent to dominant power and the status quo it has produced from her students is operating in an objective and neutral manner. Critical pedagogy wants to know who's indoctrinating whom. (Kinchloe 2005, 11)

Gorski claims, "the most dangerous dimensions of educational hegemony in the US is a culture of pragmatism" (2008a, 521). This highlights the dilemma within which teacher education finds itself, frequently losing its autonomy to a flood of education policies that work against the teaching profession while embracing a view of education as empowerment and social justice. As university professors, our autonomy and experiences become marginalized by the accreditation and licensing expectations. We are in a position where we cannot reject those mandated expectations since our candidates would then be denied access to the profession.

While we agree with Gorski's assertion that teachers need to transcend hegemony and recognize the large systems of power and control that they will be complicit participants within, we must also ensure our candidates meet the expectations of hegemonic forces of licensure. The potential solution is to engage our candidates as both future teachers and as citizens clearly demonstrating how the political system influences the professional and what actions outside of the classroom can be taken to engage the system as citizens.

Throughout our teacher education curriculum, for example, teacher candidates are made aware of the partisan implications of teaching, in that K–12 public education is driven by policy created by and codified by the democratic process. Further, several courses include opportunities for candidates to practice their potential roles as public intellectuals. One assignment asks students to write public commentary on a misconception in the public—or by political leaders—and then to frame more accurately that topic or policy.

For the teacher education program of study, the attention and focus on both the politics of education as well as the commitment to social justice require effort throughout the entire program, from the first education course, to the methods courses and internship, and continuing into the professional life of the teachers. The coherence of the program is the result of multiple faculty members sharing a commitment to social justice, a consensus that is often difficult to achieve. This is illustrated by the ways that individual professors challenging the students' misconceptions when illustrated around a crosscutting topic such as literacy.

Literacy is central to all education, regardless of grade level or content area of the teacher. For students majoring or certifying to teach, there is a commonsense view that literacy is significantly class-bound—poor children have less literacy than middle-class and affluent children. Both the media and research have both reinforced this commonsense view, a deforming myth, since nearly every public piece discussing the word gap (the claim that monolithic social class distinctions include simplistic differences among social classes in terms of the amount of vocabulary children have acquired) refers to the same study by Hart and Risley (1995).

However, virtually no one ever acknowledges the essential class-based problems with Hart and Risley's (1995) work, directly confronted by Dudley-Marling and Lucas (2009). Seeking to move future teachers away from a deficit perspective of class, race, and gender is further complicated but also supported by challenging deficit views of language—both discrediting the dualistic view of correct/incorrect as well as the class-based view of language.

Privileged students must come to understand the power of language, the role of language in the coincidence of their privilege, and the need to step away from deficit views of language in order to teach all children with equity—instead of falling into the paternalistic trap of "fixing" poor children in the image of middle-class and affluent children.

Lareau (2011) observed that middle-class children often negotiated, bargained, and whined during interactions with adults whereas working-class children rarely talked back to adults, whined, or claimed to be bored. Language in the working-class home was functional and directive.

For teacher candidates, the first step is becoming aware of the challenges to the word gap narrative and research (asking them to read Dudley-Marling and Lucas, for example), and then helping them reconsider their assumptions about language (challenging standard English and the biases against so-called dialects associated with race and social class) through a linguistic model (the history of the English language and its relationship with power). The activity with *Click, Clack, Moo* from above represents this transition from normative literacy to critical literacy.

A final and related tension involves the extension of political teaching with political scholarship and public work. While formal education and education majors/programs may serve to perpetuate—instead of dismantle—

social norms for students and teacher candidates, professors also experience the hegemony of tenure and promotion norms along with the normalization of department politics (again, often working invisibly as class privilege does when not critically confronted).

Critical scholarship and nearly all public work are often marginalized and even discouraged as "political"—without regard to the politics of normalized scholarship and the refusal to do public work. For critical working-class professors, the bureaucracy of being a professor reproduces their enculturation into formal K–12 and undergraduate schooling and then graduate school as well as life in the university.

These professional and scholarly tensions again serve as autobiography for helping undergraduate teacher candidates navigate their own, although inverted, journey into confronting their privilege so that they can better teach students unlike them. Our program includes field-based experiences throughout the program, and students are placed in high-poverty, majority-minority schools so that they can begin to practice and navigate this critical perspective while being supervised and supported in a traditional context of schooling.

Pierre Bourdieu (1988) noted that scholars like to imagine themselves as objective observers of the world. In our case, as scholars and teacher-educators, we are actively engaged in the social world. The working-class origins of professors of education create an almost continuous state of cognitive dissonance when preparing future teachers. The resolution of that dissonance is necessary in order for both the success of the future teachers and the children they will one day instruct. Although our role is to serve as gatekeepers to the teaching profession, the effectiveness and impact of our candidates dictates that we need to act more as tour guides than gatekeepers. Our dissonance has taught us how to accept the discomfort, and it is necessary for future teachers to also learn how to embrace and resolve the dissonance their future classrooms will create.

CODA: A CRITICAL OPPORTUNITY

During a May Experience course (a two-credit session designed for experience different from traditional courses) in 2015, a student typical of our students—a relatively affluent, white female—shared that while working as a university guide for Admissions, she had led a tour of all-black students from a local charter school. These students were in uniforms and attended what many call a "no excuses" charter school that has strict disciplinary and academic policies.

This May Experience course serves as a crucible by exposing students to critical pedagogy and challenges commonly held views about both traditional schooling and current education reform. While this student has been viewing documentaries and preparing her public writing about a misconception about education, she has admitted to the class in discussions and to the professor (Thomas) that she had initially believed the strict charter schools were a positive and necessary experience for the poor black students. But during the course, she had not only changed her mind, but also begun to feel badly about her previous assumptions about race and class—feelings that identify her coming to terms with her own privilege.

Although only one student, and one experience, we believe this is the beginning of how critical pedagogy can bolster our roles as working-class professors who seek ways to give privileged students the opportunities and tools to confront and then rise above their own privilege that prevents them from fully engaging with students not like them. This student had not been asked to reconsider or reject her beliefs, but had been given the opportunity made rich and possible because viewpoints unlike her own were raised and honored throughout the course viewing of critical documentaries and the classroom discussion from students with race and class diversity. For us, this is the classroom crucible that is essential for producing teachers who work in the name of their students and democracy.

Part Three

Work in the Academy

Chapter Ten

Working-Class, Teaching Class, and *Working* Class in the Academy

Krista M. Soria

Like several working-class academics, I piece together an academic career by holding many concurrent employment positions. Over the last decade, I have juggled working in full-time higher education positions concomitant with teaching in contingent adjunct faculty positions—sometimes teaching as many as six classes per semester at several different institutions.

I know I am not alone in these pursuits: 76.4% of faculty in the United States are contingent instructional staff (Curtis 2014). Furthermore, like me, over half of adjunct faculty teach at more than one institution at a time (Street et al. 2012).

I feel both grateful and lucky to serve as an adjunct instructor while earning my primary living wages through full-time employment. I am grateful because I find deep personal fulfillment in combining my full-time work as a researcher with teaching undergraduate and graduate students across a variety of academic disciplines (technical writing, student affairs, higher education, adult education, statistics, and leadership).

Like other working-class academics, I often believe I landed here by pure luck given that I feel as though I do not truly belong in academia as a working-class person (Rothe 2006). I am also lucky because, unlike some other adjuncts, I primarily earn a living wage through a full-time position that sustains my part-time teaching.

Such an intense workload resonates soundly with my working-class upbringing, which is signified—at least for me—by working excessively long hours of the day, possessing a strong work ethic, seeking to create a better life for future generations, and diligently helping others to achieve their own educational and professional goals to build a prosperous community. While I feel fulfilled by my workload, I also feel a great degree of emptiness because, like many adjunct faculty, I am systematically excluded as a legitimate member of the academy.

Through the pursuit of my doctoral degree, I became interested in studying the experiences of working-class college students, which, reflexively, enhanced my own awareness of my social class upbringing and opened my eyes to the ways in which higher education institutions reinforce middle-class and upper-class cultures, beliefs, and values. In researching the experiences of working-class college students (Soria 2012; Soria and Bultmann 2014; Soria and Stebleton 2013; Soria, Stebleton, and Huesman 2013–2014; Soria, Weiner, and Lu 2014), I also began to see how social class operated in my professional and teaching positions—and how the mechanisms of social reproduction are embodied in several organizational levels of the higher education enterprise (Bourdieu and Passeron 1977).

The purpose of this chapter is to provide a critical examination of these class-based issues as they may impact the lives of adjunct faculty in higher education. In this chapter, I argue that adjunct faculty essentially represent the working class within a hierarchical class-based system of higher education.

I also connect the experiences of working-class academics with adjunct faculty, providing parallels between each group and introducing research supporting the idea that social class still permeates higher education even though matters of class are whitewashed in these institutions.

Several of the primary issues concerning working-class academics and adjunct faculty are connected as they center on the basic elements constituting social constructions of social class: power, prestige, and income.

FRAMING THE EXPERIENCES
OF WORKING-CLASS ACADEMICS

For decades, working-class academics have detailed their challenges working in the academy and, through these narratives, have woven together themes connected to theories of cultural and social reproduction (Bourdieu and Passeron 1977). In part, the ability to navigate educational systems is dependent upon the level of one's economic capital (accumulated money or wealth), social capital (networks and resources), and cultural capital (knowledge or level of familiarity with the dominant culture), with individuals possessing greater amounts of the "right kinds" of capital more likely to achieve success in those systems (Bourdieu 1986; 1996).

Educational systems reproduce social classes by granting continued advantages to individuals from culturally (and economically) wealthy backgrounds who can successfully navigate those systems (Bourdieu 1986);

therefore, because they do not belong to elite social classes, working-class individuals are structurally disadvantaged in educational systems. These disadvantages follow them from childhood to adulthood—and persist through their professional careers.

Bourdieu's (1996) conception of these three forms of capital clearly resonates with the experiences of working-class academics. Working-class individuals often come from families with lower economic resources and several working-class scholars have detailed their challenges paying for their undergraduate and graduate degrees (Dews and Law 1995; hooks 2000; Mahoney and Zmroczek 1997; Muzzatti and Samarco 2006; Oldfield and Johnson 2008; Ryan and Sackrey 1995; Tokarczyk and Fay 1993).

Such narratives tend to be framed by several themes, including lacking knowledge about resources available to pay for tuition, "stumbling" into assistantships or scholarship opportunities, or having to work full-time while enrolled to pay for educational expenses.

Because many working-class academics are also first-generation college students, they possess limited amounts of the requisite social capital that might help them to make the best decisions related to their educational pursuits (e.g., selecting a good college, pursuing a particular academic major leading to a higher-paying career). Social capital also relates to acquiring the personal connections from faculty at elite and prestigious institutions—connections that can open doors to graduate degree programs, research partnerships, or funding, thus solidifying one's status as a member of the academy (Huxford 2006).

Working-class academics often discuss insecurities in academia because they possess "the wrong kinds" of cultural capital compared with their peers whose parents had been to college. In other words, because they were raised within a social class in which less elite forms of cultural capital were cultivated, working-class individuals are disadvantaged in higher education because they lack knowledge of "high culture." Cultural capital is "a set of cultural credentials that certify eligibility for membership in status-conferring social groups. To 'fit in' and 'look and know the part' is to possess cultural capital" (McNamee and Miller 2014, 77).

Social and cultural capital works, in part, to help students feel comfortable in the habitus of higher education. Baker (2006), for instance, noted that she would not have attended either university or graduate school had she not been acquainted with middle- and upper-class roommates, from whom she appropriated cultural and social capital. Huxford (2006) described this cultural capital as

> acquiring the patina of self-assuredness and the arrogance that comes with the knowledge of one's guaranteed place among the elite—along with the cultural appreciation of knowing good wines from bad wines, an appreciation of fine

art and classical music, and the knowledge of how to comport oneself in any social situation. (208)

Economic, social, and cultural capital remain critically important long into working-class academics' professional careers: indeed, many have written about their challenges in paying for their education, lack critical social capital for professional advancement, and generally feel out of place in the academy despite their advanced positions or academic credentials (Borrego 2008; Muzzatti and Samarco 2006; Ryan and Sackrey, 1995; Tokarczyk and Fay, 1993; Welsch 2004). Below, I provide a discussion of how the forms of capital, structural barriers, and other factors play into the experiences of working-class adjunct faculty and influence their sense of citizenship in the academy.

WORKING-CLASS ADJUNCTS IN HIGHER EDUCATION

Working-class individuals working in higher education—whether faculty or professional staff—may experience a profound sense of dissociation and estrangement as they continually navigate the working-class world of their upbringing and the middle-class world of higher education. These personal beliefs and experiences, in addition to structural forces that preserve distinctions between the social classes, bear weight on working-class academics' aspirations for faculty positions.

Accordingly, I hypothesize that working-class academics are proportionately more likely to be contingent adjunct faculty than academics from middle- and upper-class backgrounds. Thus, "in academia, lack of class privilege is a tremendous obstacle to success," especially for working-class academics (Dunbar 1999. para. 5).

Mazurek suggested that working-class academics come from backgrounds that tend to make them "sensitive to hierarchy, and those that enter academic careers tend to be clustered in colleges and universities that are lower on the academic totem pole and thus more teaching-intensive" (2009, para. 13). Working-class academics, typically "end up somewhere toward the bottom of the prestige scale of the profession, if for no other reason, they are affiliated with second rank institutions" (Ryan and Sackrey 1995, 76).

Indeed, many working-class academics gravitate to regional colleges and universities, which are more familiar and comfortable to those from working-class backgrounds (Christopher 2003). Regional colleges and universities offering primarily bachelor's and master's degrees are also more likely to carry a greater percentage of adjunct faculty compared to doctoral-granting institutions (Curtis 2014), which may mean that more working-class faculty serve as adjuncts at those types of institutions.

Similarly, since many working-class academics from low-income backgrounds attended less-elite colleges and universities for their bachelor and graduate degrees—perhaps to save costs but also because of proximity to their home communities—they are less likely to have graduated with prestigious credentials. This, of course, matters because, within higher education institutions, "prestige replaces wealth as the mediating value" (Ryan and Sackrey 1995, 74).

Furthermore, lacking the "right kinds" of social capital, working-class academics may not have letters of recommendation from faculty at prestigious universities or pursue all of the steps along the best pathways to secure tenure-track positions.

After all, the faculty job market is rooted in class-based hierarchical structures that reflect deeper social inequalities: only 25% of institutions produce 71% to 86% of all tenure-track faculty and, across disciplines, prestige hierarchies make the best predictions of faculty placement over other factors (Clauset, Arbesman, and Larremore 2015). Working-class faculty and adjunct faculty who did not earn their credentials at those most-prestigious universities therefore encounter systematic difficulties in obtaining tenure-track faculty positions (Dunbar 1999, 30).

There is also the challenge that many working-class academics are taught to believe that what constitutes "real work" is product-based. Emanating from traditions in which work is associated with hard physical labor, working-class academics often describe feeling insecure in their roles as teachers and researchers; for example, Rothe (2006) described utilizing a strategy of overproduction and teaching course overloads in attempts to compensate for feeling as though she was not producing "real" finished projects congruent with the working-class employment positions her family held throughout her upbringing.

These factors may lead many to retain full-time employment positions and teach part-time as adjuncts, a professional lifestyle that feels secure, real, and more in line with a working-class upbringing. Like working-class undergraduates who struggle to feel full membership in the academy and make concerted decisions to either withdraw or pursue vocationally oriented training (Lehmann 2007b), many working-class academics may similarly opt out of tenure-track faculty positions given that the professional identity feels foreign.

Some of these decisions may feel "natural," as they are reinforced by the scores of messages that working-class academics heard from their families and community members about the fruitlessness of their pursuits up the social class ladder. According to Rothe, working-class individuals are profoundly aware of their place in the social class hierarchy—"subordinate to the White middle- or upper-class individuals" (2006, 49)—and therefore decisions to pursue "lower-status" contingent faculty positions may feel congruent with the experiences of working-class individuals.

For working-class scholars, there is a certain futility in aspiring to success in the field of academia: dictates of humility that resonate throughout working-class culture mean that one can only ever attribute one's successes to "blind luck." Failure in academia becomes a self-fulfilling prophecy: a reminder of one's working-class status and a confirmation that, as a working-class person, one should never strive to be anything greater because of the inevitable barriers sure to block one's access to the top. Some of the expectations regarding how to be successful in academia—self-promotion, self-assurance, and visibility—are veritably antithetical to the values of humility and invisibility taught in working-class families (Rothe 2006).

Along those lines, in reflecting upon her difficulties in applying for full-time faculty positions, Dunbar wrote that "I should have listened to those in my working-class community who told me I was wasting my time, that even if I did everything I was told, when it came time for me to step up and receive my reward, they'd raise the bar, or change the rules" (1999, para. 5). Many adjuncts today likely whisper such sentiments to themselves as they consider the current conditions of their employment. It is easy to understand why such beliefs may make one reticent to aspire to upper-level or full-time faculty positions if consistent messages reinforce one's inferiority.

ADJUNCTS WORKING CLASS

In addition to being a working-class adjunct, I am also an adjunct who is at all times working class in academia. First, I am an object of social class: I am influenced by social class and in many ways compelled by social class forces outside of my control. But, I am also struggling to reach outside of the social class confines of my upbringing as I navigate my new social class surroundings; thus, I see myself as striving toward being a subject of social class with agency. Juxtaposed between social class subject and object, I am always *working class* as a working-class person in academia.

As social class objects, many working-class academics like myself are subject to subvert messages—microaggressions—related to social class in the middle- and upper-class culture of higher education. For instance, I have had a colleague tell me, "That is very classy of you!" when I wrote an unsolicited letter of recognition for another colleague on campus.

In class one day, one of my students told me I looked "so much more classy" when I put my blazer on over my Black Sabbath T-shirt in class. Both colleagues and my students have laughed openly when I tell them about my affiliation with the heavy metal subculture—I am but a working-class novelty in their middle-class culture.

By telling me that I am "classy" (but only when I symbolically and practically cover up my true working-class identity), individuals raised in the middle class validate that I have properly conformed to middle- or upper-class expectations for behavior and dress in higher education.

Yet, while praising my middle- or upper-class performance, they also remind me that I am an imposter in the ivory tower (Huxford 2006) and that I am constantly having to "work" at performing social class every day.

My influx status as a faux-middle-class faculty member is exacerbated by my illegitimate status as a contingent adjunct faculty. As a "perpetual adjunct faculty member" for over a decade now, I reside tenuously both inside and outside of the academy—mirroring my own experiences as a working-class person in a structural system clearly designed by—and for—the middle and upper classes.

As a working-class person, I am keenly aware of my outsider status in the academy—an element of my identity that informs my practice, inspires my research, and means that I am essentially always working class at any given time as I navigate the middle-class culture of higher education.

There are several ways in which I attempt to navigate these worlds and make sense of my social class experience. For one, whenever I engage in campus conversations about diversity, I remind colleagues about the importance of social class in informing students' experiences.

Furthermore, I actively work within my classrooms to tell students about my working-class background and some of the struggles I encountered as a student—both to connect with other working-class, first-generation students and also to help them frame their experiences in structural terms as they make sense of their collegiate experiences (Stephens, Hamedani, and Destin 2014). In this manner, I seek to share messages like "if I can do it, so can you" and also "you are not alone in this struggle."

I also seek to disrupt middle-class conceptions of what it means to pursue doctoral education and work as a researcher and professor. I wear a black metal T-shirt nearly every day at work: being metal is an important part of my identity. I hope to change people's conceptions of what it means to grow up working-class through my keen ability to transition, act, and speak like a middle-class person; yet it is taxing to engage in these dual roles and to always exist in the periphery of these social class boundaries. As I wrote in 2013,

> I belong and conversely do not belong in my professional community, family community, educational community, and personal community. While I like to think that my ability to code-switch and move easily between these worlds is some marker of distinction, in reality, it is a heavy burden to translate, pretend, and constantly shift identities. (para. 4)

Admittedly, though, I am also beset by the constant burden of fear: they will find out that I do not really belong in the academy, I am not supposed to be here, and I should be removed from all of my positions.

I worry about being too outspoken—especially in the presence of middle-class people in positions of power and authority. So, more often then I like to admit, I cover my black metal T-shirts with a blazer or cardigan and remain silent. In this way, too, I also *work class* by inadvertently succumbing to social class pressures and silently conforming to middle-class norms.

I am not alone in shouldering the burdens of always working class within my professional and teaching work. Below, I outline the experiences of adjunct faculty in higher education—a group of professionals in the academy who, no matter their individual social class backgrounds—embody the "working class" of faculty in higher education. Given their positions, contingent adjunct faculty members are almost always working class as they navigate the hierarchies of the academy.

The issues facing adjunct faculty on college and universities across the United States are decidedly *social class issues*. Although, on the surface, adjunct faculty positions are viewed as prestigious given the level of education required, expectations of professional or research contributions, and influence over students' learning, these positions are, in reality, the same as many working-class positions with low organizational power, limited prestige, and low wages.

Although they play important roles in teaching undergraduates and graduate students at every type of college and university, adjuncts are woefully underpaid for their work. Adjunct faculty earn a median of $2,700 for each semester-long class they teach, with adjuncts who manage to cobble together full-time (three or four) course loads earning annual wages between $18,000 and $25,000 (Curtis and Thornton 2013). At 40 hours per week, full-time adjuncts teaching three or four classes per semester earn less than federal minimum wage (Fruscione 2014).

Nearly 25% of part-time college faculty receive some form of public assistance, such as food stamps, Medicaid, or cash welfare (Jacobs, Perry, and MacGillvary 2015). It has been estimated that, because 55% of adjuncts report having doctoral degrees and 35% report having master's degrees, contingent faculty "likely make up the most highly educated and experienced workers on food stamps and other public assistance [programs] in the country" (House Committee on Education and the Workforce 2014, 26).

In the majority of cases, contingent faculty also receive no benefits or job security. Nearly 95% of adjunct faculty reported feeling as though they had no job stability whatsoever—and that they did not know whether they would be teaching courses from one semester to the next. On top of this instability, several adjuncts reported receiving extremely late notification that they would be teaching a class in a given semester: some mentioned that they were notified of their teaching schedules a day before their semester began (House Committee on Education 2014).

Adjunct faculty are highly educated employees who "overwhelmingly have post-graduate degrees" (2014, 1). As recognized by the committee, "Having played by the rules and obtained employment in a highly skilled, in-demand field, these workers should be living middle-class lives. But . . . many often live on the edge of poverty" (House Committee on Education 2014, 1). Many adjuncts, for example, report experiencing extreme difficulty in attempting to pay back their student loans while earning such low incomes (2014).

Although they work in quintessentially middle- or upper-middle-class employment positions, adjunct faculty are not only living on the economic edges of society, they are tenuously balanced at the very fringes of the academy due to their low status in institutions, liminal positions in their respective fields, and wavering grasp on full-fledged membership in the enterprise.

These harsh economic capital realities may lead some to opt out of academic careers altogether, especially if coupled with a debilitating lack of confidence in one's ability to succeed in the world of academia, cultural disconnections with the expectations of what it means to be successful in academia, or persistent feelings of dislocation in the middle-class environs of higher education. As Neal described his experience as an adjunct faculty, "my years as an adjunct have obliterated any trace of egotism and pride, not to mention confidence, I might once have had" (Neal 2001, 21).

Indeed, some have described opting out of faculty or upper-ranking administrative positions given their lack of confidence or believing that others did not have confidence or faith in their abilities to be successful in those positions (Borrego 2008). Gale reflected upon the sense of institutionalized exploitation she felt as an adjunct, recounting that "each college has its own way of humiliating you. Of letting you know that you are a second class citizen" (Gale 2001, 14). Dunbar (1999) noted feeling pressure to complete the many prerequisites to obtaining a faculty position, including serving "more time in poverty as a 'freeway flyer'—allowing not just one but several different institutions to exploit me as an adjunct" (1999, para. 3).

Similarly, adjunct faculty do not often receive opportunities to engage in collaborative research opportunities and develop mentorship relationships with their faculty colleagues. Although they may benefit from developing relationships with full-time faculty in their field, less than one in five adjuncts report having some type of mentoring relationship (Danley-Scott and Scott 2014). In higher education, adjuncts are regarded as "contractors" performing low-wage "piece work" (House Committee on Education 2014).

Few adjuncts have even offices in which to hold office hours with students, receive no pay to prepare their courses (which could be canceled at a moment's notice), and lack access to basic office supplies. All of these symbols are markers of the low-status positions conferred to adjuncts by their institutions.

Additional structural barriers can prevent adjunct faculty from participating fully in the academy; for instance, contingent faculty are rarely offered opportunities to engage in professional development or governance activities (Baldwin and Chronister 2001) although they are interested in professional activity and development (Kezar and Sam 2011). One potential barrier to this type of professional engagement in the field is time: few adjunct faculty—especially those working and teaching at multiple institutions—have time to attend staff meetings, professional development opportunities, or office hours (Danley-Scott and Scott 2014).

As a consequence, contingent faculty will be less informed about departmental or university announcements or news and become less involved with crafting policies pertinent to their students. These conditions limit adjunct faculty's opportunities to develop the types of critical social capital that might enable them to advance professionally or enter full-time positions if desired. As such, by limiting adjuncts' opportunities to acquire social capital, adjuncts remain in lower positions of power and prestige in the organization.

Given that so many adjunct faculty must obtain teaching positions at several institutions, another structural challenge prohibiting adjuncts' career opportunities is that of limited time to adequately connect with their students and provide optimal learning experiences for their students.

A national survey found that 98% of adjuncts felt that they were missing out on opportunities to better serve their students because of demands on their schedules (House Committee on Education 2014). Students' ratings of their teachers are important in hiring and promotion—and adjunct faculty sprinting from class to class (about 89% of all adjunct faculty) are not able to spend considerable time with their students (2014).

While capital certainly plays into the lived experiences of many working-class faculty, greater structural and organizational factors also shape those trajectories and continue to perpetuate conditions of inequality when considering intersections of race, ethnicity, and social class. Among white faculty, at all institutional types, 50.7% are part-time while 29.8% are full-time tenured or tenure-track and 19.5% are full-time non-tenure-track; however, among black faculty, 61.0% are part-time faculty, while 20.7% are full-time tenure or tenure-track and 17.3% are part-time non-tenure-track (Curtis 2014).

Further intersections between gender and social class should also be examined when reviewing the percentages of men and women who work in full-time tenure-track or contingent positions. Among men, 27.4% are full-time tenured or tenure-track, 14.9% full-time non-tenure-track, and 38.0%

part-time while, among women, 19.5% are full-time tenured or tenure-track, 16.5% full-time non-tenure-track, and 45.2% part-time (Curtis 2014).

Clearly, there are significant disparities among the hiring and promotion of tenure-track faculty that advantage white academics and male academics over faculty of color and women. These disparities influence students' perceptions about "who belongs" in full-time tenure-track positions. According to one adjunct survey respondent from a national survey of adjunct faculty, since the majority of adjuncts are "bright, highly educated women," female students "suffer" when they perceive that "some of the best women teachers are an underclass in higher ed" (House Committee on Education 2014, 29).

As they are situated in higher education institutions, adjunct faculty are far removed from institutional structures that could promote their status. According to Mazurek, "it is the lack of power in the workplace (without a strong union or political advocates to argue for them)" that perpetuates the low-status conditions facing adjunct faculty (2009, para. 5). If class is defined at least in part by the amount of power that one has in an occupation (Zweig 2000), then adjunct faculty represent the working class in academia.

Many contingent adjunct faculty are working in their positions because there are limited full-time tenure-track opportunities available in their field and they aspire to these positions (House Committee on Education 2014). Adjunct faculty are ultimately caught up in a "catch-22" position: because they teach so many classes, they have little time to research, publish, and attend conferences—all important steps toward securing tenure-track positions (2014).

There is also a persistent fear in discussing these types of class-based issues with students or somehow organizing to effect greater change in adjunct faculty's wages or employment conditions. Maisto (2013) described these fears as stemming from the "tension, well-documented and long-discussed, between adjuncts' nominal professional status and the actual workplace conditions that place us in the category of the working class" (para. 2). These conditions are exacerbated by a sense of shame that some adjuncts experience in personalizing the structural inequalities present in higher education:

> Naive belief in an illusory meritocracy often obstructs the ability to understand that the academic employment system is not immutable. "I had the privilege of an education and the pleasure of work I enjoy," goes this script, "so I should have 'known better,' and now deserve the conditions in which I live." (Maisto 2013, para. 4).

Then again, there is also the very real fear that speaking out about the working-class status of adjuncts will result in retaliation, of which real-world examples abound (Eisen 2009; Jaschik 2009; Moore 2013). Pressured not to disrupt the system as it stands and silently subordinating to the status quo that reinforces hierarchies excluding them from full membership in the academy, many adjunct faculty are therefore *working class* by their complicity.

Thus, in some ways, the experiences of working-class academics and adjunct faculty working class are shared in that both groups grapple with the weight of greater systemic and structural forces that they may internalize and personalize. Neither working-class academics nor adjunct faculty feel any deep sense of belonging to the academy—and it is clear that structural challenges prohibit their full membership in several respects.

CONCLUSION

The status of adjunct faculty at colleges and universities across the nation should be concerning to administrators and policymakers for several reasons. First, evidence suggests students who take more courses from non-tenure-track faculty experience lower academic success and graduation rates compared to their peers (Kezar 2013). Additionally, the poor living standards and work lives of adjuncts should be a concern because these individuals are responsible for educating the next generation for society and should therefore be compensated according to their tremendous responsibilities.

Yet there appears to be no immediate change in the current conditions: colleges and universities have increased the percentage of contingent faculty they hire every year—up 221.7% from 1975 to 2011 and 46.0% from 2001 to 2011 (Curtis 2014). Trends suggest that higher education institutions will continue down the path toward hiring more adjuncts to meet increasing enrollment demands from students and decreasing public funding for higher education.

According to Dubson, "No one else but the fast food industry allows so much of its principal work to be done by underpaid, expendable help. . . . The excessive use and abuse of adjuncts puts the grandstanding, the pontificating and the intellectualism of higher education officials into a very different light indeed" (2001, vi–vii).

It is important to note that adjuncts are not often alone in their struggles: other campus employees also experience challenges within their low-prestige and low-power positions, which can exacerbate feelings of isolation, fear, and fatalism as associated with their professional identities (Magolda and Carnaghi 2014; Magolda and O'Connell 2013). Higher education administration must consider the ramifications of these predominant labor market models—on adjunct faculty, professional staff, and students alike—and seek reforms to ensure that all faculty members are given an equal voice in the academy.

While retaining the reputation of a middle-class career pathway, the college professor occupation—especially adjunct faculty who now hold the majority of all faculty positions—has limited power and income opportunities, giving adjunct faculty working-class-like status in the social class hierarchy in higher education. Like working-class academics, the new working-class majority of adjunct skilled labor deserves full-fledged membership in the academy.

Chapter Eleven

"We're All Middle Class Here"

Privilege and the Denial of Class Inequality in the Canadian Professoriate

Timothy J. Haney

It is common in North American universities to hear faculty members and administrators proclaim that "we're all middle class here," and it is sadly a statement that I have heard far too often. Such claims serve to mask the class diversity that exists within university faculties and, more importantly, conceal the myriad ways that class inequality continues to affect the work done by professors.

Despite the silence about class, I have always felt that my own socioeconomic background continues to affect my academic work in many ways; from interactions with colleagues to the material that I teach and the topics I pursue in my research, my own socioeconomic origins matter. But is this true of other academics? And what prevents us from developing a more complete understanding of class inequalities among members of the professoriate?

Researchers are beginning to pay attention to the experiences of working-class students who navigate the educational system (Hurst 2009; Hurst 2010; Lehmann 2009a; Walpole 2003). Recent studies demonstrate how working-class students decide whether to attend a university and how their socioeconomic backgrounds matter while attending universities (Radford 2013; Stuber 2011; Armstrong and Hamilton 2013).

Still, research is lacking into how socioeconomic background may continue to matter after these individuals complete college and enter white-collar professions. And even less work has been done on the perceptions that middle-class workers in white-collar professions have of working-class colleagues.

This chapter shifts the focus to one profession in particular: the professoriate. It asks how the socioeconomic backgrounds of Canadian university professors shape the ways in which they approach their scholarly, pedagogical, and administrative work.

In this chapter I ask whether academics feel that their class-related experiences are salient or important in their work lives. If so, in what ways does class affect the ways that academics view their role in the university setting, how well do they "fit" within that environment, to what extent do they feel that the environment is welcoming of working-class individuals, and how do their classed upbringings affect their scholarly and pedagogical work?

More importantly, I ask what discursive strategies faculty members from more privileged backgrounds use to contextualize or understand class inequality in the professoriate. Building on my own reflections and buttressed by data from a nationwide sample of professors, spanning numerous disciplines and selected from all ninety-five institutions of the Association of Universities and Colleges of Canada (AUCC), the following analyses unpack the ways in which class background, though rarely talked about, continues to impact the work of professors. Further, it pays special attention to the ways that those from more privileged backgrounds overlook or conceal class difference in the professoriate.

I grew up in a family of automobile workers in the factory town of Janesville, Wisconsin. Through time spent working at the local General Motors plant, I became a third-generation automobile worker.

As the first in my family to attend college, and one of the first to work in a white-collar occupation, my experiences in college forced me to consider the many ways that my class background made me maladapted to a life of the mind. This includes a lack of tolerance for lengthy policy and bureaucratic discussions (which I view as talking about work, rather than actually doing work), a resentment of the assumption that we all have expendable income (and can donate money for every workplace event), a more passionate and emotional approach to work, and a disdain for purely theoretical work with no real-world application.

As these feelings accumulated, they led me to seek out a number of autobiographical essay collections on the experiences of working-class academics (Ryan and Sackrey 1995; Tokarczyk and Fay 1993; Dews and Law 1995), many of which confirmed that my feelings were shared by other working-class academics.

Still, I was dismayed by the lack of systematic scholarship on these issues—the type that would permit some degree of generalizability. As such, I undertook one of the first efforts to collect data from a random sample of professors, spanning Canadian universities, to help us understand the ways in which their socioeconomic backgrounds continue to matter in their professional careers.

In the following section, I briefly discuss the existing literature on working-class academics. Then, I utilize both my own reflections and data drawn from my sample of Canadian academics to examine the salience of class among the professoriate, in three main areas: (1) feelings of "fit" within the academy; (2) conflict and authority relations in the academic workplace; and (3) approaches to and motivations for teaching and research.

In each of these sections, I pay special attention to the issue of privilege, and the ways in which those faculty members hailing from middle-class origins frame or (just as often) deny the existence of class inequalities in their workplaces. Findings of the chapter demonstrate that although working-class faculty members feel profoundly affected by their class backgrounds, their middle-class colleagues are either unaware of their colleagues' origins or they argue that scholarship and teaching must remain detached from one's background.

To this end, they utilize discursive strategies that reduce differences to personality or intellect, rather than class background, while arguing that those who allow their backgrounds to affect the pursuit of knowledge are flawed or misfit academics. In doing so, this chapter demonstrates why class inequality continues to be left out of diversity discussions going on within academic spaces.

CLASS AND ACADEMIC WORK

Most existing research on class and higher education focuses on the important issue of how working-class college students navigate the middle-class space of the university (Granfield 1991; Hurst 2010; Lee and Kramer 2013; Lehmann 2007a; Lehmann 2009a) or, just as commonly, how class advantage facilitates access to a university education to begin with (Lehmann 2007b). Most of this research, however, ends upon degree attainment.

As a result, we know less about how socioeconomic background may continue to shape individuals' career trajectories, particularly in academia. There remains little empirical research on how the class backgrounds of professors affects their work, except for one study looking only at sociologists (Grimes and Morris 1997) and my own recent paper focusing on the educational, but not career, experiences of Canadian professors (Haney 2015).

There is a robust collection of essays by working-class academics. Based solely on autobiographical essays, Ryan and Sackrey (1984, 75) observe "academics from the working class have a sense of 'separateness from the academic community' of being a stranger, distance from an authentic sense of self."

Other collections of autobiographic and autoethnographic essays reach similar conclusions (Ryan and Sackrey 1984; Dews and Law 1995; Tokarczyk and Fay 1993). Probably the most significant theme emerging from the autobiographic and autoethnographic literature by working-class academics is the suggestion that academics from working-class backgrounds continue, through the duration of their careers, to feel out of place in the academic workplace. And, as I find in my previous work (Haney 2015), working-class academics often have to sacrifice close relationships to their families and home communities, as they drift farther apart culturally and geographically. This work suggests that class background continues to exert an influence over the life course and manifests itself in several ways.

First, academic work requires "a high level of politics" and networking (Grimes and Morris 1997, 100). Academics from working-class backgrounds may never properly learn or master these skills. As Langston (1993, 67) contends, "coming from a working-class background guarantees that you will feel uncomfortable in middle- and upper-class settings. . . . Keeping up with a different set of 'manners' and pretentious small talk is an exhausting experience."

Second, working-class academics report that the tone of speech and word choice they are forced to use in academic settings contrasts sharply with the language and tone they learned at home, forcing them to be extremely deliberate in choosing their speech.

Participants in Grimes and Morris's (1997) ambitious study felt that the lingering of working-class speech patterns (not to mention manners and appearance) impeded full acceptance into academia (199). And, as Tokarczyk and Fay (1993, 3) find, female academics from working-class backgrounds frequently felt "uncomfortable" with the language they used, afraid their voices would "slip into dialect or working-class patterns."

These findings suggest that, much like working-class college students (Kaufman 2003), working-class academics engage in code-switching, or the deliberate selection of one dialect and set of vocabulary in the workplace and another around working-class friends and family (Granfield 1991).

Regarding tone, Overall (1998) contends that she must deliberately tone down her "expressiveness and exuberance" as such expressiveness is seen as unprofessional or unwelcome in academic spaces. She argues that she must "be sure I know how to pronounce words that I have learned only through reading, and curb my tendency to use a relaxed, colloquial speaking style."

She further recalls that when she lapses into academic-speak around loved ones (using words like "demographics"), she is met with "incomprehension, laughter, and even contempt" (Overall 1998, 121). The inability to adjust speech patterns and modes of disagreement to the expectations of a middle-class milieu get some academics labeled as "trouble makers" (Overall

1998, 120) because they often originate from homes where there is rarely such a thing as a "civil" argument (Lubrano 2004, 65).

Third, fit within academia depends upon cultural capital (Bourdieu 1986), or knowledge about which cultural practices to engage in around middle-class academic colleagues. This includes subtleties regarding which type of drink to order at dinner (Lubrano 2004, 84), how to dress, or what books to read—all of which might potentially affect how academics relate to their colleagues in social situations. It also involves differing notions of how to conduct a meeting, how to handle conflict, and how to best accomplish collective tasks.

In one prescient example, Garger (1995) remarks that "[in meetings] we discovered the longer the argument ran, sometimes over an hour on a relatively minor issue, the more likely it was that when the motion was called it would pass unanimously. Viewed from my background, this represents a considerable waste of time and talent. . . . I am sure that my need for closure and 'to get it done' amuses my colleagues" (51).

Perhaps most importantly, existing essays assert that the ability of academics from working-class backgrounds to fit in within academia is negatively impeded by colleagues' ignorance of or unwillingness to address class difference. Middle-class colleagues "assume that you're just like them" (Lubrano 2004, 149) or "assert sameness" (Christopher 2009, 108).

Yates (2007, 160) points out, for instance, that his middle-class colleagues "had little knowledge of or sympathy for working people." As Overall (1998, 113) similarly recalls, "I have noticed that my attempts to discuss my working-class origins and their current significance within the university are often received with a certain discomfort best represented by the response, 'Why do you have to keep talking about it?'"

Feeling silenced, many working-class academics report attempting to pass as middle-class or trying to self-censor by avoiding discussions about class. Many others report existing in a culture where they are constantly bombarded with anti-working-class ideas. For instance, "[t]he prejudice against bowling alleys in departments of English is daunting" (Law 1995, 9).

These findings, culled from the autoethnographic literature, connect directly to a larger body of research on how those from privileged backgrounds understand their privilege and interact with those who are less privileged (see, for instance, Rasmussen et al. [2001] on "whiteness" or Khan [2012] on youth in an elite boarding school).

According to Nenga (2011), "little research examines the ways that individuals exercise agency in response to class privilege" (266). Nenga's study finds that privileged youth who do volunteer work use four different strategies to exercise agency discussing their work: they evade class as a topic of conversation, employ equalizing discourses that help them distance themselves from the poor, discuss the ways that their cultural capital prevents them from forming relationships with lower-income people, and in some cases, directly challenge their class privilege by forming interclass relationships and working for social justice objectives. Much like Nenga's youth, I expected that faculty members from more privileged backgrounds would adopt one or all of these strategies to explain their privileged position.

Taken together, the scattered existing evidence demonstrates that the differences in cultural capital and tastes, word choice and linguistic differences, the importance of networking and schmoozing, and the unwillingness of middle-class colleagues to discuss class serve to impede the ability of working-class academics to fit within academic spaces. But to what extent is this true across the academy? And how do both working-class and middle-class academics understand these differences? The following sections attempt to answer these questions.

UNDERSTANDING THE EFFECT OF CLASS BACKGROUND ON ACADEMIC WORK

The data analyzed in this chapter are drawn from surveys of 176 Canadian academics, selected randomly from ninety-five Canadian institutions. The 176 faculty members who responded to my survey (out of a sample of 1,000, for a response rate of 17.6 percent) span more than twenty academic disciplines.

All surveyed faculty members are full-time, tenure track or tenured (i.e., contingent and part-time faculty are not included as they are often not listed on department websites). For a detailed description of sampling and survey methodology, please consult Haney (2015).

Some references to quantitative analyses below are drawn from logistic regression models, all of which model the effect of three indicators of class background (self-identification, experiences of material deprivation, parental educational attainment), plus gender, on various class-related outcomes (the dependent variables). Although I omit regression tables for simplicity and brevity (available upon request), normally focusing on the qualitative findings, I will occasionally reference these quantitative findings below.

When attributing qualitative data to a particular individual, I will classify these individuals using the self-identification they provided in the survey (working/poverty-class vs. middle-class). Only one participant answered "upper-class/wealthy" and I have lumped this participant together with "middle-class." In most cases, I also cross-reference this self-identification with parental education, checking to see whether their parents held a bachelor's degree or higher.

"Fit" within Academia

Though I eventually learned to speak the academic language, I never feel wholly at home when doing so, and like many working-class academics, probably never will. My tone is more direct, I have less tolerance for obfuscation, and I detest long meetings over vision statements and ad nauseam discussion of the particularities of Robert's Rules of Order, which seems to happen so frequently. All of this, in my view, stems from my childhood in a lower-SES family and community. I often wonder if these feelings, normally difficult to conceal, prohibit my full participation in university life and might carry career penalties. I'm sure my more direct tone has been called "uncollegial" on more than one occasion.

The quantitative findings of my study (available upon request) indicate that faculty members from working-class backgrounds are less likely than middle-class colleagues to say they "fit in" within academia, and more likely to say they feel "different" from their colleagues, both suggesting that working-class academics perceive themselves as a bit out of place in the university. Working-class survey participants discussed their inability to articulate their ideas as well as their peers, and their general lack of "worldliness."

But how do middle-class participants understand difference and class-based heterogeneity in their workplaces? As expected, middle-class participants frequently discussed the ways in which they felt similar to their colleagues or felt that they belonged. In the words of Overall (1998), they "asserted sameness."

For instance, a male history professor notes his "similar interests and sensibilities" with his colleagues. Others refer to academics as "my people" or "my tribe." As one middle-class male psychology professor notes, "we disagree about many individual issues . . . [but] . . . we share common assumptions about how to address such disagreements (rational argument, evidence, etc.)." These accounts of shared assumptions and taken-for-granted consensus were largely missing from the accounts of working-class academics.

Though middle-class participants did note interactional differences between themselves and their colleagues, they did not typically connect these differences directly to class differences. Instead, they often attributed them to intelligence, social awareness, professionalism, or other "soft skills" that they perceive some other colleagues as lacking. In several instances, this took a judgmental tone. For instance, a middle-class male religious studies professor notes that there is a difference in speech between "me and the minority who make a socio-political point of speaking in an unprofessor-like manner." Similarly, a middle-class male English professor observes that "some colleagues are not particularly well-spoken."

Though these participants did not mention class when discussing these speech differences, one has to wonder if they are actually, perhaps unknowingly, drawing distinctions between themselves and their colleagues from working-class origins. Such comments leave me wondering whether the participants understand that they are comparing themselves to working-class colleagues, or if they fail entirely to recognize class difference.

A number of participants, almost entirely from middle-class origins, felt that class background almost certainly does not impact the way that professors fit into academic culture. One participant noted, "The main factor that determines how well one fits in is the quality and impact of one's work. To fit in, you need to do good work."

A middle-class male biology professor likewise feels that fit "has more to do with ability, drive and personality than it does with class background." And a middle-class female anthropologist feels that "fitting in [is] in some ways more about intellectual interests than class directly." Comments like these serve to actively minimize the potential importance of class background for fitting in within the academic workplace.

Others from middle-class backgrounds described class as "irrelevant," a term that appeared more than once in the qualitative data. As an extreme example, a middle-class history professor bristles at "any attempt to ennoble poverty or the struggles of working-class people." *Was this participant suggesting that my study was attempting to do that?*

The tendency to discount class as a meaningful axis of difference did not occur solely along class lines, however. As a working-class female physics professor notes, "a good academic is an independent thinker, and that means independent of their background too." This instructive comment implies that any academic who views their work as originating from or linked to their class background must not be "a good academic."

Similarly, a middle-class geographer claims that higher education is an "equalizer" so there really cannot be class differences among professors. Finally, some middle-class academics were blissfully ignorant of the class backgrounds of their colleagues. As one middle-class male biology professor reflects, "I don't know the class background of a lot of my peers, and they don't know mine."

Serving as more extreme examples, some participants typed curt, angry, or dismissive responses that critiqued the necessity and purpose of a study such as my own. A male middle-class economics professor remarked that "I am not sure why you are focusing on class. . . . I think class is a bit outdated way of thinking about things."

Others talked about their experiences in university, graduate school, and their work in academia as "meritocratic," "equalizing," or called scholarship a "homogenizer," suggesting that talent and intellect dwarf class background in determining who is successful in our chosen profession.

This dismissiveness by our middle-class colleagues toward the salience of class background in the professoriate is often hinted at in the autoethnographic literature, but these comments suggest the feelings are fairly commonly held among academics from middle-class origins.

As expected, working-class participants spoke of having to adjust their tones in the workplace, speak the academic language, and otherwise work to fit in. What is perhaps most noteworthy is that middle-class participants seem rather oblivious to these dynamics.

In other words, working-class participants discussed a rather elaborate game that they employ to allow them to better exist in an academic workplace (code-switching, adjusting their tone, looking up unfamiliar terminology after meetings, observing colleagues and modeling their behavior), yet their middle-class colleagues who inhabit the same hallways, corridors, and offices are largely unaware of these efforts—or, perhaps more perniciously, are aware but vehemently deny that these class differences matter in any meaningful way.

Conflict and Authority in the Academic Workplace

I know that I've never properly figured out how to network or "schmooze" at university functions. I've long viewed such networking as insincere and too status-driven. Hobnobbing with upper administrators and board members makes me uneasy and, where possible, I avoid these functions and instead sequester myself in my office to write or to prepare for teaching. Though I often beat myself up about my inability to play the game, I also know that it's entirely logical; nobody in my family taught me how to network, and I probably imbibed a significant amount of suspicion for those who do it.

In meetings, my tendency to flatly state my feelings on an issue has perhaps alienated some administrators who expect a particular degree of patronage or deference from faculty members. But my background seems to prevent me from properly choosing my battles, applying the right social lubricant, and disagreeing in a way that is allowable.

Prompted by my own difficulty understanding interactional rules in middle-class academic spaces, I asked participants in my study many questions about their relationships with colleagues and with authority figures. I also asked them about whether their colleagues were accepting of those from working-class backgrounds and about the classist comments they may hear in their workplaces.

Here it must also be remembered that one person's understanding of what constitutes a disparaging comment will naturally differ from another person's. For example, hearing a colleague characterize a local labor union as "greedy" may be understood by one person as a reasonable assessment of a labor dispute, while another may view it as an unnecessary, hostile attack on labor and working-class individuals. Therefore, this question measures perception as much as reality.

Still, it is worth noting that more than 40% of participants have heard disparaging comments about working-class or poverty-class people. At the same time, about 40% of participants feel that their colleagues are not accepting of those from lower-SES backgrounds, and 63% hold the belief that the university is a hostile place for those from lower-SES backgrounds.

These findings suggest that class hostilities are present in universities and the findings from logistic regression modeling (available upon request) reveal that middle-class faculty members are significantly less likely than working-class faculty to report hearing disparaging comments, again suggesting that many middle-class professors are unaware of the ways that class matters for their working-class colleagues.

As a middle-class female philosophy professor notes, "I think my colleagues assume that all their colleagues are from the same class background. There are a lot of jokes and stories told at the expense of working class and poverty class people from the area."

The qualitative data are also especially illuminating in terms of the issue of the university being hostile to working-class individuals. But here, middle-class participants tended to shift the discussion to working-class students, and away from the topic of the study: professors.

A female middle-class history professor believes that "sometimes the sense of privilege we have as academics is overlooked by colleagues who approach students hierarchically (using speech habits, theoretical lack of background or university affiliation as points of judgment)." This comment reveals that some colleagues unselfconsciously judge the merit of students or colleagues based upon criteria that are related to class background.

Similarly, one middle-class participant finds her peers "unselfconsciously classist," suggesting that some professors from more privileged backgrounds do indeed think about class inequalities, at least in terms of their relationships to students from lower-income backgrounds. Few, however, mentioned such "hierarchical" thinking or labeled their colleagues as "unselfconsciously classist" when interacting with colleagues from lower-SES backgrounds. This finding suggests to me that professors from more privileged backgrounds are, to some extent, aware of their classed interactions with students, but that this reflexivity does not normally extend to interactions with colleagues, who are generally viewed as homogenously middle class.

Among working-class participants, the rules for interacting in meetings, encapsulated by Robert's Rules of Order, were commonly maligned. This document outlines how debate and disagreement should proceed in meetings. Some working-class participants viewed this document as creating a meeting culture that is hierarchical and intimidating. Similar to my own reflections (see above), a working-class women's studies professor notes that "things like Robert's Rules continue to be completely unfamiliar to me. I find some meetings to be informal and engaging, but am very intimidated by Senate or the Board of Governors, for example." Besides the instructive comment about being intimidated by powerful individuals, this comment was common among working-class participants who noted that the rules for debate and disagreement (very formal, turn-taking, friendly amendments, etc.) conflicted with working-class practices for debate and disagreement.

The data also speak to the ability to work with, and the tendency to challenge, senior administrators. As an example of the privilege that middle-class participants feel in this arena, one economics professor notes, "I find it very easy to interact with colleagues in different disciplines, senior university administration as well as stakeholders from the private and public sector." The politicking necessary in academia is also exemplified by a comment from a middle-class female English professor who says that she got to her current position "by not making enemies—or not letting them know that they are enemies."

These notions of diplomacy, negotiation, and strategic alliance-building were largely missing from the working-class participants' responses; instead, they spoke of fear and trepidation. This fear was noted by several middle-class academics who were critical of their colleagues' "timidity," in some cases describing them as "deathly afraid of opposing policies or agendas that I know they feel to be insidious."

The findings do seem to suggest that those from middle-class backgrounds possess ease in dealing with administrators, while also exhibiting somewhat less trepidation in challenging those administrators—likely because they understand the ritualized, standard rules for how to do so without alienating that individual. By contrast, perhaps socialized into the ubiquitous fear of job loss, and not fully understanding these rules, many working-class academics report feeling intimidated and silenced when speaking with those in power.

Scholarly Praxis

At the start of each semester, I find myself scanning my classroom, looking for students who may come from lower-SES backgrounds, and trying to think of ways that I can help those students to be successful in their studies. A few times in my career, students have opened up to me about their class backgrounds—a brave and unusual thing to do in Alberta (an oil-rich province) and Canada (a place where we're eager to dismiss class inequality as a US problem). Those have been some of the most meaningful exchanges of my career.

In my research, I try to tackle problems whose solutions will materially benefit lower-SES people. Although I don't call myself an applied sociologist, I don't like to divorce myself from the real concerns of real people. I frequently listen to sociologist colleagues discuss their work on obscure texts, far-removed historical events, or purely theoretical problems, and when I ask them the "who gives a damn?" question, many are unable to articulate how their research matters for real people living in the real world.

I find this deeply problematic and have to believe my skepticism and intolerance stem from my own background—a background where few in my family had the luxury of pondering esoteric problems far detached from a material reality.

Any study on the work of professors should naturally include analysis of teaching and research—the two most important activities undertaken by an academic. The participants in my study opened up about their work in these two arenas. They also described their views on activism in the academy (an important arena for understanding professors' praxis) or their ability and willingness to put empirical knowledge to work in encouraging social change.

On this topic, working-class academics in the sample wrote passionately about the ways in which their class backgrounds impacted their teaching, typically prompting them to both incorporate discussions of inequality and power in their teaching and to be more sensitive to the struggles of working-class students.

A working-class female political scientist believes that because of her class background, she has "more empathy for students who are working their way through university than people who have not done so themselves. . . . I also participate in a work study program for students who are the first in their families to go to university."

Similarly, a working-class female philosopher tries to "watch out for students from a poor or working-class background and provide them with extra encouragement and mentoring." She believes this is a difficult task because "my university gives them every reason to be closeted." Participants often discussed their teaching as a potential vehicle for social change, and often select topics and examples strategically in order to encourage such change.

Although such responses did occur among middle-class participants, they appeared somewhat less commonly. Among middle-class participants, many expressed surprise that class considerations may be salient for university-level teaching. Middle-class participants tended to say "I don't know" or "I haven't thought about it before." As a middle-class male biologist reveals, "I would like to think that my approach to individual students is affected by their interest and academic ability, and not specifically by their socioeconomic background, which in most cases is not evident."

Similarly, a middle-class female historian says that her "primary concern is about student attitude and quality of their work. Their class background may impact that, but I do not tend to be aware of it." Others use phrases such as "as far as I am aware" or say flatly that "that question never entered my mind," which suggest only limited reflection into how their classrooms are affected by socioeconomic differences.

In even more extreme examples, several middle-class participants asserted that class considerations are totally irrelevant, or in some cases, seized the opportunity to answer the question about teaching with a condemnation of students who prioritize paid employment over their studies, something working-class students often must do. As one male philosopher argues, "I do not approach university teaching on the assumption that my students are working full time, but that they are full-time students."

A male historian likewise gets "impatient with students who don't want to put in the necessary hours at their studies because they are working (or have to work) to pay their way and try to do both at the same time, instead of working first and studying when they've saved up."

In an interesting contrast, the pattern emerging from the qualitative data is one where working-class faculty members discuss their tendency to watch for students from working-class backgrounds, spend extra time with them, provide mentorship, adopt perspectives (political economy, etc.) that will resonate with them, and work toward ameliorating existing inequalities through their teaching. Middle-class professors, by contrast, were more likely to say they do not think about class considerations in their teaching, cannot identify working-class students and, in several cases, are frustrated by students who do not prioritize their studies because of their employment schedules.

When asked whether class might affect their research endeavors, participants provided several insightful comments. In particular, working-class academics discussed the ways in which their class backgrounds impeded their ability to develop as researchers.

As one female English professor from a contradictory class background (mother is university educated, father worked as a tradesperson) indicates, "I don't think I had as much opportunity to learn how to properly do research, or the money to do it, because so much of my time was spent trying to make ends meet in grad school. I feel those from more wealthy backgrounds have better opportunities, contacts, and feel more entitled to travel or take semesters off from working [teaching] in grad school to do it."

Other working-class academics discussed how their class backgrounds prompted them to be more "practical" in their research and less theory driven; for these participants, research, like teaching, should work as a tool for social change and should not be disconnected from everyday concerns.

By contrast, middle-class participants often contend that they pursue more basic, less applied research agendas. As one middle-class male psychologist believes, he is "less concerned about the 'practicality' of my research topics because I accept academic research as valuable in its own right, and that might come from my upbringing in an academic household."

Though he acknowledges that his research questions might be informed by his class background, many other middle-class academics failed to make this connection, believing that they take a more detached, purportedly objective, approach to their research.

As a middle-class male historian indicates, "class does not affect the questions or the answers. It does not shape the writing. It does not enter how I act at conferences." A middle-class male aboriginal studies professor believes that his approach to research is entirely "careerist," presumably indicating that he envisions his work as advancing his own career, first and foremost. Similarly, a middle-class female English professor indicates "mainly what I'm doing here is making a living—a very, very nice living."

That said, there were also certainly middle-class academics who were concerned with the practical application of knowledge. As one middle-class male chemist believes, "I focus on research topics that have a very real practical purpose. I always say if I can't explain it to my mother in three sentences . . . then it's not worth doing."

Whereas many working-class academics acknowledged the ways that their political commitments affected their teaching and research, as well as the ways that activism was an integral part of their work, these reflections were largely missing from the accounts of their middle-class colleagues. A number of middle-class participants felt strongly that the academic mission of the university should remain distinct from activism.

Some, like a middle-class male professor of languages, believe we should not "use teaching to promote a specific activism that you're engaged in. . . . We should not use our privileged status (in the classroom) to promote a certain specific position that we hold personally." More bluntly, a middle-class male English professor remarks that "anyone who collapses research/ teaching and activism is not an academic."

In short, the qualitative data demonstrate that coming from a working-class background encourages faculty members to leverage their teaching and research responsibilities in ways that they hope will promote social change. This change, they hope, will create a more just, egalitarian world.

On the other hand, colleagues from middle-class backgrounds attempt to remain more objective in their teaching and research, while at the same time fearing that the insertion of activism into academic work may somehow corrupt the core mission of the university. Those from middle-class backgrounds also say they tend to not be aware of the class backgrounds of their students, and on the contrary, report feeling frustrated with students from working-class backgrounds (although their backgrounds are never mentioned explicitly) who have less time to commit to their studies.

CONCLUSION

I've often had colleagues tell me that as a white male, I can't properly understand social inequalities and shouldn't be teaching about them. I've always found this puzzling, as someone who came from a working-class family and community, and as the first in my family to attend college. It is even more puzzling when the colleagues who make such remarks are second- or third-generation academics, inheritors of intellectual and economic capital to which I never had access.

These interactions suggest to me that in an environment rife with identity politics, race and gender take priority, and class falls off the map. Though we must continue to investigate and understand race, gender, sexualities, and all other types of inequality, and how they intersect, there very clearly needs to be a more comprehensive understanding of the ways that class background shapes the experiences of professors and affects the work that we do.

This chapter presents an exploratory analysis of the ways in which professors' socioeconomic backgrounds impact their academic work and their workplace interactions. It also finds a strong current through which academics from more privileged backgrounds discount class as a potential marker of difference between themselves and their colleagues.

Much like Nenga's (2011) high-SES youth, participants in the study at times avoided class backgrounds of colleagues as a topic of conversation (switching instead to topics such as the class background of students, where there is more empirical literature and a more sustained discourse) and, at other times, applied equalizing discourses that erased class difference, instead attributing differences between colleagues to individual traits. They discuss differences in interest, work ethic, academic ability, intelligence, or professionalism—in short, personal, individual differences not related to socioeconomic status.

This finding suggests that some professors are blind to the ways that their own backgrounds advantage them vis-à-vis their working-class colleagues, while others may possibly see these inequalities but refuse to acknowledge them. Either way, this cluelessness about class difference prohibits a more robust discussion of class inequality within the professoriate.

Yet we must not forget that working-class faculty members are acutely aware of their middle-class colleagues' presumptions of privilege and a homogenous workplace culture. As Michael Schwalbe (1995) recalls, for instance:

> One time the conversation in the mailroom turned to sailing in the Mediterranean. I had nothing to say. For a moment I felt ashamed of my deficient background. But then I felt angry at the casual presumption of class privilege that I was witnessing. This one episode is like academia as a whole. Acquiring

what's necessary to participate is expensive. But some people begin with enough resources to pay the price with no pain at all. Those of us who pay dearly, and perhaps can never buy all that we need, may always have mixed feelings about our purchase. (329)

It is my hope that this chapter is a first step in knocking down these silent and exclusionary walls of privilege, and I'm hopeful that more working-class academics will move beyond feelings of shame and actively challenge such "casual presumption[s] of class privilege."

It is also entirely possible that much conflict in the academy occurs because of cultural or interactional differences related to class background, but books on conflict or "incivility" in academia often make little or no mention of class (i.e., Twale and De Luca 2008), meaning that a great deal of conflict is instead chalked up to simple interpersonal differences. Yet my findings suggest that creating an explicit dialogue about class inequality in the academy might do much to assuage workplace conflict and create better working conditions for professors from all socioeconomic backgrounds.

The findings discussed above also indicate the need for more robust discussions of diversity in the academy. Though universities often maintain task forces dedicated to ending sexism, racism, or homophobia in institutional processes such as hiring or tenure/promotion, few of these groups make efforts to diversify the academy in terms of socioeconomic origins (Oldfield 2007).

In my previous work, I have advocated for the inclusion of socioeconomic background in university hiring statements and even for a class-based program of affirmative action in white-collar professions (Haney 2015, 182).

Hopefully by demonstrating that class background still matters in the lives of today's academics, and by demonstrating the mechanisms by which middle-class faculty members sometimes resist this more inclusive discussion, this chapter and this volume can help to generate more inclusive policies and practices in North American colleges and universities.

Chapter Twelve

Narrating the Job Crisis

Self-Development or Collective Action?

Gretchen Braun

The summer before my first of several forays into the academic job market, I casually mentioned to my dissertation director that I planned to participate in a sympathy strike with the union representing campus custodial and food service staff. His reaction was not disapproval, but puzzlement.

He recognized the practical value of graduate student unionization, as a means to ensure reasonable workloads so that teaching assistants could successfully complete their studies. But he couldn't fathom why I would walk a picket line with the janitor who cleaned our building.

I was equally confused by his response. After years of teaching composition at wages that qualified me for Lifeline telephone service, entering a depressed job market and uncertain I would ever find tenure-track stability, my connection with the experience of working-class employees lacking job security seemed obvious.

Neither my perspective nor my director's was unreasonable. Graduate students and recent PhDs who enter the academic job market find themselves poised between two class identities.

Several years later, newly settled in a tenure-track position, I became curious about the professional discourse surrounding this moment of transition: the years when a graduate student becomes a job seeker.

This chapter suggests that when academics in the humanities discuss the ongoing "job crisis" and the resultant adjunctification of the academy, their discourse is influenced by the narrative traditions that are their objects of scholarly study. Simply put, when reflecting on the experiences of graduate students and job seekers in a precarious academic workplace, scholars of literature often turn to the genre of the *Bildungsroman*, the novel of self-development. This move has classed implications, and may impede productive concrete and systemic responses to the growing inequality within the professoriate.

While engaging to some degree the broad problem of contingency within academic workplaces, my analysis targets the discourse about employment in humanities programs and particularly among English, literature, and foreign language faculty.

There are two rationales for this focus. The first is quite simply practical: departments of English, in staffing composition courses, and departments of modern foreign languages and literatures, in seeking instructors for introductory language classes, have increasingly turned to contingent faculty to fill these unglamorous and labor-intensive assignments. [1]

In addition to the growing reliance on degreed adjunct instructors within the humanities, it is widely known that at research universities, graduate students in English and related fields teach many if not most introductory composition courses, and a growing number of literature courses. [2]

English professor and former union activist Marc Bousquet, whose research on academic labor systems informs my analysis, has argued that "the holders of the doctoral degree are not so much the *products* of the graduate student labor system as its *by-products*," ironically less likely to find stable employment in the academy once they complete the PhD (Bousquet 2008, 21). Problems associated with a casualized academic workforce and a depressed market facing seekers of stable tenure-track jobs are most visible within humanities fields.

The second rationale concerns not the sheer numbers of contingent faculty, but the way their experiences within the humanities job market and workplace are narrativized in professional publications. Specifically, the focus on individual growth or disillusionment inadvertently deflects attention away from systemic analysis and collaborative responses to exploitation and hardship.

After outlining how narrative functions as a means of understanding and providing a framework for thinking about class within the academic hierarchy, this chapter considers how the "job crisis" is addressed by humanities scholars in their professional forums. My interest lies in how literature faculty dialogue with one another about the consequences of and possible solutions to the shortage of tenure-track positions, the increasingly marked disparity between tenure-track and non-tenure-track instructors, and the related experiences of seekers of tenure-track jobs.

My analysis is deliberately focused upon how these problems are narrativized and debated within mainstream professional publications, recognizing that alternative venues, such as online activist communities, can produce a different discourse. Narratives of and perspectives on contingency under discussion include essays from Modern Language Association publications

(*PMLA*, *ADE/ADFL Bulletin*), *Women in German Yearbook*, and both the *Chronicle of Higher Education* and *Inside Higher Ed* (online professional news sources). These essays document and may unintentionally reproduce faculty resistance to collective action as a possible solution.

NARRATIVE AS MEANS OF UNDERSTANDING

Narrative is not simply entertainment: according to the literary critic and theorist Peter Brooks, plot is "the organizing dynamic of a specific mode of human understanding" (1984, 7). We particularly turn to storytelling in the face of events we find challenging or unacceptable, he argues, because "the ordering of the inexplicable and impossible situation as narrative . . . somehow mediates and forcefully connects its discrete elements," allowing speaker/writer and audience/reader to comprehend circumstances that defy logical reasoning (Brooks 1984, 10). We tell stories to make sense of our world and achieve intellectual mastery over life events.

The influential Marxist critic Franco Moretti calls the *Bildungsroman*, nascent in the eighteenth century and dominant in Western society through the nineteenth, "the symbolic form of modernity," defining it as a subgenre of narrative fiction particularly concerned with youth and characterized by "mobility" and "interiority" (Moretti 2000, 4). *Bildungsromans* (literally, "novel of formation" in German) trace the progress of an adolescent as he or she leaves the security of the originating home, encounters a broader socioeconomic environment, and finds a place in it. Mistakes made and challenges met along the way develop insight.

Within the traditional form of this genre, "self-development and integration are complementary and convergent trajectories" (Moretti 2000, 18–19). The protagonist's discovery of authentic identity is linked to finding her place within a community, and maturity is marked by professional accomplishment (men), marriage (women, sometimes also men), or meaningful death (either). Charlotte Brontë's *Jane Eyre*, Charles Dickens's *David Copperfield*, and Stendhal's *Le Rouge et le noir* can all be considered within this framework: they prioritize individuality, documenting a psychological as well as a temporal and physical journey.

Moretti associates the classical *Bildungsroman* both practically and thematically with the advent of industrial capitalism. It is an explicitly bourgeois story, not suited to working-class protagonists, who lack the economic and social means to actualize individual aspirations (Moretti 2000, ix). Similarly, Brooks, whose analysis of the nineteenth-century European *Bildungsroman* focuses on "the ambitious hero" (1984, 39), ties the genre to public aspiration and self-betterment. Why is the traditional *Bildungsroman* exclusively a bourgeois genre, and primarily a masculine one?

Moretti locates these limitations in the historical moment of its genesis. During the eighteenth and nineteenth centuries, he argues, "the west European middle-class man held a virtual monopoly" on the "wide cultural formation, professional mobility, [and] full social freedom" essential to this narrative arc (Moretti 2000, ix). Unlike the aristocrat, he has something to aspire toward; unlike the working-class man or any woman, he has formal education, ease of physical and geographical mobility, and control over economic resources, not to mention a cultural mandate to take leadership roles in the public sphere (2000, viii–x).

A few examples will be illustrative. In Dickens's *Oliver Twist*, the hero's childhood begins in abject poverty, first in a workhouse and then as a petty thief under the control of vicious career criminals. He always feels at odds with the morals and pleasures of his fellows, gravitating instead toward the genteel lifestyle he fleetingly experiences with upper-class benefactors. The novel closes with the discovery that Oliver is a gentleman's son cheated of his inheritance by a wicked half-brother, and he enters adolescence safely ensconced in the class to which he was born. In this paradigm, the authentic self is the middle-class self.

Similarly, the title characters of both *David Copperfield* and *Jane Eyre* experience privation, but reconnect with well-to-do relatives at key moments in the plot; these connections enable their class ascension. David earns public respect as a writer; his marriage to the "right" domestic woman crowns his success but does not define it.

Jane's fate illustrates the limitations of the form for female protagonists: while she rises from charity-school governess to land-owning lady, her marriage to Rochester ends her economic participation and sequesters her in rural life. Both David and Jane demonstrate industry, but benefit from preexisting bourgeois ties.

In these novels, a youth earns respect and economic advancement through social challenges that develop character, proving that his or her disposition aligns with the values of the ruling class, thus warranting a happy ending. Modern coming-of-age stories reimagine this core narrative to accommodate a greater variety of class positions and ethnicities, to convey a wider range of female experience, and to recognize different modes of mature belonging. But the traditional *Bildungsroman* retains its imaginative sway, as demonstrated by the numerous filmic adaptions and cultural appropriations of Dickens and Austen novels, and of Brontë's *Jane Eyre*.

Crucially for my analysis, the traditional *Bildungsroman* neither cultivates class solidarity nor ends well for protagonists whose proletarian roots run too deep. David Copperfield works in a factory, but he does not build meaningful friendships there. Jane Eyre as governess maintains hierarchical social distance from the other servants in Rochester's home. Those nineteenth-century *Bildungsromans* that feature a truly working-class protagonist often end not only in tragedy, but in alienation.

Among traditional nineteenth-century novels of self-development, genuinely working-class protagonists are less common and fare less well, seldom achieving full social integration. For instance, Pip of Dickens's *Great Expectations* is a workingman's orphan articled as a blacksmith when a secret benefactor gratifies his wish to be a gentleman, providing him an inheritance and education.

However, he squanders the inheritance and closes the novel awkwardly and unhappily middle class, working as a merchant, trapped between his affection for the working-class family that raised him and his hopeless love for a wealthy woman.

Pip does better than some of his working-class literary peers. The title character of Thomas Hardy's *Jude the Obscure* dies alienated both from the stonemasons among whom he worked and the dons and university students with whom he aspired to study.

Charlotte Elizabeth Tonna's *Helen Fleetwood* tells of a resolutely virtuous working-class protagonist worn down and finally killed by factory life. The heroine of Elizabeth Gaskell's *Mary Barton* achieves happiness only by marrying a man whose ingenuity and industry have brought him into the middle class. She distances herself from her Chartist factory worker father and her fellow seamstresses, who are portrayed as morally flawed.

The implicit message: ambition among the working classes is self-destructive, ending in early death, shame, or both, and it is particularly dangerous when individual aspiration is coupled with a strong allegiance to working-class interests.

Relatedly, even as *Bildungsromans* document mature community integration through professional success and/or marriage, they teach readers that individuality is preferable to a notion of selfhood defined through commonalities with peers. The first-person narration of both *David Copperfield* and *Jane Eyre* celebrates interiority almost to the point of self-absorption, and the plots of these novels implicitly demonstrate the incompatibility of personal ambition with group allegiance (although family bonds are generally affirmed).[3]

Thus we see the potential pitfalls of imposing *Bildungsroman* conventions upon professional discussion of the alleged humanities "job crisis." We are telling the story of diverse individuals facing poverty in a middle-class, Eurocentric, largely masculinized narrative form. Regardless of our intentions, we are shifting attention from structural impediments to seekers of tenure-track employment and focusing on their feelings, personal transformation, and individual success or failure. We are placing their experiences in a narrative context that constructs individual success as achieving a middle-

class professional status *against* competitors, not *through* collaborative networks of equals.

CLASSED IDENTITIES WITHIN LITERATURE,
LANGUAGE, AND WRITING PROGRAMS

As any college teacher knows—but college students may fail to discern—the
middle-class or even elite lifestyle widely attributed to professors by the
general public does not accord with the lived experience of many faculty
teaching on contemporary campuses in the United States. The reality of
marginalization and economic instability some contingent faculty undergo
conflicts with our deeply ingrained American cultural association of education with opportunity and class ascension.

It is useful here briefly to review terminology specific to the labor structure of American academia. The crucial distinction is that between tenure-
track faculty (full, associate, or assistant professor), who enjoy degrees of
employment stability, and contingent faculty, who are employed either on a
contract basis for one or more years, often with benefits (lecturers), or on a
per-course basis, without any benefits (adjuncts or "part-time" faculty). Ironically, to eke out a living, so-called part-time faculty generally must teach far
more courses per year than their tenure-track colleagues, unless they have
other income.

It is common knowledge that across academic disciplines, research-
focused tenure-track appointments with lower teaching loads that comprise
fewer general education courses are considered most prestigious and are
typically most remunerative.

Specifically within departments of English, positions focused on particular literary or theoretical fields are overwhelmingly (though not exclusively)
more respected, better paid, and, crucially, more stable than those devoted
primarily to the teaching of literature surveys and/or undergraduate writing.
Positions in rhetoric and composition are desirable only if they are tenure-
track, research-focused jobs, as in the expanding field of digital scholarship
(Bousquet 2014, 1).[4]

Similarly, in modern foreign language programs, introductory composition and conversation courses are likeliest to be taught either by graduate
student instructors or other contingent faculty, while more advanced courses
in literature and culture will fall to the tenure-track professors. Even if the
number of students majoring in languages decreases, demand for introductory conversation courses—as French scholar Joseph Mai terms them, "'*Bon-
jour, ça va*' classes"—holds steady, ensuring a need for contingent labor
(Mai 2007, 53).

Between the mid-1970s and the mid-1990s, feminism attained prominence in humanities research, ethnic studies programs were instituted following student demands, and postcolonial studies became recognized as an interdisciplinary field. These two decades (1975–1995) coincide with the rise of composition studies and the related explosion of low-paid, contingent instructorships statistically likeliest to be staffed by women, in which faculty of color are overrepresented (Bousquet 2008, 165–66, 171).[5]

For female and nonwhite faculty, gains in terms of shaping academic discourse have not clearly translated into material gains.[6] Bousquet insists that higher education workforce "casualization is an issue of racial, gendered, and class justice" (2008, 43).

Quite reasonably, contingent faculty discuss their experiences within the academy as classed experiences, in primarily negative ways. In her analysis of "the rhetorics and realities of contingent writing instructors," rhetoric and composition scholar Eileen Schell—herself a former adjunct composition teacher—observes that "in hierarchical, stratified cultures such as the military or academia, ranks and titles affect every aspect of a professional's life" (Schell 1998, 62).

One's position within the hierarchy has implications economically (salary and eligibility for health and retirement benefits), materially (office space and access to technology), and socially (professional and personal inclusion).

An anonymous humanities career adjunct who considers faculty like himself or herself "second-class citizens" describes both limited access to resources (research grants, facilities, preferred courses) and social exclusion from tenure-track colleagues: "I always wanted to feel part of a university. Going to graduation ceremonies just makes one feel on the margins" (Anonymous 2015, 1). More polemically, an adjunct writing instructor thus characterizes her isolation and exploitation: "Adjuncts, separate and unequal. South Africa has abandoned its policy of apartheid, but academic apartheid still exists in the United States" (Hahn 2001, 69).

Contingent faculty in contract positions may in fact have both middle-class incomes and the institutional resources to excel as teachers (even as they may regret the lack of support, and indeed time, for research). Adjuncts, by contrast, find every aspect of their professional lives stymied by the terms of their employment.

Public discussions of why adjuncts remain in academia despite low wages often fall back on the notion that they regard teaching as a calling worthy of the sacrifice. But the conditions of their labor undermine both effective pedagogy and meaningful connections with students. Spreading a heavy course load across multiple campuses makes it difficult to provide individualized attention. Shared or nonexistent office space impedes effective student conferencing. Uncertain employment complicates long-term mentoring, and when poverty-level adjuncts instruct children of privilege, they doubtless feel uncomfortable dissonance.

When humanities faculty discuss the academic job market, either as graduate students embarking upon it or as tenured faculty reflecting on hiring patterns, this bleak specter of contingency looms over the conversation. Anxiety and anger over adjunctification have begun to spread beyond the academy. The 2013 death of eighty-three-year-old Margaret Mary Vojtko, a cancer-stricken career adjunct in French who could not afford to fix her furnace, provoked public outrage when covered in online forums such as *Slate* and *Huffington Post*.

It is noteworthy, however, that outcry over Vojtko's demise conveys shock not simply at her exploitation, but that someone so *educated* could decline to such dire straits. Daniel Kovalik, the union representative whose *Pittsburgh Post-Gazette* op-ed ignited interest in Vojtko's case, describes fielding an inquiry from Adult Protective Services, weeks before her collapse.

After he explained that the ailing woman's poverty resulted from a layoff from her university teaching job, Kovalik reports, "the caseworker paused and asked with incredulity, 'She was a professor?' . . . This was not the usual type of person for whom she was called in to help" (Kovalik 2013, 1).

Public outrage over the hardships of contingent faculty—however justified and even necessary—is inextricable from Americans' ingrained valuation of education as the means to class ascension. William Pannapacker, an English professor from a working-class background who has written extensively, scathingly, and often insightfully about the problem of contingency, observes that "for most of us, graduate school in the humanities is about the implicit promise of the life of a middle-class professional, about being respected, about not hating your job and wasting your life" (Pannapacker 2010, 1). Hence the shock when it is instead a preface to poverty.

NARRATING THE JOB MARKET: SELF-DEVELOPMENT

The job market, and the seemingly interminable job crisis, figures prominently in publications focused on higher education. This is understandable: the issue is central to the working conditions of all instructional staff, from adjuncts to full professors, and to the future of humanities scholarship as we know it. What is less clear at first glance is why language and literature faculty so often turn to *Bildungsroman* conventions to engage this problem. As more humanities PhDs will find themselves in the proletarian position of adjunct than the bourgeois position of tenured professor, this narrative choice is problematic.

In the twenty-first century, the job market essay has become a definable genre, particularly within advice and opinion columns in venues such as *The Chronicle of Higher Education*. It shares several key characteristics with the traditional *Bildungsroman*. Both generally relate, in first or third person, the story of one or several idealistic and ambitious young people seeking their place in a broader community. Like the *Bildungsroman* protagonist, the typical job seeker is cast as wanting not only material advancement and status, but also emotional fulfillment.

References to specific novels can serve as shorthand for emotional experience. Tasked with producing an advice column for job seekers, Mai abjures clichéd dictums in favor of a nuanced analogy to Gustave Flaubert's *A Sentimental Education* (Mai 2007). Dialoging back with faculty who advise undergraduates to forgo the PhD, English professor Gina Barreca (2010) invokes Thomas Hardy's *Jude the Obscure* to make the case for access across socioeconomic class.

In a wry meditation on leaving an Ivy League position when faced with impending tenure denial, German literature scholar Eric Jarosinski (2014) sardonically name-checks that prototypical *Bildungsroman* of intellectual angst, *The Sorrows of Young Werther*, which concludes in suicide. In a still bleaker account, the amusingly pseudonymed Atlas Odinshoot (2014) envisions the academic job seeker as a tribute fighting his fellows to the death in the dystopic world of *The Hunger Games*.

Even when specific novels of self-development are not invoked, the focus on individual psychological growth through professional challenge persists. Soo Jin Pate (2014) and Rebecca Schuman (2014), recent PhDs whose promising graduate careers have not yet led to the anticipated tenure-track appointment, have each written *Chronicle* essays on how adjuncting changed their attitude toward teaching and their understanding of success and failure. In *Inside Higher Ed*, William Bradley (2014) has reflected on how a feared recurrence of Hodgkin's lymphoma provided much-needed perspective during the anxiety-ridden job search process.

Adjunct colleagues and fellow job seekers are noticeably absent from the day-to-day world depicted in these stories. Interactions with students (or in Bradley's case, fellow patients and physicians) are depicted in detail; beloved family and/or distant mentors are sketched in the background. Schuman quotes adjuncts at other institutions to support her analysis, but does not describe her colleagues. These essays prioritize the narrating adjunct/job seeker's internal struggles with ambition, self-doubt, persistent hope, and awareness of injustice, to the exclusion of portraying any community among contingent faculty. And they are typical of the genre.

All of the essays referenced anchor their analyses in actual *Bildungsroman* narratives and/or employ recognizable elements of the traditional genre as it has been handed down to us from the nineteenth century. These rhetorical choices are not culpable in themselves, and indeed may be illuminating, but they do influence how both the authors, and their wide readership within professional publications, conceptualize personal experience within the humanities job market. The *Bildungsroman* typically envisions peer groups as competitive rather than collaborative, and to achieve formal cohesion, such novels tell one story at the expense of others.

Zeroing in on the psychological development of a particular academic may vividly evoke the material conditions of his or her labor, but it does not promote practical connections between individuals facing the same structural impediments to well-being. As narrative theorist Alex Woloch argues, the nineteenth-century realist novel (by which these contemporary narratives are informed) implicitly teaches readers that while many characters *can* emerge as hero, only one *will*; this novelistic tension between *recognizing* multiple valid claims and *privileging* one resonates with ambivalence about widespread political enfranchisement (Woloch 2003, 31).[7]

Not entirely unlike the nineteenth-century British ruling class, many contemporary American academics—those who have or harbor hopes of acquiring a tenure-track position—retain a deep ambivalence about sharing institutional and professional leadership with less privileged colleagues (long-term lecturers and career adjuncts). In focusing on individual accomplishment, whether defined as stable employment or a more enlightened perspective, the job market essay can unintentionally reproduce an ethos of self-protection and competition and undercut potential for solidarity.

Pannapacker might perhaps be credited (or blamed, depending on one's perspective) with developing or at least popularizing the job market essay genre. He places the psychological state of the job seeker front and center: his first *Chronicle* publication is a 1998 piece that opens with the line, "Graduate school is not just learning a discipline; it's internalizing a permanent sense of inadequacy and dread" (Pannapacker 1998, 1).

Pannapacker's essays—first published under his own name, then, after he began a tenure-track position, sometimes under the pen name Thomas H. Benton—address a range of topics within academic life. Early on, he related first-person impressions as a labor activist on the job market. But he is best known for his impassioned (and some might say embittered) essays warning undergraduates away from graduate school, written from the security of a tenured position, in pained awareness that most young people entering the profession will have a different fate.

An early example entitled "Hope, or a New Life on the Tenure Track" (Pannapacker 2000) describes the transformative moment when, on his daughter's first birthday, he was finally offered a tenure-track position at Hope College. He reflects upon his earlier anger at the academic establishment and his own mentors, which he judges sometimes justified and sometimes ungrateful, and he contemplates his journey from Harvard graduate student and labor activist to one of the fortunate few tenure-track college faculty.

Despite its conscious engagement with contingency as a structural problem of the academy, and stated aspiration to correct it, the essay focuses upon its author's self-development, even describing his relief at the job placement as a sense that "my life had become a Pilgrim's Progress" (Pannapacker 2000, 1).

Ten years later, writing as a tenured professor, Pannapacker would craft a searing indictment of the academy that reversed this optimistic narrative. "The Big Lie about the 'Life of the Mind'" (Pannapacker 2010) provoked even more outrage than the controversial "Graduate School in the Humanities: Just Don't Go" (Pannapacker 2009). "The Big Lie about the 'Life of the Mind'" tells the story of a hypothetical graduate student who seems rather like a female version of Pannapacker: from working-class origins, initially delighted to attend an Ivy League graduate program, and eventually disillusioned by years of unsuccessful academic job searching.[8]

Here the fictional version diverges: rather than getting that call from Hope that restores hope, "she continues as an adjunct who qualifies for food stamps, increasingly isolating herself to avoid feelings of being judged" (Pannapacker 2010, 1).

Pannapacker tells us, "Such people sometimes write to me about their thoughts of suicide, and I think nothing separates me from them but luck" (2010, 1). He argues that universities profit at the expense of graduate students like this one, whose working-class or middle-class families taught them to regard education as a path to advancement, who lack the networks and resources that allow students from more elite backgrounds to excel on the academic job market, and who have become so deeply "identified with academic life" (Pannapacker 2010, 1) that they cannot envision themselves either happy or professionally successful outside of it.

This is a story of unraveling rather than maturation, but it is still concerned primarily with the effects of economic injustice on an *individual* psyche. The essay briefly calls for collective action from graduate students, and the American Association of University Professors, to demand universities release comprehensive data about PhD placement. But it does not imagine what such action would look like. Its only clear mandates are negative: that undergraduates don't go to graduate school in the humanities, that their professors don't advise them to do so.

Pannapacker is far from alone in evincing uncertainty about the efficacy of collective action as a feasible solution. Graduate student Katharine Polak crafted a 1,287-word reply to "The Big Lie about 'The Life of the Mind'" that calls on tenure-track faculty to partner in developing concrete responses to the job crisis; she dismisses unionization in a brief parenthetical comment that blames tenured faculty for their lack of "commitment" to it (Polak 2010, 1).

Perhaps the most extreme articulation of the position that the dismal job market should be an opportunity for self-development comes from A. W. Strouse, a doctoral student in English. Contextualizing the hardships of contemporary academics within the history of scholarly renunciation from the Middle Ages onward, he suggests that "today's labor crisis could be considered part of our heritage as academics," pointing out that "poverty and self-sacrifice" have long been associated with the life of the mind (Strouse 2015, 1). He suggests, "instead of seeing our bad wages as a sign of shame, we might wear them as a badge of honor" (2015, 1).

Strouse concludes that "spiritualizing the cruelty of the job crisis could, at least, offer some philosophical consolation" (2015, 1). One might reasonably inquire whether this consolation would still be adequate were the author to face a medical emergency or any other circumstance in which economic stability and health benefits are crucial. Does embracing one's intellectual forefathers (and their maleness is implicit, though unacknowledged, in Strouse's essay) impede political and economic alliances with contemporary colleagues in higher education?

It is telling that perspectives so opposed as Pannapacker's and Strouse's both focus on the job seeker's individual psyche. The culture of humanities scholarship encourages this inward turn, which may in part explain reluctance to act collectively.

THINKING STRUCTURALLY, ACTING COLLECTIVELY

Many tenured and tenure-track faculty remain distrustful of unionization and other forms of collective action. But as universities corporatize, this opposition erodes as the practical value of collaborative solutions becomes evident. When more than two-thirds of college teachers are not in tenurable positions, how can we maintain academic freedom?

In the late 1990s, reflecting on her recent stint as a dean at Arizona State University, prominent feminist theorist Annette Kolodny observed that "university faculty have traditionally been reluctant to blur the boundaries between blue-collar wage earning and salaried professional status" but, like physicians and nurses, began turning to unionization in the face of corporatized pressure for increased productivity with limited resources (Kolodny 1998, 205). Almost twenty years later, however, labor movements still meet with resistance among tenure-line faculty. Michael Bérubé confronted that reluctance head-on as MLA president.

Bérubé opened his convention address calling 2012–2013 "a watershed, the year when the working conditions of most of our colleagues in higher education moved from the margin to the center of discussion" (Bérubé 2013, 530). Noting several meaningful accomplishments, most importantly a first-ever MLA per-course wage recommendation for adjunct faculty, he nonetheless expressed concern that the very nature of intellectual work within language and literature studies—defined by increasing specialization within subdisciplines over the course of one's career—discourages thinking collectively about the field as a whole (539).

Perhaps the most intractable impediment to effective organizing is the resistance of many university faculty to embracing the identity of "worker" with its implication of interdependence with others. As history professor David Perry suggests, "Academics—even many adjuncts—continue to think they belong to a loosely meritocratic system in which the best work rises to the top, peer review remains the optimal way to judge the quality of work, and if you work hard enough, you'll be fine" (Perry 2014, 1). The individualized nature of academic research within the humanities, where coauthoring is rare, solidifies the self-image of autonomous professional.

But professional organizations and their publications can articulate and embody solidarity. Brigetta Abel's recent essay in *Women in German Yearbook*, "Activism and Academia" (2014), provides one model of incorporating personal experience into professional dialogue in a way that fosters collaboration rather than solipsism. Throughout Abel's essay, we meet with descriptions of faculty engaging in thoughtful debate and mutual support, across academic rank.

Abel segues from her own decision to cease tenure-track job searching and remain in a lectureship into analysis of the two-tier academic labor system and the role professional organizations can play in combating its hazards (Abel 2014, 187–92). The security of tenure, she points out, enables faculty to engage controversial issues in meaningful ways without fear of reprisal (190–91). To emphasize the importance of such engagement, Abel then describes her own involvement in Minnesota's 2012 election battle over marriage equality, and how groups of faculty and students confronted these civil rights questions (192–95).

The essay's argument about the threat contingency poses to both faculty well-being and academic freedom connects the author's personal experience to goal-directed action among faculty colleagues, student populations, and the community beyond the college gates. And it calls readers to action, not just individually but collectively: "We need to create pressure from within; we need to use the structures and organizations that already exist within academia to fight for a fairer system" (191). There are encouraging recent examples of faculty thinking, acting, and even *writing* collectively, in line with what Abel models and envisions.

In a recent *Chronicle* commentary addressed to administrators who seek to reduce operating costs, Scott Schneider, a higher education attorney who represents employers, warns that socioeconomic and legal conditions are now favorable for faculty organizing. He notes the recent National Labor Relations Board (NLRB) ruling in favor of full-time faculty organizing at Pacific Lutheran University and the contract victories of adjuncts at Tufts University, and one detects a tone of anxiety when he opines, "colleges are perhaps more vulnerable now to organizing drives and pressure to improve working conditions of their faculty members than they have ever been" (Schneider 2015, 1).

Increasingly, contingent faculty are working together—sometimes within or alongside mainstream professional organizations—to share information and ideas toward the goal of achieving a more equitable workplace. For instance, as Bérubé noted in his 2013 address, Josh Boldt, a member of the adjunct advocacy organization New Faculty Majority, spearheaded a collaborative website called The Adjunct Project that enables contingent faculty to share employment data (Bérubé 2013, 531).

Now partnered with the *Chronicle* and supported by the MLA and AHA, this site allows adjuncts to submit per-course salaries by institution, search salary data by geographical area, and blog about their experiences.[9] A July 29, 2014, blog submission from Joseph Fruscione asks readers to sign a petition calling on the US Department of Labor to investigate faculty working conditions in light of adjunctification. While many blog posts relate personal narratives, they invite advice and dialogue; for instance, "How do you respond to requests like this from students? And why?"[10] Site design promotes communication and action on concrete issues.

A similar ethos of collective action governs the MLA "subconference," a "shadow" convention run by and for job seekers and contingents in 2014 and 2015. The subconference describes itself as "an autonomous gathering of graduate workers, adjunct and contingent faculty, and unemployed or independent intellectuals who are interested in creating a new kind of conference environment for ourselves and our peers" (Subconference of the MLA Community, 1).[11]

Most panels have focused on labor conditions in the academy, including practical issues of use to organizers, such as "University Finances 101." Unlike the MLA conference itself, registration was free and meals were provided.

The Adjunct Project and the MLA subconference entail turning away from the private interiority of the beleaguered adjunct. For more than a decade, adjuncts and job seekers have employed the self-focused narrative model descended from the *Bildungsroman* to relate their progress through a precarious, corporatized academic workplace. While this rhetorical move is understandable, it can inadvertently undermine coalition building between workers in academe.

Contingent faculty have recently shifted the discourse and reinvigorated collective action within higher education, challenging the stratification that still characterizes American university teaching. Notwithstanding the necessarily individualistic nature of some research, academics can and arguably must find ways to imagine, enact, and narrate autonomy without perpetuating rank-based division or self-isolation.

NOTES

1. David Laurence's (2013) MLA study finds a higher percentage of humanities faculty teaching off the tenure track, as opposed to social sciences and natural sciences faculty, and that the majority of these contingent faculty personnel hold (less stable and remunerative) part-time teaching assignments. According to this study, 50.3% of all humanities faculty members are now in non-tenure-track positions (with an additional 8.5% working at institutions without any tenure system) (Laurence 2013, 15). By contrast, in the social sciences 41.8% are non-tenure-track and in the natural sciences 45.5%. This study indicates that 79.3% of non-tenure-track humanities faculty teach on a part-time, meaning per-course, basis (Laurence 2013, 8), and of those, 37.1% have no other employment to support themselves (2013, 22). It should be noted that these numbers *do not* include graduate students teaching courses, only individuals classified as faculty members by their employer.

2. A 1996–1997 survey found that only 61% of English courses were staffed by tenure-line faculty, with that number falling to 41% in departments that employ graduate student teaching assistants (ADE Ad Hoc Committee on Staffing 2008, 1). National Study of Postsecondary Faculty surveys found a decline in tenure-line faculty in English between 1993 and 2004, with only 32% of college and university instructors of English holding tenurable positions in 2004 (ADE Ad Hoc Committee on Staffing 2008, 3–4).

3. A young man rising in school or business, or a young lady on the marriage market, must necessarily define him- or herself *against* others, through competition, as David and Jane do.

4. Of course, the resurgence of interest in rhetoric and composition studies fueled by new media of the digital age has begun to shift this dynamic in that many English departments are adding tenure-track, research-focused appointments in fields such as digital humanities and composition rather than the traditional literary disciplines that have long dominated (for example, British Romanticism or Twentieth-Century American Literature). Marc Bousquet argues that these new tenure-track lines reflect "the rational, reasonable, and growing interest in fields specializing in the conditions of textual production at a moment when textual production is undergoing the greatest shift since Gutenberg" (Bousquet 2014, 1). However, what is important to my argument is that any growing prestige—or increased financial compensation—associated with rhetoric and composition accrues not to faculty teaching the bulk of undergraduate writing courses, who are mostly contingent, but to research-focused tenure-track rhet/comp hires whose limited teaching comprises mainly advanced and graduate-level courses.

5. The AAUP finds that in 1975, 57% of all faculty positions were tenure track and 43% were contingent. By 1993, those numbers were exactly reversed (Curtis 2013). For a detailed statistical breakdown of faculty employment status by academic rank, race, and gender, see Curtis (2014). For statistical analysis of the status of women in modern languages and literature programs in US higher education, see Committee on the Status of Women in the Profession (2000).

6. The overrepresentation of women in the lower-status, underpaid field of writing instruction has deep roots in the history and culture of the American university. For a historical analysis of this problem and its background in early twentieth-century changes to the goals and labor structure of the American university, see Schell 1998, 29–33. English scholar Katie J. Hogan asserts that "despite a handful of female academic stars (whose exceptional prominence is evoked as evidence that women have stormed the academy)" in the years following second-wave feminism, most academic women have seen little improvement in conditions from "sala-

ries to working conditions to promotion" since the MLA first investigated the status of women in the profession in 1971 (Hogan 2010, 56–57).

7. Woloch explains, "In my reading of the realist aesthetic, a dialectical literary form is generated out of the relationship between inequality and democracy. The realist novel is infused with a sense that any character is a potential hero, but simultaneously enchanted with the freestanding individual, defined through his or her interior consciousness. In the paradigmatic character-structure of the realist novel, any character *can* be a protagonist, but only one character is: just as increasing political equality, and a maturing logic of human rights, develop amid acute economic and social stratification" (2003, 31). He then draws an analogy between George Eliot's multiplot realist novel and John Stuart Mill's political philosophy: "Eliot's desire to preserve a singular protagonist *and* to extend narrative attention to a broad mass of characters evocatively parallels John Stuart Mill's strange compromise position on universal suffrage, which idealistically insists on democratic principles (both morally and politically) *and* tries to preserve basic structures of class privilege" (Woloch 2003, 31).

8. In an earlier column, "A Class Traitor in Academe" (2007), Pannapacker thoughtfully examines his own discomfort as an academic of working-class family background teaching at an elite liberal arts college.

9. The website can be accessed at http://adjunct.chronicle.com. Details about its history and methodology are located at http://adjunct.chronicle.com/about/. The site features the byline, "The Adjunct Project is by adjuncts, for adjuncts." Administrators and departments are invited to submit additional or corrective salary data if they wish, but that information supplements, rather than replaces, adjunct self-reporting.

10. See Hay (2014).

11. The organization's Facebook page, which contains this statement, can be found at https://www.facebook.com/MLAsubconference?fref=ts. Its website, which includes past programs, is accessible at http://mlasubconference.org.

Chapter Thirteen

Capitalizing Class

*An Examination of Socioeconomic Diversity
on the Contemporary Campus*

Deborah M. Warnock

I began my academic career as a visiting assistant professor at a private liberal arts college in the Northeast. While I greatly enjoyed working with the student body there, I was troubled by the fact that there seemed to be few students from working-class backgrounds like mine.

Having attended a similar institution as an undergraduate, I was eager to find ways to support working-class and first-generation students on campus. Doing so proved to be a complicated task.

Together with a first-generation student of mine, we sought to publicize and recruit members for a low-income, first-generation, working-class student group. Our first obstacle was in even finding a way to communicate to this part of the student body, as the admissions office kept no statistics on its socioeconomic composition.

We finally were able to contact students through the Office of Financial Aid, which e-mailed a message to all of the students on Pell grants. However, this solution was not perfect because not all first-generation students come from Pell-eligible backgrounds.

The response was overwhelming. Over twenty students attended the first meeting, which was held midway through the fall semester. As the school year went on, the group faced obstacles and membership dwindled.

Part of the problem stemmed from the hurdles of achieving formal club status and, along with it, recognition and a budget. The process demanded that group members solicit a minimum number of signatures from the student body, a task many of the first-generation and low-income students found to be humiliating and prohibitive. Though some members tried to gather signatures and I distributed the signature sheets in my classes, the students ultimately fell short of the target and did not achieve formal club status.

Despite all of the work we had done to raise awareness about socioeconomic diversity and the events we had organized, including a social class dialogue workshop through Class Action and a student-led panel discussion on social class on campus, the group was in danger of dissolving without formal campus recognition. Indeed, without club status and with a contingent faculty advisor near the end of her contract, the group ceased to exist when the student founder graduated and I left for a tenure-track position.

While I was able to secure financial support through my department for some of the group's endeavors, I rarely felt as though other faculty in my department or on campus considered my investment in the group to be important or relevant to diversity on campus. Socioeconomic class, the relative dearth of low-income students on campus (only 12% of the student body were Pell-eligible), the increased reliance on contingent faculty, and the shortage of working-class background faculty mentors for low-income and first-generation students were rarely mentioned in campus dialogues on diversity.

While brainstorming with the student founder and other members of the group one night about how we could garner more support on campus, I had an epiphany: the reason our efforts were not supported was that we were directly challenging the bottom line of the institution.

At a liberal arts college with a relatively small endowment that sought to climb in the rankings, there was no incentive to increase socioeconomic diversity. Not only are low-income students expensive, their college entrance exam scores are lower on average and they are less likely to graduate within four years (two criteria central to the rankings system) than their more privileged peers.

It dawned on me that our demands for increased socioeconomic diversity were in stark contrast to the goals of the institution—goals that were defined in part by external influences. In order to better understand what seemed to be one institution's reluctance to support one group of students in search of recognition on campus, I find it important to better understand the extent to which higher education in general is adhering to a mission of social mobility or to one of social reproduction.

In this volume that seeks to draw attention to the role that social class plays in contemporary academic work, it is vital to draw attention to the troubling trends in higher education of the past few decades. Earning a college degree is central to the American dream of upward mobility, yet access has remained largely restricted to the socioeconomically privileged.

During the past few decades even as college enrollment rates have grown, the social class gap has remained stable. From the lowest income quartile only 54% of high school graduates enroll in college compared to 82% of students from the top quartile (Bowen, Kurzweil, and Tobin 2005).

This gap is most striking at the nation's most prestigious colleges and universities, where 70% of the student body comes from the highest income quartile and only 5% can be found from the lowest (Carnevale and Strohl 2010). Indeed, recent research suggests that academically strong students from low-income backgrounds have less access to higher education now than they did forty years ago (Kahlenberg 2004).

Unsurprisingly, college graduation rates are also heavily stratified by family income. The percentage of people from the top income quartile who earn four-year degrees (71%) is more than that of the three bottom income quartiles combined (Mortenson 2012). Another study showed that almost all students from the highest income quartile who begin college (97%) earn a degree by age twenty-four compared to less than one in four students from the bottom quartile (Lewin 2011).

These gaps cannot be explained away by achievement or ability differences. High-scoring, low-income students are equally as likely to graduate college as low-scoring, high-income students (US Department of Education 2000).

When low-income students do enroll in college, they are overrepresented in for-profit institutions with high student loan default rates that are funded almost exclusively through governmental aid (Mettler 2014). Clearly, there is an information and recruiting problem wherein for-profits are aggressively targeting low-income students and nonprofit four-year colleges and universities are not doing their part to appeal to these students.

While there has been a recent push among some elite colleges and universities to recruit students from low socioeconomic backgrounds (Hill and Levy 2015), I argue here that increasing socioeconomic diversity is not a desirable goal for the vast majority of campuses. Due to the reduction of governmental funding and corresponding rise in tuition rates along with the flawed system of college rankings, colleges and universities have little incentive to increase socioeconomic diversity.

DECREASING GOVERNMENTAL SUPPORT AND INCREASING TUITION RATES

Because governmental support for public institutions has been drastically cut in the past few decades, public colleges and universities are increasingly reliant upon tuition.

In turn, the failure of Pell and other governmental grants to keep pace with these tuition increases necessitates that families from the lower and middle range of the income spectrum must rely increasingly on loans as a method of paying for college.

For example, the Pell grant, which was designed to aid low-income students in attending college, has not kept stride with increasing tuition rates. While the maximum Pell grant covered 87% of average public four-year tuition and fees in 2003–2004, ten years later it only covers 63% (College Board 2013). The corresponding contemporary percentage for private non-profit colleges is a measly 19%.

Public colleges and universities, which were historically funded in large part by federal and state governments, have been raising tuition fees to make up the deficit in recent dwindling governmental support (Ehrenberg 2006). Indeed, the percentage of state funding allocated to higher education has been reduced by more than a third over the last few decades (2006).

Meanwhile, private colleges strive to find families who can pay full tuition, and spend large portions of their budgets on building state-of-the-art dining halls and dorms in order to attract the "country club" set (Jacob et al. 2013). Students who cannot pay for college out of pocket have been forced to rely more heavily on student loans as federal and state funding for low-income students have decreased as well (St. John 2003).

The shift from government-based financing to a reliance on families to pay the college bills has resulted in an ironic shift of funding among private and public institutions. Most private institutions are able to draw on their endowments and governmental aid sources to offer students a discounted tuition rate, while public institutions have been relying in larger part on families to foot the bill and taking out more and more loans to do so. The funding limitations at public colleges and universities are especially troubling because 80% of all college students attend public institutions (Ehrenberg 2006).

Problematically, the governmental financial aid that remains has shifted in large part from being need-based (i.e., distributed on the basis of financial need) to merit-based (distributed on the basis of "merit," measured on the basis of grades and/or test scores). As need-based aid has declined, state-based merit aid programs have gained support across the country (Heller 2006).

While some research suggests that the transparent guidelines of these programs have helped low-income students gain access (Ness and Tucker 2008), other studies suggest that these programs are providing funding for students whose families would have been able to pay for college while shutting out those who could not (Heller 2006). Indeed, concurrent with an increase in non-need aid in the form of state grants in 1995–2004, data show that high-income student aid grew by more than 200% while aid for low-income students grew by only 50%, a troubling pattern across both private *and* public institutions (Haycock 2006).

Needy students who do not receive enough aid to pay the sticker price often make up the difference by taking out student loan debt, which currently is the largest type of debt in American society, having surpassed credit card debt in 2010 (Kantrowitz 2010). The majority of students borrow to pay college costs with the average debt amount upon graduation topping out at more than $26,000 (Avery and Turner 2012; Reed and Cochrane 2012).

Low-income students are more likely to take out loans and hold more debt than their high-income peers (Kesterman 2006; Warnock and Hurst 2015). Students who attended for-profit colleges, a demographic dominated by low-income students, are more likely to default on these loans (Hillman 2014).

Another change in response to declining governmental funding is the shifting composition of campus faculty, which has evolved from being mostly tenured or tenure-track to a majority of contingent faculty labor (AAUP 2015).

Seeking to cut costs in the face of reduced governmental funding, public colleges and universities in particular have eliminated tenure-track lines in favor of hiring contingent faculty, who are paid significantly less and are often ineligible for benefits. In one study of the State University of New York system, researchers found that the percentage of classes taught by tenure-track or tenured instructors had declined by 22 percentage points during the 1990s (Ehrenberg and Klaff 2003).

Research suggests that the increasing reliance on contingent faculty has come at a cost to the student body. One study found that first-year students with an "adjunct-heavy" course schedule were less likely to continue to their sophomore year (Bettinger and Long 2006). Another suggests that the increase in contingent faculty is associated with declining four-year graduation rates overall (Ehrenberg and Zhang 2006).

Colleges and universities have increasingly adopted corporate lingo as they seek to find "customers" and keep them happy (Saunders 2014). Implicit in this language is the financial relationship between college and student, a relationship that has become more akin to a transaction in recent years than the learning and apprenticeship it should be. Campuses are being designed in order to attract the "country club" set and along with them the vital dollars they need to remain viable.

Where is there room within this context for the working-class and/or first-generation student who seeks upward mobility through higher education? Where is there room for the working-class academic who seeks to foster and encourage socioeconomic diversity on college campuses? Both are a rarity on the contemporary college campus and, when they are present and vocal, they bump up against the commitment to the bottom line.

THE INCENTIVE STRUCTURE OF THE RANKINGS SYSTEM

Part of the problem has to do not only with the hostile economic climate these institutions face, but also with the ways in which they seek to maintain status among their peers. *U.S. News & World Report* rankings are one of the ways institutions (and their prospective clientele) gauge their place. [1]

The *U.S. News & World Report* has published college and university rankings since 1983. Their rankings are the most widely quoted of their kind in the United States and there is evidence that parents and students consider them when making decisions on where to enroll (Griffith and Rask 2007).

The influence of rankings on enrollment decisions does not go unnoticed by college and university administrators who alter their behavior in an attempt to increase them (Ehrenberg 2003b). Universities have raised tuition rates in an attempt to seem more "elite," have sought applications from unqualified students in order to lower their acceptance rate, increased merit aid to lure high-scoring students, and have mailed out expensive publications to administrators at peer institutions to increase their reputation scores, the most heavily weighted subfactor in the rankings (Ehrenberg 2003b).

When colleges and universities do rise in the rankings, they are rewarded with more applications, higher enrollments, and improved test scores (Ehrenberg 2003a). Some research suggests that a university's ranking is even more important in drawing coveted high-income, high-scoring students than merit aid scholarships (Griffith and Rask 2007).

How are these rankings calculated? The factor weighed most heavily (and equally to student retention) in the *U.S. News & World Report* rankings is academic reputation, which is measured by soliciting evaluations from college and university administrators of all institutions in their same category (i.e., administration at a "national university" rank all other national universities on nebulous factors such as "faculty dedication to teaching") and by polling counselors at the top public and independent schools.

Regardless of the questionable likelihood that these evaluators would be able to accurately gauge how well each institution truly performs, research has shown that previously published rankings significantly influence these peer assessments, net of any institutional changes in performance (Bastedo and Bowman 2010). The past rankings influence present reputation scores which then influence future rankings, indicating that rankings are, in part, a "self-fulfilling prophecy," or a prediction that becomes true simply by virtue of its definition.

Focused on raising their rankings, all colleges and universities compete for students with high SAT scores, a measure which has repeatedly been found to correlate highly with social class background (Balf 2014; Rampell 2009; Soares 2011). The race to recruit top-scoring students has arguably led to the aforementioned shift in aid from need-based to merit-based (Burd 2013).

U.S. News & World Report has recently introduced an additional component to the rankings called graduation rate performance, which takes into account student graduation rate net of student test scores and the percentage of the student body receiving Pell grants. While this is meant to be a measure of how well institutions serve low-income and lower-scoring students, it is worth only one-third of the nebulous reputation score in determining the overall ranking and ranks less than the measure of financial resources based upon per student spending.

The incentive structure to score high in these widely used rankings is thus based upon cultivating a reputation for success, recruiting high-scoring students who are also more likely to graduate in four years, and generous spending on "student services."

The faculty component of the rankings also does not account for the growth in the percentage of contingent faculty. The closest the rankings come is to account for the proportion of the faculty who are full-time, a number that accounts for 1% of the total score.

Along with building incentives into the rankings to recruit students from low socioeconomic backgrounds, incentives to hire and employ more tenure-track faculty, and especially tenure-track faculty from working-class backgrounds, are also needed. Indeed, there have been calls for the proportion of classes taught by adjunct faculty to be included in the rankings (Rollins 2012).

As the rankings are currently calculated, there is little to no incentive to colleges and universities to recruit low-income students and, in fact, there are arguably disincentives to do so. Institutions are rewarded in the rankings for maintaining close relationships with top-ranked high schools (where low-income students are less likely to be found), for recruiting students with high SAT/ACT scores, for retaining students into the sophomore year, for graduating students within four years, and for spending on student facilities.

Although a higher proportion of contingent faculty on campus decreases graduation and retention rates, colleges and universities are not directly penalized in the rankings for increasing reliance on these underpaid and overworked faculty. Finally, there is also no incentive among the rankings for colleges and universities to identify and recruit faculty from working-class backgrounds, a point I will return to later.

THE LOW-INCOME AND/OR FIRST-GENERATION
STUDENT EXPERIENCE

For first-generation students and those from low-income backgrounds, campus priorities are all too clear. These students often feel unacknowledged and unsupported in their struggles to acclimate to a climate built for their more privileged peers (Foster 2015; Hurst 2010; Hurst and Warnock 2015; Lee and Kramer 2013; Soria 2015). When they do seek to acclimate to a campus climate that too often privileges partying as a way of life, they see far greater consequences for sloughing off academically (Armstrong and Hamilton 2013).

Students from low- and middle-income families are more likely to work and work more hours per week than those from more economically privileged families (Choy and Berker 2003). For students who must work their way through college and who view higher education as their ticket to upward mobility, they often find the social landscape of the college campus to be an alienating and strange place with confused priorities (Hurst and Warnock 2015).

Studies show that first-generation and working-class students are less likely to be socially involved on campus than students from more class privileged families (Nuñez and Cuccaro-Alamin 1998; Stuber 2011). This lack of social integration results in the greater likelihood that first-generation and low-income students will leave college with debt and no degree (Howard and Levine 2004).

Because socioeconomic diversity is not a clearly stated goal on many campuses and socioeconomic status tends to be an invisible and often stigmatized identity, these students often feel alone on campuses. Their comparatively low numbers at the nation's most selective colleges and universities can trigger awareness of their marginal positions on campus (D. Smith 2009) and the invisible nature of social class can make finding like-minded peers a challenge (Warnock and Hurst 2014).

While some campuses have programs to support first-generation and low-income students and some student-led groups have popped up on campuses around the country (Pappano 2015), the problem of upward social mobility on the contemporary college campus is too often painted as an individual journey (Hurst and Warnock 2015). This individualist rhetoric reinforces the neoliberal policies touting education as a private good that families and students should shoulder the burden for, as well as the merit-based aid policies that too often reward success on measures that have clearly been demonstrated to be class biased.

Low-income and first-generation students are often also at a loss for visible role models. Socioeconomic diversity among faculty has been largely ignored in the literature on diversifying faculty, although research suggests that faculty from working-class backgrounds differ in important ways from their more privileged academic peers (Haney 2015). Specifically, working-class academics remain hyperaware of their class background, reporting the need to work harder to compensate for their comparative lack of cultural and social capital. The sacrifices working-class people make by joining the academy, such as the guilt suffered at leaving behind friends and family, are real and often go unacknowledged.

Detailing the unique contributions of working-class academics to pedagogy and scholarship, including making class visible on campus by revealing their class backgrounds in the classroom and using their experiential knowledge of social class to shape their research agendas, Stricker (2011) makes a compelling argument for recognizing and recruiting for social class diversity within the professoriate. College can be an alienating and even hostile environment for first-generation and working-class students.

The presence of working-class faculty can help these students to realize that someone like them can be successful in this environment. In addition, working-class students are more likely to seek out mentor relationships with faculty who come from similar backgrounds and are, thus, more likely to understand the challenges they face. The support that these students receive from similar background faculty could make the difference between leaving and staying.

Finally, working-class academics are more likely to pursue research agendas informed by their social class backgrounds and are more likely to be sensitive to the needs of working-class and first-generation students in the classroom. All of these components are a win for the retention and support of students who are too often overlooked on campus.

THE STRUGGLE AGAINST STATUS INCONGRUITY

What does all of this mean for the working-class academic? It is difficult to reconcile the goals of facilitating upward mobility for students from similar backgrounds while being aware that the goals of many colleges and universities stand in contrast to the recruitment and support of these students. This, combined with the fact that campuses are increasingly reliant on adjunct labor, makes it difficult for the contemporary tenure-track or tenured working-class academic to reconcile his or her position in the academy.

Working-class academics already suffer from "status incongruity," or a sense of being caught between two worlds, their working-class origin and their middle-class destination in academe (Sennett and Cobb 1972). Adding to this sense of unease is the realization that one's work in the academy may be contributing much more to the social reproduction of class stratification in society than to the desired goal of aiding in students' upward mobility that many working-class academics share (Stricker 2011).

If the goals of higher education truly are to provide the chance for upward mobility, then much work remains to be done. Central to this task is the working-class academic and likeminded allies who understand the importance of recruiting low-income and first-generation students to four-year institutions and making sure that they receive the recognition and support they deserve once there. College ranking systems like the *U.S. News & World Report* should reward institutions that seek to increase socioeconomic diversity not only in the student body but in the tenured and tenure-track faculty as well.

Part of this also means acknowledging and seeking to reduce stratification among the faculty. Institutions of higher education must examine their goals of prestige and consider those who are being sacrificed in their quest to rise in the rankings. Finally, state and federal policymakers crafting decisions in higher education funding must consider the consequences for the low-income and first-generation students of this country.

All of these goals are difficult in the current sociopolitical and economic climate of higher education, among rising tuition rates, declining governmental aid, and students' necessarily increasing reliance on loans to pay for college. However, change is essential.

Rather than capitalizing on class by profiting from the loans of students who seek upward mobility through higher education and seeking to increase prestige through paying high-scoring (and all too often high-income) students to enroll, institutions should be capitalizing (or prioritizing) social class on campus, recruiting and supporting students and faculty from underrepresented low-income and/or first-generation backgrounds.

According to Soria (2015), concrete steps that campuses can take to recruit and support working-class students include

- Restructuring admissions policies

  - Eliminating legacy preferences and early decision admissions
  - Reducing the emphasis on test scores
  - Practicing need-blind admissions

- Increasing and better publicizing need-based financial aid
- Recruiting students from low-income public high schools
- Reaching out to families of first-generation and/or working-class students
- Implementing precollege bridge programs
- Diversifying tenure-track faculty on the basis of socioeconomic background
- Including social class as an important form of campus diversity

• Providing a safe space for students to explore their social class identities

Had these priorities been emphasized at the campus described in the opening vignette, the student group, and all working-class, first-generation, and/or low-income students and faculty on campus would have found crucially needed support.

These goals are not easy to attain in the current political and economic climate. However, colleges and universities must begin to demonstrate a commitment to socioeconomic diversity among the student body and the professoriate if we are to continue to identify higher education as a pathway to upward mobility.

NOTE

1. In the analysis of the *U.S. News & World Report* rankings reported here, I am using the 2014 criteria that were used to calculate the rankings for the 2015 issue, released on September 9, 2014. Information on the measures used can be found at http://www.usnews.com/education/best-colleges/articles/2014/09/08/best-colleges-ranking-criteria-and-weights.

References

Abel, Brigetta. 2014. "Activism and Academia." *Women in German Yearbook.* 30: 186–96.

Abelev, Melissa S. 2009. "Advancing Out of Poverty: Social Class Worldview and its Relation to Resilience." *Journal of Adolescent Research* 24(1): 114–41.

ADE Ad Hoc Committee on Staffing. 2008. "Education in the Balance: A Report on the Academic Workforce in English." *Modern Language Association.* Accessed June 22, 2015. http://www.mla.org/pdf/workforce_rpt03.pdf.

Adichie, Chimamanda Ngozi. *Americanah.* 2013. New York: Random House.

Adler, Nancy E., Thomas Boyce, Margaret Chesney, Sheldon Cohen, Susan Folkman, Robert Kahn, and S. Leonard Syme. 1994. "Socioeconomic Status and Health: The Challenge of the Gradient." *American Psychologist* 49(1):15–24.

Adler, Nancy E., Elissa Epel, Grace Castellazzo, and Jeanette R. Ickovics. 2000. "Relationship of Subjective and Objective Social Status with Psychological and Physiological Functioning: Preliminary Data in Healthy White Women." *Health Psychology* 19(6):586–92.

Akkerman, Sanne F., and Arthur Bakker. 2011. "Boundary Crossing and Boundary Objects." *Review of Educational Research* 81(2): 132–69.

Alcoff, Linda Martín. 1995. "The Problem of Speaking for Others." In *Who Can Speak? Authority and Critical Identity,* ed. Judith Roof and Robyn Wiegman, 97–119. Urbana: University of Illinois Press.

Allison, Dorothy. 2002. *Trash: Stories.* New York: Plume.

American Association of University Professors (AAUP). 2015. "Contingent Faculty Positions." Accessed May 27, 2015. http://www.aaup.org/issues/contingency.

American Psychological Association (APA). 2015a. "About APA." Last modified June 7, 2015. http://www.apa.org/about/.

———. 2015b. "How Does the APA Define 'Psychology'?" Last modified June 3, 2015. http://www.apa.org/support/about/apa/psychology.aspx#answer.

Anonymous. "Treadmill to Oblivion." 2015. *Inside Higher Ed,* May 11. Accessed May 14, 2015. https://www.insidehighered.com/advice/2015/05/11/essay-instructor-who-has-taught-adjunct-25-years.

Anyon, Jean. 1980. "Social Class and the Hidden Curriculum of Work." *Journal of Education* 162 (1): 67–92.

Anzaldúa, Gloria. 1987. *Borderlands/La Frontera: The New Mestiza.* San Francisco: Aunt Lute Books.

Appel, Margaret. 2014. "World Traveler." Paper written for "Writing/Writing Process" education course. Portland, OR: Lewis and Clark College.

Aranda, Elizabeth. 2007. "Struggles of Incorporation among the Puerto Rican Middle Class." *Sociological Quarterly* 48:198–228.

Armstrong, Elizabeth A., and Laura T. Hamilton. 2013. *Paying for the Party: How College Maintains Inequality.* Cambridge, MA: Harvard University Press.

Arner, Lynn. 2014. "Working-Class Women at the MLA Interview." *Rhizomes* 27.

Arnett, Jeffrey J. 2008. "The Neglected 95%: Why American Psychology Needs to Become Less American." *American Psychologist* 63 (7): 602–14.

Arum, Richard, and Josipa Roska. 2014. *Aspiring Adults Adrift: Tentative Transitions of College Graduates.* Chicago: University of Chicago Press.

Astin, Alexander, and Leticia Oseguera. 2004. "The Declining 'Equity' of American Higher Education." *Review of Higher Education* 27(3): 321–41.

Avery, Christopher, and Sarah Turner. 2012. "Student Loans: Do College Students Borrow Too Much—Or Not Enough?" *Journal of Economic Perspectives* 26(1): 165–92.

Baker, Kelly. 2012. "Evidentiary Boundaries, and Improper Interventions: Evidence, Implications, and Illegitimacy in American Religious Studies." *Bulletin for the Study of Religion* 41(4): 2–11.

Baker, Phyllis L. 2006. "Trajectory and Transformation of a Working-Class Girl into an Upper-Middle-Class Associate Dean." In *Reflections from the Wrong Side of the Tracks: Class, Identity, and the Working Class Experience in Academe*, ed. Stephen. L. Muzzatti and C. Vincent Samarco, 197–206. Lanham, MD: Rowman & Littlefield Publishers.

Baldwin, Roger G., and Jay L. Chronister. 2001. *Teaching without Tenure.* Baltimore: Johns Hopkins University Press.

Balf, Todd. 2014. "The Story behind the SAT Overhaul." *New York Times Magazine*, March 6.

Barreca, Gina. 2010. "Jude, Eliza, and Access." *Chronicle of Higher Education,* January 9. Accessed May 27, 2015. http://chronicle.com/blogs/brainstorm/jude-elizaaccess/20415.

Barth, Frederick. 1969. *Ethnic Groups and Boundaries: The Social Organization of Culture Difference.* Boston: Little, Brown and Company.

Bastedo, Michael N., and Nicholas A. Bowman. 2010. "U.S. News & World Report College Rankings: Modeling Institutional Effects on Organizational Reputation." *American Journal of Education* 116(2): 163–83.

Benedict, Mary Ellen, and Louis Benedict. 2014. "What Faculty Unions Can Learn from Workload Policy in Ohio." *Academe* 100.2 (Mar/Apr): 18–38.

Berlinerblau, Jacques. 2001. "Toward a Sociology of Heresy, Orthodoxy, and Doxa." *History of Religions* 40(4): 327–51.

Bernstein, Basil. 1971. "Social Class, Language, and Socialization." In *Power and Ideology in Education,* eds. Jerome Karabel and A. H. Halsey, 473–86. New York: Oxford University Press.

Bérubé, Michael. 2013. "Presidential Address 2013: How We Got Here." *PMLA* 28(3): 530–41.

Bettinger, Eric P., and Bridget Terry Long. 2006. "The Increasing Use of Adjunct Instructors at Public Institutions: Are We Hurting Students?" In *What's Happening to Public Higher Education? The Shifting Financial Burden*, ed. Ronald G. Ehrenberg, 51–70. Baltimore: Johns Hopkins University Press.

Borrego, Susan E. 2008. "Hate Is Not a Family Value." In *Resilience: Queer Professors from the Working Class,* ed. Kenneth Oldfield and Richard Greggory Johnson, III, 223–45. Albany: State University of New York.

Boshers, Danielle, Anna Garcia, Melody Ng, Christopher Reynolds, and Dwight Lang. 2013. "First-Generation College Students at Michigan Share Their Stories." *Ann Arbor News*, April 19.

Bourdieu, Pierre. 1977. *Outline of a Theory of Practice.* Translated by Richard Nice. New York: Cambridge University Press.

———. 1984. *Distinction: A Social Critique of the Judgment of Taste.* Cambridge, MA: Harvard University Press.

———. 1985. "Social Space and the Genesis of Groups." *Theory and Society* 14(6): 723–44.

———. 1986. "The Forms of Capital." In *Handbook of Theory and Research for the Sociology of Education,* ed. J. G. Richardson, 241–58. Westport, CT: Greenwood Press.

———. 1988. *Homo Academicus.* Translated by Peter Collier. Stanford: Stanford University Press.

———. 1990. *The Logic of Practice*. Translated by Richard Nice. Stanford: Stanford University Press.

———. 1991. *Language and Symbolic Power*. Cambridge, MA: Harvard University Press.

———. 1996. *The State Nobility: Elite Schools in the Field of Power*. Cambridge: Polity.

———. 2000. *Pascalian Meditations*. Translated by Richard Nice. Stanford: Stanford University Press.

———. 2001. "The Sociology of Economic Life." In *Handbook of Theory of Research for the Sociology of Education*, 46–58. New York: Greenwood Press.

———. 2002. "The Forms of Capital." In *Economic Sociology*, ed. Nicole Woolsey Biggart, 280–91. Malden, MA: Blackwell.

———. 2004. *Science of Science and Reflexivity*. Chicago: University of Chicago Press.

———. 2007. *Sketch for a Self-Analysis*. Translated by Richard Nice. Chicago: University of Chicago Press.

Bourdieu, Pierre, and Terry Eagleton. 1992. "Doxa and Common Life." *New Left Review* 191(1): 111–21.

Bourdieu, Pierre, and Jean-Claude Passeron. 1977. *Reproduction in Education, Society, and Culture*. London: Sage.

———. 1979. *The Inheritors: French Students and Their Relation to Culture*. Translated by Richard Nice. Chicago: University of Chicago Press.

———. 1990. *Reproduction in Education, Society and Culture*, 2nd ed. Thousand Oaks, CA: Sage.

Bourdieu, Pierre, and Loïc J. D. Wacquant. 1992. *An Invitation to Reflexive Sociology*. Chicago: University of Chicago Press.

Bousquet, Marc. 2008. *How the University Works: Higher Education and the Low-Wage Nation*. New York: New York University Press.

———. 2014. "The Moral Panic in Literary Studies." *Chronicle of Higher Education*, April 7. Accessed May 5, 2015. http://chronicle.com/article/The-Moral-Panic-in-Literary/145757/.

Bowen, William G., Martin A. Kurzweil, and Eugene M. Tobin. 2005. *Equity and Excellence in American Higher Education*. Charlottesville: University of Virginia Press.

Bradbury, Barbara, and Peter Mather. 2009. "The Integration of First-Year, First-Generation College Students from Ohio Appalachia." *NASPA Journal* 46: 258–8I.

Bradley, William. 2014. "The Worst That Can Happen." *Inside Higher Ed*, October 3. Accessed May 14, 2015. https://www.insidehighered.com/advice/2014/10/03/essay-finding-perspective-about-tough-academic-job-market.

Bramen, Carrie Tirado. 2000. "Minority Hiring in the Age of Downsizing." In *Power, Race, and Gender in Academe: Strangers in the Tower?*, ed. Shirley Geok-Lin Lim and María Herrera-Sobek, 112–31. New York: Modern Language Association.

Brooks, Peter. 1984. *Reading for the Plot: Design and Intention in Narrative*. Cambridge, MA: Harvard University Press.

Brunner, Edmund de Schweinitz. 1927. *Village Communities*. New York: George H. Doran and Company.

Burawoy, Michael, and Karl von Holdt. 2012. *Conversations with Bourdieu: The Johannesburg Moment*. Johannesburg, South Africa: Wits University Press.

Burd, Stephen. 2013. "Merit Aid Madness." *Washington Monthly,* October 2013.

Burton, Linda, and Belinda Tucker. 2009. "Romantic Unions in an Era of Uncertainty: A Post-Moynihan Perspective on African American Women and Marriage." *The Annals of the American Academy of Political and Social Science* 621:132–48.

Butler, Judith. 1997. *Excitable Speech: A Politics of the Performative*. New York: Routledge.

Calarco, Jessica. 2011. "'I Need Help!' Social Class and Children's Help-Seeking in Elementary School." *American Sociological Review* 76(6): 862–82.

———. 2014. "Coached for the Classroom: Parents' Cultural Transmission and Children's Reproduction of Inequalities." *American Sociological Review* 79(5):1015–37.

Callaghan, Dympna. 1995. "The Vicar and Virago: Feminism and the Problem of Identity." In *Who Can Speak?,* eds. R. Wiegman and J. Roof, 195–207. Chicago: University of Illinois Press.

Cannata, Marisa. 2010. "Understanding the Teacher Job Search Process: Espoused Preferences and Preferences in Use." *Teachers College Record* 112(12): 2889–934.

Carlsen, Elof Axel. 2001. *The Unfit: A History of a Bad Idea.* Cold Harbor Spring, NY: Cold Harbor Spring Laboratory Press.

Carnevale, Anthony P., and Stephen J. Rose. 2004. "Socioeconomic Status, Race/Ethnicity, and Selective College Admission." In *America's Untapped Resource: Low-Income Students in Higher Education,* ed. Richard D. Kahlenberg, 101–56. New York: Century Foundation Press.

Carnevale, Anthony P., and Jeff Strohl. 2010. "How Increasing College Access Is Increasing Inequality, and What to Do about It." In *Rewarding Strivers: Helping Low-Income Students Succeed in College,* ed. Richard D. Kahlenberg, 71–190. New York: Century Foundation Press.

Cheah, Pheng. 2006. "Cosmopolitanism." *Theory, Culture & Society* 23(2–3): 486–96.

Chen, Edith, and Miller, George E. 2012. "'Shift-and-Persist' Strategies: Why Low Socioeconomic Status Isn't Always Bad for Health." *Perspectives on Psychological Science* 7(2): 135–58. doi: 10.1177/1745691612436694.

———. 2013. "Socioeconomic Status and Health: Mediating and Moderating Factors." *Annual Review of Clinical Psychology* 9:723–49. doi: 10.1146/annurev-clinpsy-050212–185634.

Childers, Mary M. 2002. "The Parrot or the Pit Bull: Trying to Explain Working Class Life." *Signs* 28(1): 201–20.

Choy, Susan P., and Ali M. Berker. 2003. "How Families of Low- and Middle-Income Undergraduates Pay for College: Full-Time Dependent Students in 1999–2000." *Education Statistics Quarterly* 5(2): 7–13.

Christopher, Renny. 2003. "Damned If You Do, Damned If You Don't." *Academe* 89 (4): 37–40.

———. 2009. *A Carpenter's Daughter: A Working Class Woman in Higher Education.* Boston: Sense Publishers.

Cisneros, Sandra. 1984. *The House on Mango Street.* New York: Vintage Books.

Clauset, Aaron, Samuel Arbesman, and David B. Larremore. 2015. "Systematic Inequality and Hierarchy in Faculty Hiring Networks." *Science Advances* 1(1): e1400005.

Clifford, James. 1998. "Mixed Feelings." In *Cosmopolitics: Thinking and Feeling Beyond the Nation,* ed. Pheng Cheah and Bruce Robbins, 362–70. Minneapolis: University of Minnesota Press.

Colander, David, with Daisy Zhuo. 2015. "Where Do PhDs in English Get Jobs? An Economist's View of the English PhD Market." *Pedagogy: Critical Approaches to Teaching Literature, Language, Composition, and Culture* 15.1 (Jan.): 139–56.

Cole, Elizabeth R., and Safiya R. Omari. 2003. "Race, Class and the Dilemmas of Upward Mobility for African Americans." *Journal of Social Issues* 59(4): 785–802.

College Board. *Rethinking Pell Grants.* 2013. Accessed June 1, 2015.

Committee on the Status of Women in the Profession. 2000. "Women in the Profession, 2000." *Profession.* New York: Modern Language Association, 191–217.

Corsaro, William. *The Sociology of Childhood,* 4th ed. 2015. Thousand Oaks, CA: Pine Forge.

Crane, Diana. 1969. "Social Class Origin and Academic Success: The Influence of Two Stratification Systems on Academic Careers." *Sociology of Education* 42(1): 1–17.

Cunliffe, Ann L. 2004. "On Becoming a Critically Reflexive Practitioner." *Journal of Management Education* 28(4): 407–26.

Curtis, John W. 2013. "Trends in Faculty Employment Status, 1975–2011." *American Association of University Professors.* Accessed June 23, 2015. http://www.aaup.org/sites/default/files/Faculty_Trends_0.pdf.

———. 2014. "The Employment Status of Instructional Staff Members in Higher Education, Fall 2011." *American Association of University Professors.* Accessed June 23, 2015. http://www.aaup.org/sites/default/files/files/AAUP-InstrStaff2011-April2014.pdf.

Curtis, John W., and Saranna Thornton. 2013. "Here's the News: Annual Report on the Economic Status of the Profession, 2012–2013." *Academe* (Mar–Apr): 4–19.

Cutten, George Barton. 1927. *Speaking with Tongues: Historically and Psychologically Considered.* New York: Yale University Press.

Dahl, Espen, Jon Ivar Elstad, Dag Hofoss, and Melissa Martin-Mollard. 2006. "For Whom Is Income Inequality Most Harmful? A Multi-level Analysis of Income Inequality and Mortality in Norway." *Social Science & Medicine* 63(10): 2562–74.

Danley-Scott, Jennifer, and Gray Scott. 2014. "The Other Half: Non-tenure Track Faculty Thoughts on Student Learning Outcomes Assessment." *Research & Practice in Assessment* 9: 31–44.

Davenport, Frederick Morgan. 1905. *Primitive Traits in Religious Revivals: A Study in Mental and Social Evolution.* New York: MacMillan.

Day, Katy, Bridgette Rickett, and Maxine Woolhouse. 2014. "Class Dismissed: Putting Social Class on the Critical Psychological Agenda." *Social and Personality Psychology Compass* 8(8): 397–407.

Delpit, Lisa. 2006. *Other People's Children: Cultural Conflict in the Classroom.* New York: The New Press.

deMarrais, Kathleen Bennett, and Margaret LeCompte. 1999. *The Way Schools Work: A Sociological Analysis of Education*, 3rd ed. New York: Addison Wesley Longman.

Dews, C. L. Barney, and Carolyn Leste Law, eds. 1995. *This Fine Place So Far from Home: Voices of Academics from the Working Class.* Philadelphia: Temple University Press.

Diemer, Matthew A., Rashmita Mistry, Martha Wadsworth, Irene López, and Faye Reimers. 2012. "Best Practices in Conceptualizing and Measuring Social Class in Psychological Research." *Analyses of Social Issues & Public Policy.* Advance online publication: doi: 10.1111/asap.12001.

Downs, Valerie C., Manoochehr Mitch Javidi, and Jon F. Nussbaum. 1988. "An Analysis of Teachers' Verbal Communication within the College Classroom: Use of Humor, Self-Disclosure, and Narratives." *Communication Education* 37(2): 127–41.

Duany, Jorge. 2002. *The Puerto Rican Nation on the Move: Identities on the Island and in the United States.* Chapel Hill: University of North Carolina Press.

Dubson, Michael, ed. 2001. *Ghosts in the Classroom: Stories of College Adjunct Faculty—and the Price We All Pay.* Boston: Camel's Back Books.

Dudley-Marling. Curt. 2007. "Return of the Deficit." *Journal of Educational Controversy* 2(1). http://cedar.wwu.edu/jec/vol2/iss1/5.

Dudley-Marling, Curt, and Krista Lucas. 2009. "Pathologizing the Language and Culture of Poor Children." *Language Arts* 86(5): 362–70.

Dunbar, Kathleen. 1999. "For Sale: One Phi Beta Kappa Key (A Working-Class Woman's Experience in Academe)." *Transformations* 10(2): 30–41.

Ehrenberg, Ronald G. 2003a. "Method or Madness? Inside USNWR College Rankings." *Cornell Higher Education Research Institute (CHERI).* Paper 39. Accessed June 1, 2015. http://digitalcommons.ilr.cornell.edu/workingpapers/42/.

———. 2003b. "Reaching for the Brass Ring: The U.S. News and World Report Rankings and Competition." *Review of Higher Education* 26(2): 145.

———. ed. 2006. *What's Happening to Public Higher Education? The Shifting Financial Burden.* Baltimore: Johns Hopkins University Press.

Ehrenberg, Ronald G., and Daniel B. Klaff. 2003. "Changes in Faculty Composition within the State University of New York System: 1985–2001." Unpublished manuscript.

Ehrenberg, Ronald G., and Liang Zhang. 2006. "Do Tenured and Tenure-Track Faculty Matter?" In *What's Happening to Public Higher Education? The Shifting Financial Burden*, ed. Ronald G. Ehrenberg, 37–50. Baltimore: Johns Hopkins University Press.

Eisen, Ben. 2009. "Shooting the Messenger?" *Inside Higher Education*, June 12. https://www.insidehighered.com/news/2009/06/12/adjunct.

Elam, Diane. 1995. "Speak for Yourself." In *Who Can Speak?*, eds. R. Wiegman and J. Roof, 231–37. Chicago: University of Illinois Press.

Engle, Jennifer, Adolfo Bermeo, and Collen O'Brien. 2006. "Straight from the Source: What Works for First-Generation College Students." Pell Institute for the Study of Opportunity in Higher Education. ERIC Document Reproduction Service No. ED501693.

Ferfolja, Tania, Christine Jones-Diaz, and Jacqueline Ullman. 2015. *Understanding Sociological Theory for Educational Practices.* London: Cambridge University Press.

Finnegan, Dorothy E. 1993. "Segmentation in the Academic Labor Force: Hiring Cohorts in Comprehensive Universities." *Journal of Higher Education* 64.8 (Nov/Dec): 621–56.

Fiske, Susan T, and Hazel Rose Markus. 2012. *Facing Social Class: How Societal Rank Influences Interaction.* New York: Russell Sage Foundation.

Fone, David, Frank Dunstan, Gareth Williams, Keith Lloyd, and Stephen Palmer. 2007. "Places, People and Mental Health: A Multilevel Analysis of Economic Inactivity." *Social Science & Medicine* 64(3): 633–45. doi:10.1016/j.socscimed.2006.09.020.

Foster, Brooke L. 2015. "What Is It Like to Be Poor at an Ivy League School?" *Boston Globe Magazine*, April 9.

Foster, Jennifer, and Kari Stanek. 2007. "Cross-cultural Considerations in the Conduct of Community-Based Participatory Research." *Family & Community Health: The Journal of Health Promotion & Maintenance* 30(1): 42–49.

Freire, Paulo. 1970, 1983. *Pedagogy of the Oppressed.* New York: Continuum.

———. 2005. *Teachers as Cultural Workers: Letters to Those Who Dare Teach.* Boulder, CO: Westview Press.

Freud, Sigmund. 1936. "'A Disturbance of Memory on the Acropolis': An Open Letter to Romain Rolland."

Fruscione, Joseph. 2014. "When a College Contracts 'Adjunctivitis,' It's the Students Who Lose." *PBS NewsHour*, July 25. http://www.pbs.org/newshour/making-sense/when-a-college-contracts-adjunctivitis-its-the-students-who-lose/.

Gale, Kate. 2001. "Adjuncts Are Not People." In *Ghosts in the Classroom: Stories of College Adjunct Faculty—and the Price We All Pay,* ed. Michael Dubson. Boston: Camel's Back Books.

Gardner, Saundra. 1993. "What's a Nice Working-Class Girl Like You Doing in a Place Like This?" In *Working-Class Women in the Academy: Laborers in the Knowledge Factory,* eds. Michelle M. Tokarczyk and Elizabeth A. Fay, 49–59. Amherst: University of Massachusetts Press.

Garger, Stephen. 1995. "Bronx Syndrome." In *This Fine Place So Far from Home: Voices of Academics from the Working Class,* eds. C. L. Barney Dews and Carolyn Leste Law, 41–53. Philadelphia: Temple University Press.

Gianaros, Peter J., and Stephen B. Manuck. 2010. "Neurobiological Pathways Linking Socioeconomic Position and Health." *Psychosomatic Medicine* 72(5): 450–61.

Giddens, Anthony. 1991. *Modernity and Self-Identity: Self and Society in the Late Modern Age.* Stanford: Stanford University Press.

Godoy, Ricardo, Victoria Reyes-García, Susan Tanner, William R. Leonard, Thomas W. McDade, and Thomas Huanca. 2008. "Can We Trust an Adult's Estimate of Parental School Attainment? Disentangling Social Desirability Bias and Random Measurement Error." *Field Methods* 20(1): 26–45.

Goldrick-Rab, Sara. 2006. "Following Their Every Move: An Investigation of Social-Class Differences in College Pathways." *Sociology of Education* 79(1): 67–79.

Gordon, David George. 1998. *Eat-a-bug Cookbook: 33 Ways to Cook Grasshoppers, Ants, Water Bugs, Spiders, Centipedes, and Their Kin.* Berkeley: Ten Speed Press.

Gorski, Paul C. 2008a. "Good intentions Are Not Enough: A Decolonizing Intercultural Education." *Intercultural Education* 19(6): 515–25.

———. 2008b. "The Myth of the 'Culture of Poverty.'" *Educational Leadership* 65(7): 32–36.

———. 2013. *Reaching and Teaching Students in Poverty: Strategies for Erasing the Opportunity Gap.* New York: Teachers College Press.

Graham, Sandra. 1992. "'Most of the Subjects Were White and Middle Class': Trends in Published Research on African Americans in Selected APA Journals, 1970–1989." *American Psychologist* 47(5): 629–39.

Granfield, Robert. 1991. "Making It by Faking It: Working-Class Students in an Elite Academic Environment." *Journal of Contemporary Ethnography* 20: 331–51.

Griffith, Amanda, and Kevin Rask. 2007. "The Influence of the US News and World Report Collegiate Rankings on the Matriculation Decision of High-Ability Students: 1995–2004." *Economics of Education Review* 26(2): 244–55.

Grimes, Michael D., and Joan M. Morris. 1997. *Caught in the Middle: Contradictions in the Lives of Sociologists from Working Class Backgrounds*. Westport, CT: Praeger.

Grusky, David. B. 2014. "4 Myths about Poverty." *The Chronicle of Higher Education: The Chronicle Review,* February 24.

Guba, Egon, and Yvonna S. Lincoln. 1994. "Competing Paradigms in Qualitative Research." In *Handbook of Qualitative Research*, eds. N. K. Denzin and Y. S. Lincoln, 105–17. London: Sage.

Gutiérrez y Muhs, Gabriella. 2012. *Presumed Incompetent: The Intersections of Race and Class for Women in Academia*. Boulder: University Press of Colorado.

Hahn, Barbara Wilson. 2001. "Adjunct Apartheid." In *Ghosts in the Classroom: Stories of College Adjunct Faculty—and the Price We All Pay*, ed. Michael Dubson. Boston: Camel's Back Books: 61–69.

Hall, Gordon C. Nagayama, Bansal, Anita, and López, Irene R. 1999. "Ethnicity and Psychopathology: A Metaanalytic Review of 31 Years of Comparative MMPI/MMPI2 Research." *Psychological Assessment* 11(2): 186–97.

Hall, Gordon C. Nagayama, López, Irene R., and Bansal, Anita. 2001. "Academic Acculturation: Race, Gender, and Class Issues." In *The Intersection of Race, Class, and Gender: Implications for Multicultural Counseling*, eds. H. L. K. Coleman & D. Pope-Davis, 171–88. Thousand Oaks, CA: Sage.

Hammerback, John, and Richard Jensen. 2003. *The Rhetorical Career of Cesar Chavez*. College Station: Texas A&M University Press.

Haney, Timothy J. 2015. "Factory to Faculty: Socioeconomic Difference and the Educational Experiences of University Professors." *Canadian Review of Sociology* 52(2): 160–86.

Hardt, Michael, and Antonio Negri. 2004. *Multitude: War and Democracy in the Age of Empire*. New York: Penguin Books.

Hart, Betty, and Todd R. Risley. 1995. *Meaningful Differences in the Everyday Experiences of Young American Children*. Baltimore: Brookes.

Hay, Victoria. 2014. "On Working for Free." Accessed June 22, 2015. http://adjunct.chronicle.com/on-working-for-free/.

Haycock, Kati. 2006. *Promise Abandoned: How Policy Choices and Institutional Practices Restrict College Opportunities*. Washington, DC: The Education Trust.

Heller, Donald E. 2006. "Merit Aid and College Access." Unpublished manuscript.

Hertel, James. 2002. "College Student Generational Status: Similarities, Differences, and Factors in College Adjustment." *Psychological Record* 52: 3–18.

Hill, Catherine B., and Harold Levy. 2015. "Elite Colleges Need Economic Diversity." *USA Today*, May 12.

Hilliard, Asa G. 2001. "Teacher's Packet: Kentucky Educational Television Professional Development Workshop for Educators Approved for Professional Development Training by the Kentucky Department of Education." http://www.ket.org/education/guides/pd/asa_hilliard.pdf.

Hillman, Nicholas W. 2014. "College on Credit: A Multilevel Analysis of Student Loan Default." *Review of Higher Education* 37(2): 169–95.

Hogan, Katie. 2010. "Superserviceable Feminism." In *Over Ten Million Served: Gendered Service in Language and Literature Workplaces,* eds. Michelle Massé and Katie J. Hogan, 55–71. Albany: SUNY Press.

hooks, bell. 2000. *Where We Stand: Class Matters.* New York: Routledge.

House Committee on Education and the Workforce. 2014. *The Just-in-Time Professor: A Staff Report Summarizing eForum Responses on the Work Conditions of Contingent Faculty in Higher Education*. Washington, DC: US House of Representatives.

Howard, Adam, and Arthur Levine. 2004. "Where Are the Poor Students? A Conversation about Social Class and College Attendance." *About Campus* 9(4): 19–24.

Hsiao, Karin. 1992. "First-Generation College Students." *ERIC Clearinghouse for Junior Colleges.* ERIC Document Reproduction Service No. ED351079.

Hunter-Boykin, Harriet S. 1992. "Responses to the African American Teacher Shortage: 'We Grow Our Own' Through the Teacher Preparation Program at Coolidge High School." *The Journal of Negro Education* 61(4): 483–95.

Huntington, Ellsworth, and Leon Whitney. 1928. *The Builders of America.* London: Chapman and Hall.

Hurst, Allison L. 2009. "The Path to College: Stories of Students from the Working Class." *Race, Gender, and Class* 16(1–2): 257–81.

———. 2010. *The Burden of Academic Success: Loyalists, Renegades, and Double Agents.* Lanham, MD: Rowman & Littlefield.

———. 2012. *College and the Working Class.* Rotterdam: Sense Publishers.

Hurst, Allison L., and Deborah M. Warnock. 2015. *"Les Miracules:* 'The Magical Image of the Permanent Miracle'—Constructed Narratives of Self and Mobility from Working-Class Students at an Elite College." In *College Students' Experiences of Power and Marginality: Sharing Spaces and Negotiating Differences,* eds. Elizabeth M. Lee and Chaise LaDousa, 102–17. New York: Routledge.

Hutcheon, Linda et al. 2002. "Professionalization in Perspective: MLA Ad Hoc Committee on the Professionalization of PhDs." *Profession.* 187–210.

Huxford, Lyn. 2006. "Making the Grade: Imposters in the Ivory Tower." In *Reflections from the Wrong Side of the Tracks: Class, Identity, and the Working Class Experience in Academe,* eds. Stephen. L. Muzzatti and C. Vincent Samarco, 207–20. Lanham, MD: Rowman & Littlefield Publishers.

Illouz, Eva. 2008. *Saving the Modern Soul: Therapy, Emotions, and the Culture of Self-Help.* Berkeley: University of California Press.

Inkelas, Karen, Zaneeta Daver, Kristen Vogt, and Jeannie Leonard. 2007. "Living-Learning Programs and First Generation College Students' Academic and Social Transition to College." *Research in Higher Education* 48: 403–33.

Jackson, Michelle, John Goldthorpe, and Colin Mills. 2005. "Education, Employers and Class Mobility." *Research in Social Stratification and Mobility* 23:3–33.

Jacob, Brian, Brian McCall, and Kevin M. Stange. 2015. "College as Country Club." National Bureau of Economic Research Working Paper No. 18745, 2013. Accessed May 27, 2015. http://www.nber.org/papers/w18745

Jacobs, Ken, Perry, Ian, and MacGillvary, Jenifer. 2015. *The High Public Cost of Low Wages: Poverty-level Wages Cost U.S. Taxpayers $152.8 Billion Each Year in Public Support for Working Families.* Berkeley, CA: UC Berkeley Center for Labor Research and Education.

Jarosinski, Eric. 2014. "#failedintellectual: @NeinQuarterly Says Goodbye to Academe and Hello to Whatever." *Chronicle of Higher Education,* June 30. Accessed May 27, 2015. http://chronicle.com/article/failedintellectual/147353/.

Jaschik, Scott. 2009. "Punishing a Whistle Blower?" *Inside Higher Education,* August 25. https://www.insidehighered.com/news/2009/08/25/davey.

Jensen, Eric. 2009. *Teaching with Poverty in Mind: What Being Poor Does to Kids' Brains and What Schools Can Do about It.* Alexandria, VA: ASCD.

Kadi, Joanna. 1999. *Thinking Class: Sketches from a Cultural Worker.* Boston: South End Press.

Kahlenberg, Richard D. 2004. *America's Untapped Resource: Low-Income Students in Higher Education.* New York: The Century Foundation Press.

Kantrowitz, Mark. 2010. "Total College Debt Now Exceeds Total Credit Card Debt." Fastweb, August 11. http://www.fastweb.com/financial-aid/articles/total-college-debt-now-exceeds-total-credit-card-debt.

Kaufman, Peter. 2003. "Learning to Not Labor: How Working-Class Individuals Construct Middle-Class Identities." *Sociological Quarterly* 44(3): 481–504.

Kesterman, Frank. 2006. "Student Borrowing in America: Metrics, Demographics, Default Aversion Strategies." *Journal of Student Financial Aid* 36(1): 34–52.

Kevles, Daniel J. 1985. *In the Name of Eugenics: Genetics and the Uses of Human Heredity.* Berkeley: University of California Press.

Kezar, Adrianna. 2013. *Changing Faculty Workforce Models.* TIAA-CREF Institute. http://www.uscrossier.org/pullias/wp-content/uploads/2013/11/KezarPaper_fin_lr.pdf.

Kezar, Adrianna, and Cecile Sam. 2011. "Understanding Non-Tenure Track Faculty: New Assumptions and Theories for Conceptualizing Behavior." *American Behavioral Scientist* 55: 1419–42.

Khan, Shamus. 2012. *Privilege: The Making of an Adolescent Elite at St. Paul's School*. Princeton, NJ: Princeton University Press.

Kincheloe, Joe. 2005. *Critical Pedagogy Primer*. New York: Peter Lang USA.

Kohn, Melvin. 1969. *Class and Conformity: A Study in Values*. Homewood, IL: Dorsey Press.

Kolodny, Annette. 1998. *Failing the Future: A Dean Looks at Higher Education*. Durham: Duke University Press.

Kovalik, Daniel. 2013. "Death of an Adjunct." *Pittsburgh Post-Gazette,* September 18. Accessed May 19, 2015. http://www.post-gazette.com/opinion/Op-Ed/2013/09/18/Death-of-an-adjunct/stories/201309180224.

Kraus, Michael W., and, Wendy Berry Mendes. 2014. "Sartorial Symbols of Social Class Elicit Class-consistent Behavioral and Physiological Responses: A Dyadic Approach." *Journal of Experimental Psychology* 143(6): 2330–40.

Kraus, Michael W., and Nicole M. Stephens. 2012. "A Road Map for an Emerging Psychology of Social Class." *Social and Personality Psychology Compass* 6: 642–56.

Krivo, Lauren J., and Robert L. Kaufman. 2004. "Housing and Wealth Inequality: Racial-Ethnic Differences in Home Equity in the United States." *Demography* 41(3): 585–605.

Kunjufu, Jawanza. 2002. *Black Students. Middle Class Teachers*. Chicago: African American Images.

Kusserow, Adrie. 2004. *American Individualisms: Child Rearing and Social Class*. New York: Palgrave MacMillan.

Ladson-Billings, Gloria. 1995. "Toward a Theory of Culturally Relevant Pedagogy." *American Educational Research Journal* 32(3): 465–91.

———. 2001. *Crossing Over to Canaan: The Journey of New Teachers in Diverse Classrooms*. San Francisco: Jossey-Bass.

Lang, Dwight. 1987. "Equality, Prestige, and Controlled Mobility in the Academic Hierarchy," *American Journal of Education* 95(3): 441–67.

———. 1995. "The Social Construction of a Working Class Academic." In *This Fine Place So Far from Home: Voices of Academics from the Working Class*, eds. C. L. Barney Dews and Carolyn Leste Law. Philadelphia: Temple University Press.

———. 2012. "A Troubling Silence on Poverty," *Detroit Free Press*, November 11.

———. 2015. "Singing the First Generation Blues." *The Chronicle of Higher Education: Diversity in Academe—The Challenge of the First-Generation Student.* 60(36): 18–19.

Lang, Dwight, and Vanessa Lang. 2013. "Teachers Appreciate Diverse Backgrounds, Life-Changing Decisions of Their Students." *Ann Arbor News*, October 20.

Langston, Donna. 1993. "Who Am I Now? The Politics of Class Identity." In *Working-Class Women in the Academy: Laborers in the Knowledge Factory*, eds. Michelle M. Tokarczyk and Elizabeth A. Fay, 60–72. Amherst: University of Massachusetts Press.

———. 2000. "Tired of Playing Monopoly?" In *Readings for Diversity and Social Justice*, eds. Maurianne Adams et al., 397–406. New York: Routledge.

Lareau, Annette. 1987. "Social Class Differences in Family-School Relationships: The Importance of Cultural Capital." *Sociology of Education* 60(2): 73–85.

———. 1989. *Home Advantage: Social Class and Parental Intervention in Elementary Education*. Lanham, MD: Rowman & Littlefield.

———. 2003. *Unequal Childhoods*. Berkeley: University of California Press.

———. 2011. *Unequal Childhoods: Class, Race, and Family Life,* 2nd ed. Berkeley: University of California Press.

Lareau, Annette, and Dalton Conley, eds. 2008. *Social Class: How Does It Work?* New York: Russell Sage Foundation.

Laurence, David. 2013. "A Profile of the Non-Tenure-Track Academic Workforce." *ADE Bulletin* 153: 6–22.

Law, Carolyn Leste. 1995. "Introduction." In *This Fine Place So Far from Home: Voices of Academics from the Working Class*, eds. C. L. Barney Dews and Carolyn Leste Law, 1–12. Philadelphia: Temple University Press.

Lee, Elizabeth M., and Rory Kramer. 2013. "Out with the Old, In with the New? Habitus and Social Mobility at Selective Colleges." *Sociology of Education* 86(1): 18–35.

Leeb, Claudia. 2004. *Working-Class Women in Elite Academia: A Philosophical Inquiry.* Brussels: Peter Lang.

Lehmann, Wolfgang. 2007a. *Choosing to Labour? School-Work Transitions and Social Class.* Montreal: McGill-Queens University Press.

———. 2007b. "'I Just Didn't Feel Like I Fit In': The Role of Habitus in University Dropout Decisions." *Canadian Journal of Higher Education* 37(2): 89–110.

———. 2009a. "Becoming Middle-Class: How Working-Class University Students Draw and Transgress Moral Class Boundaries." *Sociology* 43(4): 631–47.

———. 2009b. "Class Encounters: Working Class Students at University." In *Canadian Perspectives on the Sociology of Education,* eds. Cynthia Levine-Rasky and Don Mills, 93–111. Ontario: Oxford University Press.

———. 2013. "Habitus Transformation and Hidden Injuries: Successful Working-Class University Students." *Sociology of Education* 87(1): 1–15.

Lemert, Charles. 2012. *Social Things: An Introduction to the Sociological Life,* 5th ed. Lanham, MD: Rowman & Littlefield.

Lewin, Tamar. 2011. "College Graduation Rates Are Stagnant Even as Enrollment Rises, a Study Finds." *New York Times,* September 27.

Lightweis, Susan. 2014. "The Challenges, Persistence, and Success of White, Working-Class First-Generation College Students." *College Student Journal* 48(3): 461–67.

Lipset, Seymour Martin, and Everett C. Ladd Jr. 1979. "The Changing Social Origins of American Academics." In *Qualitative and Quantitative Social Research,* eds. Robert K. Merton et al., 319–38. New York: The Free Press.

Liu, William Ming. 2011. *Social Class and Classism in the Helping Professions: Research, Theory and Practice.* Thousand Oaks, CA: Sage Publications.

Liu, William Ming, Alis Saba Rasheed, Geoff Soleck, Joshua Hopps, Kwesi Dunsong, and Theodore Pickett, Jr. 2004a. "Using Social Class in Counseling Psychology Research." *Journal of Counseling Psychology* 51: 3–18.

Liu, William Ming, Geoff Soleck, Joshua Hopps, Kwesi Dunsong, and Theodore Pickett, Jr. 2004b. "A New Framework to Understand Social Class in Counseling: The Social Class Worldview Model and Modern Classism Theory." *Journal of Multicultural Counseling and Development* 32(2): 95–122.

López, Irene R. 2008a. "'But You Don't Look Puerto Rican': The Buffering Effects of Ethnic Identity on the Relation between Skin Color and Self-esteem among Puerto Rican Women." *Cultural Diversity & Ethnic Minority Psychology* 14(2): 102–8.

———. 2008b. "Puerto Rican Phenotype: Understanding Its Historical Underpinnings and Psychological Associations." *Hispanic Journal of Behavioral Sciences* 30(2): 161–80.

López, Irene R., and Josefina C. Contreras. 2005. "The Best of Both Worlds: Biculturality, Acculturation, and Psychological Adjustment among Mainland Puerto Rican Adolescent Mothers." *Journal of Cross-Cultural Psychology* 36(2): 192–208.

López, Irene, Analise N. Gonzalez, and Avril Ho. "Skin Color." 2012. In *Encyclopedia of Body Image and Human Appearance,* ed. Thomas F. Cash. Vol. 2: 730–37. San Diego: Academic Press.

López, Irene, Fernando Rivera, Rafael Ramirez, Peter Guarnaccia, Glorisa Canino, and Hector Bird. 2009. "*Ataques de Nervios* and Their Psychiatric Correlates in Puerto Rican Children from Two Different Contexts." *Journal of Nervous and Mental Disease,* iii–x, 12: 923–29.

López, Irene, Lovey H. M. Walker, and Melek Yildiz Spinel. 2015. "Understanding the Association between Phenotype and Ethnic Identity." In *Studying Ethnic Identity: Methodological and Conceptual Approaches across Disciplines,* eds. Carlos E. Santos and Adriana Umaña-Taylor, 119–48. Washington, DC: American Psychological Association.

Lott, Beatrice. 2014. "Social Class Myopia: The Case of Psychology and Labor Unions." *Analyses of Social Issues & Public Policy* 14(1). doi:10.1111/asap.12029.

Lubrano, Alfred. 2004. *Limbo: Blue-Collar Roots, White-Collar Dreams.* Hoboken, NJ: John Wiley and Sons.

Mabokela, Reitumetse O., and Jean A. Madsen. 2003. "Crossing Boundaries: African American Teachers in Suburban Schools." *Comparative Education Review* 47(1): 90–111.

Magolda, Peter M., and Jill E. Carnaghi. 2014. *Job One 2.0: Understanding the Next Generation of Student Affairs Professionals.* Lanham, MD: UPA.

Magolda, Peter M., and Sarah O'Connell. 2013. *Unsanitized Tales of the Corporate University through the Eyes of Campus Custodians.* Association for the Study of Higher Education Annual Conference, St. Louis, MO, November 2013.

Mahoney, Pat, and Christine Zmroczek, eds. 1997. *Class Matters: Working-Class Women's Perspectives on Social Class.* London: Taylor & Francis.

Mai, Joseph. 2007. "A Sentimental Reeducation: Flaubert and the Job Market." *ADFL Bulletin* 38(1–2): 52–55.

Maisto, Maria. 2013. "Adjuncts, Class, and Fear." *Working-Class Perspectives: Commentary on Working-Class Culture, Education, and Politics.* September 23. https://workingclassstudies.wordpress.com/2013/09/23/adjuncts-class-and-fear/.

Mar, Elaine M. 1995. "Blue Collar, Crimson Blazer: Recollections of Class on Campus." *Harvard Magazine,* Nov/Dec, 47–51.

Martin, Jane Roland. 2000. *Coming of Age in Academe: Rekindling Women's Hopes and Reforming the Academy.* New York: Routledge.

Marx, Karl, and Friedrich Engels. 1964. *On Religion.* Introduced by Reinhold Niebuhr. New York: Schocken.

Massé, Michelle A., and Katie J. Hogan, eds. 2010. *Over Ten Million Served: Gendered Service in Language and Literature Workplaces.* Albany: SUNY Press.

Mazurek, Raymond A. 2009. "Work and Class in the Box Store University: Autobiographies of Working-Class Academics." *College Literature* 36(4): 147–78.

McCaskill, Barbara et al. 2000. "Women in the Profession, 2000: MLA Committee on the Status of Women in the Profession." *Profession,* 191–217.

McDougall, William. 1977. *Is America Safe for Democracy?* New York: Arno Press.

McGinnis, Robert, and J. Scott Long. 1997. "Entry into Academia: Effects of Stratification, Geography and Ecology." In *The Academic Profession: The Professoriate in Crisis,* eds. Martin J. Finkelstein and Philip G. Altbach, 342–66. New York: Garland.

McGrath, Jennifer J., Karen A. Matthews, and Sonya S. Brady. 2006. "Individual versus Neighborhood Socioeconomic Status and Race as Predictors of Adolescent Ambulatory Blood Pressure and Heart Rate." *Social Science & Medicine* 63(6): 1442–53.

McKinney.com. 2011. "Spent." *Urban Ministries of Durham.* Release date 2011. http://playspent.org.

McNamee, Stephen J., and Robert K. Miller, Jr. 2014. *The Meritocracy Myth,* 3rd ed. Lanham, MD: Rowman & Littlefield.

Messer-Davidow, Ellen. 2002. "Playing by the New Rules." In *Disciplining Feminism: From Social Activism to Academic Discourse,* 269–89. Durham, NC: Duke University Press.

Mettler, Suzanne. 2014. *Degrees of Inequality: How the Politics of Higher Education Sabotaged the American Dream.* New York: Basic Books.

Miething, Alexander. 2013. "The Relevance of Objective and Subjective Social Position for Self-Rated Health: A Combined Approach for the Swedish Context." *Social Indicators Research* 111(1): 161–73.

Mills, C. Wright. (1959) 2000. *The Sociological Imagination.* New York: Oxford.

MLA Office of Research. 2010. "Midyear Report on the 2009–10 MLA *Job Information List.*" March. http://www.mla.org/pdf/jil_midyear_update2009_lg.pdf.

MLA Subconference. Accessed June 22, 2015. http://mlasubconference.org.

Monsters, Inc. 2001. Directed by Pete Docter, Lee Unkrich, and David Silverman. Emeryville, CA: Pixar Animation Studios, 2002. DVD.

Moore, Mary. 2013. "Adjunct Union Accuses UMass Lowell of Retaliation Against Its Leader." *Boston Business Journal,* August 20. http://www.bizjournals.com/boston/news/2013/08/20/umass-lowell-under-fire-from-union.html.

Moretti, Franco. 1987, 2000. *The Way of the World: The Bildungsroman in European Culture.* London: Verso.

Mortenson, Thomas G. 2012. "Family Income and Unequal Education Opportunity, 1970–2011." *Postsecondary Education Opportunity* 245 (November)

Mulder, Clara, and William Clark. 2002. "Leaving Home for College and Gaining Independence." *Environment and Planning A* 34(6): 981–99.

Mullen, Ann L. 2010. *Degrees of Inequality: Culture, Class, and Gender in American Higher Education.* Baltimore: John Hopkins University Press.

Muzzatti, Stephen L., and C. Vincent Samarco, eds. 2006. *Reflections from the Wrong Side of the Tracks: Class, Identity, and the Working Class Experience in Academe.* Lanham, MD: Rowman & Littlefield.

National Center for Education Statistics. 2012. "Table 286: Employees in degree-granting institutions, by employment status, sex, control and level of institution, and primary occupation: Fall 2011." Survey of Earned Doctorates. https://nces.ed.gov/programs/digest/d12/tables/dt12_286.asp.

———. 2013. "Table 325.50: Degrees in English Language and Literature/Letters conferred by postsecondary institutions, by level of degree and sex of student: Selected years, 1949–50 through 2011–12." https://nces.ed.gov/programs/digest/d13/tables/dt13_325.50.asp.

———. 2014. "Table 315.20: Full-time faculty in degree-granting postsecondary institutions, by race/ethnicity, sex, and academic rank: Fall 2009, fall 2011, and fall 2013."https://nces.ed.gov/programs/digest/d14/tables/dt14_315.20.asp.

National Science Foundation. 2014. Survey of Earned Doctorates (SED). "Table 33: Educational attainment of doctorate recipients' parents, by sex, citizenship status, ethnicity, race, and broad field of study: 2013."www.nsf.gov/statistics/sed/2013/data/tab33.pdf.

Neal, Jim. 2001. "No Exit, or My Life as a Gypsy on the Part-Time Circuit." In *Ghosts in the Classroom: Stories of College Adjunct Faculty—and the Price We All Pay,* ed. Michael Dubson. Boston: Camel's Back Books.

Nelson, Jr., William J. 1985. "Notes and Brief Reports: Employment Covered Under the Social Security Program, 1935–1984." *Social Security Bulletin* 48(4): 33–39.

Nenga, Sandi Kawecka. 2003. "Social Class and Structures of Feeling in Women's Childhood Memories of Clothing, Food and Leisure." *Journal of Contemporary Ethnography* 32 (2):167–99.

———. 2011. "Volunteering to Give up Privilege? How Affluent Youth Volunteers Respond to Class Privilege." *Journal of Contemporary Ethnography* 40(3): 264–89.

Ness, Erik C., and Richard Tucker. 2008. "Eligibility Effects on College Access: Underrepresented Student Perceptions of Tennessee's Merit Aid Program." *Research in Higher Education* 49(7): 569–88.

Nieto, Sonia. 2006. "Teaching as Political Work: Learning from Courageous and Caring Teachers." A Longfellow Lecture at the Child Development Institute, Yonkers, NY.

Nuñez, Anne-Marie, and Stephanie Cuccaro-Alamin. 1998. *First-Generation Students: Undergraduates Whose Parents Never Enrolled in Postsecondary Education. Statistical Analysis Report. Postsecondary Education Descriptive Analysis Reports.* Washington, DC: National Center for Education Statistics.

Oberdeck, Kathryn. 1999. *The Evangelist and the Impresario: Religion, Entertainment, and Cultural Politics in America, 1884–1914.* Baltimore: Johns Hopkins University Press.

Odinshoot, Atlas. 2014. "The Odds Are Never in Your Favor: Why the Academic Job Market is Like *The Hunger Games.*" *The Chronicle of Higher Education.* January 20. Accessed May 27, 2015. http://chronicle.com/article/The-Odds-Are-Never-in-Your/144079/.

Oldfield, Kenneth. 2007. "Expending Economic Democracy in American Higher Education: A Two-Step Approach to Hiring More Teachers from Poverty- and Working-Class Backgrounds." *Journal of Higher Education Policy and Management* 29(2): 217–30.

Oldfield, Kenneth, and Richard F. Conant, 2001. "Professors, Social Class, and Affirmative Action: A Pilot Study." *Journal of Public Affairs Education* 7.3 (July): 171–85.

Oldfield, Kenneth, and Richard Greggory Johnson III, eds. 2008. *Resilience: Queer Professors from the Working Class.* Albany: State University of New York.

Ostrove, Joan M., and Elizabeth R. Cole. 2003. "Privileging Class: Toward a Critical Psychology of Social Class in the Context of Education." *Journal of Social Issues* 59(4): 677–92.

Overall, Christine. 1998. *A Feminist I: Reflections from Academia.* Peterborough, ON: Broadview Press.

Pannapacker, William. 1998. "A Graduate Student's Life: 'A Permanent Sense of Inadequacy and Dread.'" *Chronicle of Higher Education,* October 16. Accessed May 27, 2015. http://chronicle.com/article/A-Graduate-Students-Life-a/46415/.

———. 2000. "Hope, or a New Life on the Tenure Track." *Chronicle of Higher Education,* June 16. Accessed May 14, 2015. http://chronicle.com/article/Hope-or-a-New-Life-on-the/46344/.

———. 2007. "A Class Traitor in Academe." *Chronicle of Higher Education,* November 9. Accessed May 27, 2015. http://chronicle.com/article/A-Class-Traitor-in-Academe/46556/.

———. 2009. "Graduate School in the Humanities: Just Don't Go." *Chronicle of Higher Education,* January 30. Accessed May 27, 2015. http://chronicle.com/article/Graduate-School-in-the/44846/.

———. 2010. "The Big Lie about the 'Life of the Mind.'" *Chronicle of Higher Education,* February 8. Accessed May 27, 2015. http://chronicle.com/article/The-Big-Lie-About-the-Life-of/63937/.

Pappano, Laura. 2015. "First Generation Students Unite." *New York Times,* April 8.

Pascarella, Ernest, Christopher Pierson, Gregory Wolniak, and Patrick Terenzini. 2004. "First Generation College Students: Additional Evidence on College Experiences and Outcomes." *Journal of Higher Education* 75(3): 204–84.

Pate, Soo Jin. 2014. "'What's Next for You?' A Ph.D. Decides to Leave Behind Both Academe and Its Self-Defeating Notions of Success." *Chronicle of Higher Education,* April 7. Accessed May 27, 2015. http://chronicle.com/article/What-s-Next-for-You-/145763/.

Pattillo-McCoy, Mary E. 1999. *Black Picket Fences: Privilege and Peril among the Black Middle Class.* Chicago: University of Chicago Press.

Paulsen, Michael B., and Edward P. St. John. 2002. "Social Class and College Costs: Examining the Financial Nexus between College Choice and Persistence." *Journal of Higher Education* 73(2): 189–236.

Pearce, Jane. 2012. "Unsettling Class: Standpoint Pedagogies, Knowledge and Privileges." In *Critical Voices in Teacher Education: Teaching for Social Justice in Conservative Times,* eds. Barry Down and John Smyth, 99–110. Netherlands: Springer.

Pérez, Gina. 2004. *The Near Northwest Side Story.* Berkeley: University of California Press.

Perry, David. 2014. "Faculty Refuse to See Themselves as Workers. Why?" *Chronicle Vitae,* May 22. Accessed May 27, 2015. https://chroniclevitae.com/news/509-faculty-refuse-to-see-themselves-as-workers-why.

Pew Hispanic Research Center. 2002. *Billions in Motion : Latino Immigrants, Remittances and Banking*

Polak, Katherine. 2010. "A Letter from a Graduate Student in the Humanities: Please Stop Your Condescension." *Chronicle of Higher Education,* April 4. Accessed May 27, 2015. http://chronicle.com/article/A-Letter-From-a-Graduate/64889/.

Popenoe, Paul, and Roswell Hill Johnson. 1933. *Applied Eugenics.* Revised edition. New York: MacMillan.

Quon, Elizabeth C., and Jennifer J. McGrath. 2014. "Subjective Socioeconomic Status and Adolescent Health: A Meta-Analysis." *Health Psychology* 33(5): 433–47.

Radford, Alexandria Walton. 2013. *Top Student, Top School? How Social Class Shapes Where Valedictorians Go to College.* Chicago: University of Chicago Press.

Rampell, Catherine. 2009. "SAT Scores and Family Income." *New York Times Economix Blog,* August 27. Accessed May 27, 2015. http://economix.blogs.nytimes.com/2009/08/27/sat-scores-and-family-income/.

Rasmussen, Birgit Brander, Eric Klinenberg, and Irene J. Nexica, eds. 2001. *The Making and Unmaking of Whiteness.* Durham, NC: Duke University Press.

Reay, Diane, Gill Crozier, and John Clayton. 2009. "Strangers in Paradise? Working-Class Students in Elite Universities." *Sociology* 43(4): 1103–21.

Reed, Matthew, and Debbie Cochrane. 2012. *Student Debt and the Class of 2011.* Washington, DC: The Institute for College Access and Success.

Reimers, Faye Ann. 2007. "Putting It All Together: A Content Analysis and Methodological Review of the Intersection of Class, Race, and Gender in the Counseling Psychology Literature." Dissertation Abstracts International. PsycINFO, EBSCOhost. Accessed June 26, 2015.

Rist, Ray. 1970. "Student Social Class and Teacher Expectations: The Self-Fulfilling Prophecy in Ghetto Education." *Harvard Educational Review* 40:411–51.

Ritterman, Miranda Lucia, Lia C. Fernal, Emily J. Ozer, Nancy E. Adler, Juan Pablo Gutierrez, Juan Pablo, and Leonard Syme. 2009. "Objective and Subjective Social Class Gradients for Substance Use among Mexican Adolescents." *Social Science & Medicine* 68(10): 1843–51.

Rivera, Lauren. 2015. *Pedigree: How Elite Students Get Elite Jobs.* Princeton: Princeton University Press.

Robbins, Bruce. "Comparative Cosmopolitanisms." 1998. In *Cosmopolitics: Thinking and Feeling Beyond the Nation,* eds. Pheng Cheah and Bruce Robbins, 246–64. Minneapolis: University of Minnesota Press.

Robertson, Tony, Michaela Benzeval, Elise Whitley, and Frank Popham. 2015. "The Role of Material, Psychosocial and Behavioral Factors in Mediating the Association between Socioeconomic Position and Allostatic Load (Measured by Cardiovascular, Metabolic and Inflammatory Markers)." *Brain, Behavior, and Immunity* 45: 41–49.

Rodgers, Daniel T. 2011. *Age of Fracture.* Cambridge, MA: Belknap/Harvard University Press.

Rollins, Michael John. 2012. "Hit Them Where It Hurts—Right in the Rankings." *The Adjunct Blog,* April 4. Accessed May 27, 2015. http://adjunct.chronicle.com/hit-them-where-it-hurts-right-in-the-rankings/.

Roscigno, Vincent J., and James W. Ainsworth-Darnell. 1999. "Race, Cultural Capital, and Educational Resources: Persistent Inequalities and Achievement Returns." *Sociology of Education* 72(3): 158–78.

Rothe, Dawn. 2006. "A Stranger to Paradise: Working-Class Graduate in the Culture of Academia." In *Reflections from the Wrong Side of the Tracks: Class, Identity, and the Working Class Experience in Academe,* eds. Stephen. L. Muzzatti and C. Vincent Samarco, 49–59. Lanham, MD: Rowman & Littlefield.

Rothenberg, Molly Anne. 2010. *The Excessive Subject: A New Theory of Social Change.* Malden, MA: Polity Press.

Rubin, Mark, Nida Denson, Sue Kilpatrick, Kelly E. Matthews, Tom Stehlik, and David Zyngier. 2014. "'I Am Working-Class': Subjective Self-Definition as a Missing Measure of Social Class and Socioeconomic Status in Higher Education Research." *Educational Researcher* 43(4):196–200. doi: 10.3102/0013189X1452837.

Ryan, Jake, and Charles Sackrey. 1984, 1995. *Strangers in Paradise: Academics from the Working Class.* Lanham, MD: UPA.

Saenz, Victor, and Doug Barrera. 2007. "What We Can Learn from UCLA's 'First in My Family' Data." *Retention in Higher Education* 21(9):1–3.

Saunders, Daniel B. 2014. "Exploring a Customer Orientation: Free-Market Logic and College Students." *Review of Higher Education* 37(2): 197–219.

Sawhney, Sabina. 1995. "The Joke and the Hoax: (Not) Speaking as the Other." In *Who Can Speak?,* eds. R. Wiegman and J. Roof, 208–20. Chicago: University of Illinois Press.

Schell, Eileen. 1998. *Gypsy Academics and Mother-Teachers: Gender, Contingent Labor, and Writing Instruction.* Portsmouth, NH: Boynton/Cook Heinemann.

Schneider, Scott. 2015. "It's Time to Review Your Adjunct Employment Policies." *Chronicle of Higher Education,* February 16. Accessed May 15, 2015. http://chronicle.com/article/Its-Time-to-Review-Your/190035/.

Schuman, Rebecca. 2014. "Hanging Up on a Calling." *Chronicle of Higher Education,* January 27. Accessed May 27, 2015. http://chronicle.com/article/Hanging-Up-on-a-Calling/144197/.

Schwalbe, Michael. 1995. "The Work of Professing (A Letter to Home)." In *This Fine Place So Far From Home: Voices of Academics from the Working Class,* eds. C.L. Barney Dews and Carolyn Leste Law, 309–331. Philadelphia: Temple University Press.

Scott, Kate M. 2014. "Associations between Subjective Social Status and *DSM-IV* Mental Disorders: Results from the World Mental Health Surveys." *Journal of American Medical Association Psychiatry* 71(12): 1400–1408.

Sedgwick, Eve Kosofsky. 1990. *Epistemology of the Closet.* Berkeley: University of California Press.

Seiter, David M. 2003. "The Growth of the Suburbs—and the Racial Wealth Gap." *Public Broadcasting System (PBS)*. 2003. http://www.pbs.org/race/000_About/002_04-teachers-07.htm.

Sennett, Richard, and Jonathan Cobb. 1972. *The Hidden Injuries of Class*. New York: Vintage Books.

Shavers, Vickie L. 2007. "Measurement of Socioeconomic Status in Health Disparities Research." *Journal of the National Medical Association* 99(9): 1013–20.

Shoemaker, Pamela J., Martin Eichholz, and Elizabeth A. Skewes. 2002. "Item Nonresponse: Distinguishing Between Don't Know and Refuse." *International Journal of Public Opinion Research* 14(2): 193–201.

Shott, Michael J. 2006. "An Unwashed's Knowledge of Archeaology: Class and Merit in Academic Placement." In *Reflections from the Wrong Side of the Tracks: Class, Identity, and the Working Class Experience in Academe*, eds. Stephen L. Muzzatti and C. Vincent Samarco, 221–39. Lanham, MD: Rowman & Littlefield.

Shpungin, Elaine, and Mikhail Lyubansky. 2006. "Navigating Social Class Roles in Research." *American Journal of Community Psychology* 37(3–4): 227–35.

Siskind, Mariano. 2014. *Cosmopolitan Desires*. Chicago: Northwestern University Press.

Sleeter, Christine. 1992. "Resisting Racial Awareness: How Teachers Understand the Social Order from Their Racial, Gender, and Social Class Locations." *Educational Foundations* 6(2): 7–32.

Smith, Daryl G. 2009. *Diversity's Promise for Higher Education: Making It Work*. Baltimore: Johns Hopkins University Press.

Smith, Laura. 2009. "Enhancing Training and Practice in the Context of Poverty." *Training and Education in Professional Psychology* 3(2): 84–93.

Soares, Joseph A. 2011. *SAT Wars*. New York: Teachers College Press.

Soria, Krista M. 2012. "Creating a Successful Transition for Working-Class First-Year Students." *Journal of College Orientation and Transition* 20(1): 44–55.

———. 2013. "Why Getting a PhD Was the Most Metal Thing I've Ever Done." Association of Working Class Academics blog. http://awcaonline.org/wordpress/why-getting-a-phd-was-the-most-metal-thing-ive-ever-done/.

———. 2015. *Welcoming Blue Collar Scholars into the Ivory Tower: Developing Class-Conscious Strategies for Student Success*. National Resource Center for The First-Year Experience and Students in Transition. Columbia: University of South Carolina.

Soria, Krista M., and Mark Bultmann. 2014. "Advising Scholars from Blue Collar Backgrounds: Supporting Working-Class Students' Success in Higher Education." *NACADA Journal* 34(2): 51–62.

Soria, Krista M., and Michael J. Stebleton. 2013. "Social Capital, Academic Engagement, and Sense of Belonging among Working-Class College Students." *College Student Affairs Journal* 31(2): 139–53.

Soria, Krista M., Michael J. Stebleton, and Ronald L. Huesman Jr. 2013–2014. "Class Counts: Exploring Differences in Academic and Social Integration between Working-Class and Middle/Upper-Class Students at Large, Public Research Universities." *Journal of College Student Retention: Research, Theory, and Practice* 15(2): 215–42.

Soria, Krista M., Brad Weiner, and Elissa C. Lu. 2014. "Examining Financial Decisions among Undergraduate Students from Different Social Class Backgrounds." *Journal of Student Financial Aid* 44(1): 2–23.

Soto, Rhonda. 2008. "Race and Class: Taking Action at the Intersections." *Diversity and Democracy: Civic Learning for Shared Futures* 11(3): 12–13.

St. John, Edward P. 2003. *Refinancing the College Dream*. Baltimore: Johns Hopkins University Press.

Stanton-Salazar, Ricardo D., and Sanford M. Dornbusch. 1995. "Social Capital and the Reproduction of Inequality: Information Networks among Mexican-Origin High School Students." *Sociology of Education* 68(2): 116–35.

Stephens, Nicole M., MarYam G. Hamedani, and Mesmin Destin. 2014. "Closing the Social-Class Achievement Gap: A Difference-Education Intervention Improves First-Generation

Students' Academic Performance and All Students' College Transition." *Psychological Science*: 1–11. doi: 10.1177/0956797613518349.

Stephens, Nicole, Stephanie Fryberg, Hazel Rose Markus, Camille Johnson and Rebecca Covarrubias. 2012. "Unseen Disadvantage: How American Universities' Focus on Independence Undermines the Academic Performance of First-Generation College Students." *Journal of Personality and Social Psychology* 102(6): 1178–97.

Stocking, Jr., George W. *Race, Culture, and Evolution: Essays in the History of Anthropology*. New York: The Free Press, 1968.

Street, Steve, Maria Maisto, Esther E. Merves, and Gary Rhoades. 2012. "Who Is Professor 'Staff' and How Can This Person Teach So Many Classes?" Center for the Future of Higher Education. http://futureofhighered.org//wp-content/uploads/2012/08/ProfStaffFinal1.pdf.

Streib, Jessi. 2011. "Class Reproduction by Four Year Olds." *Qualitative Sociology* 34(2):337–52.

———. 2015. *The Power of the Past: Understanding Cross-Class Marriages*. New York: Oxford University Press.

Stricker, Kristi. 2011. "Class Consciousness and Critical Mass; Exploring the Practice and Scholarship of Academics from the Working Class." *Race, Gender & Class* 18(3–4): 372–84.

Strouse, A. W. 2015. "The Consolation of Asceticism." *Chronicle of Higher Education*, April 13. Accessed May 14, 2015. http://chronicle.com/article/The-Consolation-of-Asceticism/229181/.

Stuber, Jenny M. 2011. *Inside the College Gates: How Class and Culture Matter in Higher Education*. Lanham, MD: Lexington Books.

———. 2015. "Pulled In or Pushed Out? How Organizational Factors Shape the Social and Extra-Curricular Experiences of First-Generation Students." In *College Students' Experiences of Power and Marginality: Sharing Spaces and Negotiating Differences,* eds. Elizabeth Lee and Chaise LaDousa, 118–35. New York: Routledge.

Subconference of the MLA Community. Facebook page. Accessed June 22, 2015. https://www.facebook.com/MLAsubconference/info?tab=page_info.

Svec, Michael. 2013. "Empowerment through Cultural Inquiries." In *Becoming and Being a Teacher: Confronting Traditional Norms to Create New Democratic Realities*, ed. Paul Thomas. New York: Peter Lang.

Terry, D. F., and S. R. Wilson. 2005. *Beyond Small Change: Making Migrant Remittances Count*. Inter-American Development Bank.

Thomas, Paul L. 2014. "UPDATED (Again): Grit, Education Narratives Veneer for White, Wealth Privilege." *The Becoming Radical blog*, December 4. https://radicalscholarship.wordpress.com/2014/12/04/grit-education-narratives-veneer-for-white-wealth-privilege/.

Tinto, Vincent. 1999. "Taking Retention Seriously: Rethinking the First Year of College." *NACADA Journal* 19: 5–9.

Tokarczyk, Michelle M., and Elizabeth A. Fay, eds. 1993. *Working-Class Women in the Academy: Laborers in the Knowledge Factory*. Amherst: University of Massachusetts Press.

Toporek, Rebecca L., and Donald B. Pope-Davis. 2005. "Exploring the Relationships between Multicultural Training, Racist Attitudes, and Attributions of Poverty among Graduate Counseling Trainees." *Cultural Diversity and Ethnic Minority Psychology* 11(3): 259–71.

Townsend, Robert B. 2005a. "New Study Highlights Prominence of Elite PhD Programs in History." *Perspectives on History* 43.7 (Oct.).

———. 2005b. "Privileging History: Trends in the Undergraduate Origins of History PhDs." *Perspectives on History* 43.6 (Sept.): 14–20.

Tyndale Holy Bible. 1996. Wheaton, IL: Tyndale House.

Twale, Darla J., and Barbara M. De Luca. 2008. *Faculty Incivility: The Rise of the Academic Bully Culture and What to do About It*. San Francisco: Jossey-Bass.

US Department of Education. 2000. *National Education Longitudinal Study of 1988, Fourth Follow-up*. Washington, DC: National Center for Education Statistics.

Valencia, R. R. 2010. *Dismantling Contemporary Deficit Thinking: Education Thought and Practice*. New York: Routledge.

Vallejo, Jody. 2012. *Barrios to Burbs: The Making of the Mexican-American Middle Class.* Palo Alto: Stanford University Press.

Vonnegut, Kurt. 1963. *Cat's Cradle.* New York: Delta.

Walkerdine, Valerie, Helen Lucey, and June Melody. 2001. *Growing Up Girl: Psychosocial Explorations of Gender and Class.* New York: New York University Press.

Wallace, Michelle. 1990. "Invisibility Blues." In *Invisibility Blues: From Pop to Theory,* 91–99. London: Verso.

Walpole, MaryBeth. 2003. "Socioeconomic Status and College: How SES Affects College Experiences and Outcomes." *Review of Higher Education* 27(1): 45–73.

Walsh, Richard T. G., Thomas Teo, and Angelina Baydala. 2014. *A Critical History and Philosophy of Psychology: Diversity of Context, Thought, and Practice.* Cambridge: Cambridge University Press.

Warnock, Deborah M., and Allison L. Hurst. 2014. "The Poor Kids' Table: Liberal Arts Students Organizing around a Stigmatized Identity in Flux." Paper presented at the Annual meeting of the Association for the Study of Higher Education, Washington, DC, November 2014.

Warnock, Deborah M., and Allison L. Hurst. 2015. "Debt Regret and Concerns: Examining the Effects of Social Class Background and Debt Amount among Liberal Arts Graduates." Paper presented at the Annual meeting of the Working Class Studies Association, Washington, DC, May 2015.

Weber, Max. 2001. *The Protestant Ethic and the Spirit of Capitalism.* New York: Routledge.

Welsch, Kathleen A., ed. 2004. *Those Winter Sundays: Female Academics and Their Working-Class Parents.* Lanham, MD: University Press of America.

Wiegman, Robyn. 1999. "What Ails Feminist Criticism? A Second Opinion." *Critical Inquiry* 25.2 (Winter): 362–79.

Wiggins, Robert A., Eric J. Follo, and Mary B. Eberly. 2007. "The Impact of a Field Immersion Program on Pre-service Teachers' Attitudes toward Teaching in Culturally Diverse Classrooms." *Teaching and Teacher Education* 23(5): 653–63.

Wilson, Amos N. 1978. *The Developmental Psychology of the Black Child.* New York: Africana Research Publications

Wilson, Warren. 1925. *The Farmer's Church.* New York: The Century Company.

Woloch, Alex. 2003. *The One vs. The Many: Minor Characters and the Space of the Protagonist in the Novel.* Princeton: Princeton University Press.

Woosley, Sherry, and Dustin Shepler. 2011. "Understanding the Early Integration Experiences of First-Generation College Students." *College Student Journal* 45(4): 700–714.

World Health Organization and Calouste Gulbenkian Foundation. 2014. *Social Determinants of Mental Health.* Geneva: World Health Organization.

Wu, Stephen. 2005. "Where Do Faculty Receive their PhDs?" *Academe* 91.4 (July–Aug.): 53–54.

Yates, Michael. 2007. *More Unequal: Aspects of Class in the United States.* New York: Monthly Review Press.

Zeder, Melinda A. 1997. *The American Archaeologist: A Profile.* Walnut Creek, CA: AltaMira Press.

Zweig, Michael. 2000. *The Working-Class Majority: America's Best Kept Secret.* Ithaca, NY: Cornell University Press.

Index

About the Contributors

Sara Appel is a Dietrich School Postdoctoral Fellow in the English Department at the University of Pittsburgh. Her recent essays include "Postfeminist Puritanism: Teaching (and Learning from) *The Lowell Offering* in the 21st Century" (*Radical Teacher* July 2015) and "A Ruckus in My Kindergarten Heart: Class, Academia, and Anxious Times" (*Rhizomes* 2014). Her dissertation, "Football Wishes and Fashion Fair Dreams: Class and the Problem of Upward Mobility in Contemporary U.S. Literature and Culture," received the 2013 Constance Coiner dissertation prize from the Working Class Studies Association.

Lynn Arner is an associate professor of English at Brock University in Canada. Lynn's first monograph was *Chaucer, Gower, and the Vernacular Rising: Poetry and the Problem of the Populace After 1381* (2013), and she is currently writing a theorized book on working-class women in the professoriate. Trained in late medieval English literature, gender studies, and contemporary theory, Lynn earned her PhD at the University of Rochester, after which she held visiting posts at a liberal arts college and at the University of Pittsburgh.

Gretchen Braun received her PhD from the University of California at Davis and is currently assistant professor of English at Furman University in Greenville, South Carolina. She teaches classes on Victorian literature and culture and within the Women's, Gender, and Sexuality Studies interdisciplinary minor. Her research in these fields has appeared in *ELH, Women's Studies: An Interdisciplinary Journal*, and *Genre: Forms of Discourse and Culture*, among other scholarly venues. As a lecturer in the UC system she was active in the American Federation of Teachers, and she now serves as an officer in her campus chapter of the American Association of University Professors.

Timothy J. Haney is associate professor of sociology at Mount Royal University and director of the Centre for Community Disaster Research. Dr. Haney's work focuses on how families, neighborhoods, and communities prepare for, respond to, and recover from catastrophic events such as hurricanes, floods, and oil spills. Besides his work on disasters, Dr. Haney's research also focuses on the experiences of professors from lower-SES backgrounds, a project motivated by his own upbringing in a family of automobile workers in Janesville, Wisconsin. His recent work on the educational experiences of faculty members from working-class backgrounds was published in *Canadian Review of Sociology*, and his other work has appeared in outlets such as *Social Science Research, Journal of Urban Affairs, Sociological Quarterly, Critical Sociology,* and *Teaching Sociology*.

Allison L. Hurst is an assistant professor of sociology at Oregon State University, where she teaches courses on the sociology of education and theory. She is also one of the founders and the current acting president of the Association of Working-Class Academics, an organization composed of college faculty and staff who were the first in their families to graduate from college. She has written two books on the experiences and identity reformations of working-class college students, *The Burden of Academic Success: Loyalists, Renegades, and Double Agents* (2010) and *College and the Working Class* (2012). Her current research focuses on the outcomes of college graduates, specifically the role of class and the impact of student debt.

Dwight Lang is a lecturer in the Sociology Department at the University of Michigan, Ann Arbor. His recent essay "Those of Us from Rio Linda" appears in *Class Lives: Stories from Across Our Economic Divide* (2014). He taught his first sociology class in 1980.

Olivia Legan is a student at Kenyon College in Gambier, Ohio. She is majoring in psychology with a concentration in Latino studies. She has worked at an NGO to the United Nations, Doctors without Borders, and most recently, at the Child Life and Creative Arts Therapy Department at Kravis Children's Hospital at Mount Sinai in New York City. Olivia is interested in cross-cultural and developmental psychology and plans to pursue a career in clinical psychology.

Andrea Lewis is an early childhood educator who values and models academic excellence. A graduate of Spelman College, University of Pennsylvania, and Georgia State University, her professional experiences include elementary school teacher, public school administrator, child development center director, and college professor. Currently as chair and assistant professor of education studies at Spelman College, Lewis instills passion and purpose in her students. Her research interests include the effects of social class in teacher preparation, the history of school segregation, and racial identity in young children.

Irene López is an associate professor of psychology. She teaches in the Psychology Department and for the women's and gender studies and Latino studies concentrations. Born and raised in the Bronx, Dr. López is the first in her family to ever go to college or graduate school. She is a clinical psychologist who studies the impact of acculturation on mental health, cross-cultural psychopathology, phenotype, and socioeconomic status, all of which she seeks to understand within the tradition of liberation psychology. An avid photographer, Dr. López is married to Dr. Thomas Hawks, a poet who teaches creative writing. They are the proud parents of Spencer and Sabina Hawks.

Sean McCloud is professor of religious studies (and American studies and communication studies faculty affiliate) at the University of North Carolina at Charlotte. He teaches, publishes, and researches in the fields of American religions, religion and culture, and social theory. His publications include *American Possessions: Fighting Demons in the Contemporary United States* (2015); *Divine Hierarchies: Class in American Religion and Religious Studies* (2007); and *Making the American Religious Fringe: Exotics, Subversives, and Journalists, 1955–1993* (2004).

Sandi Kawecka Nenga is an associate professor of sociology at Southwestern University in Georgetown, Texas. Her research interests include the sociology of youth, middle school peer cultures, youth engagement, social class as a lived experience, and the educational experiences of first-generation college students. Her research has been published in *Journal of Contemporary Ethnography, Qualitative Sociology Review, Sociological Studies of Children and Youth, Journal of Youth Studies,* and *Childhood: A Global Journal of Child Research.* Her current research interests are the experiences of first-generation Latino high school students in a college readiness program.

Melissa Quintela has taught sociology, behavioral sciences, and feminist studies courses on race and ethnicity, social psychology, immigration, and culture in Indiana, New Jersey, Massachusetts, and Texas. She has written and presented on academic engagement, immigrant youth experiences in emerging ethnic communities, youth activism, and social justice development. Her current research encompasses active pedagogical techniques, critical ethnographic methods, and the social psychology of ethnic minority identity. She is active in her local community in areas of cross racial/ethnic dialogue and projects empowering women and youth.

Krista M. Soria is an analyst with the Office of Institutional Research at the University of Minnesota. She is also adjunct faculty at Hamline University, St. Cloud State University, St. Mary's University, and the University of Minnesota. When not teaching, she focuses on researching the experience of working-class and first-generation college students, college students' leadership development, and the benefits of participation in high-impact practices on students' developmental outcomes. She is author of over thirty peer-reviewed journal articles, coeditor of two volumes, and author of the forthcoming text, *Welcoming Blue Collar Scholars into the Ivory Tower: Developing Class-Conscious Strategies for Students' Success.*

Jessi Streib is an assistant professor of sociology at Duke University. She is the author of *The Power of the Past: Understanding Cross-Class Marriages,* as well as articles on how class reproduction occurs through schools, parenting styles, and marriages.

Michael Svec is a professor of education at Furman University in Greenville, South Carolina. He earned a PhD in curriculum and instruction from Indiana University, focusing on secondary science education. Dr. Svec teaches science methods, perspectives on American education, and the culture of American schooling. Recent research has examined using science fiction in the classroom, teacher beliefs as expressed in metaphors, and cultural inquiries for teacher professional development. Dr. Svec was awarded a 2005 Fulbright to teach science education in the Czech Republic.

P. L. Thomas is professor of education at Furman University. The National Council of Teachers of English recognized his blogging with the 2013 George Orwell Award, and he is currently a column editor for *English Journal.* His newest book is *Beware the Roadbuilders* (2015). Follow his work on Twitter (@plthomasEdD) and at The Becoming Radical blog (http://radicalscholarship.wordpress.com/).

Deborah M. Warnock is an assistant professor of sociology at SUNY Cortland, where she teaches classes in social statistics and the sociology of education. She holds a PhD in sociology from the University of Washington. Her work focuses on socioeconomic inequalities in the transitions to and from, as well as in experiences of, higher education. Her research has appeared in *Innovative Higher Education* and *Rhizomes* and is forthcoming in the *Jour-*

nal of College Student Development. Having experienced the alienation that can come from being a low-income student on a college campus, she is committed to working with and supporting working-class and first-generation students.